PRO FOOTBALL'S GREAT MOMENTS

PRO FOOTBALL'S GREAT MOMENTS

by Jack Clary

A Brookside Book

Bonanza Books
New York, New York

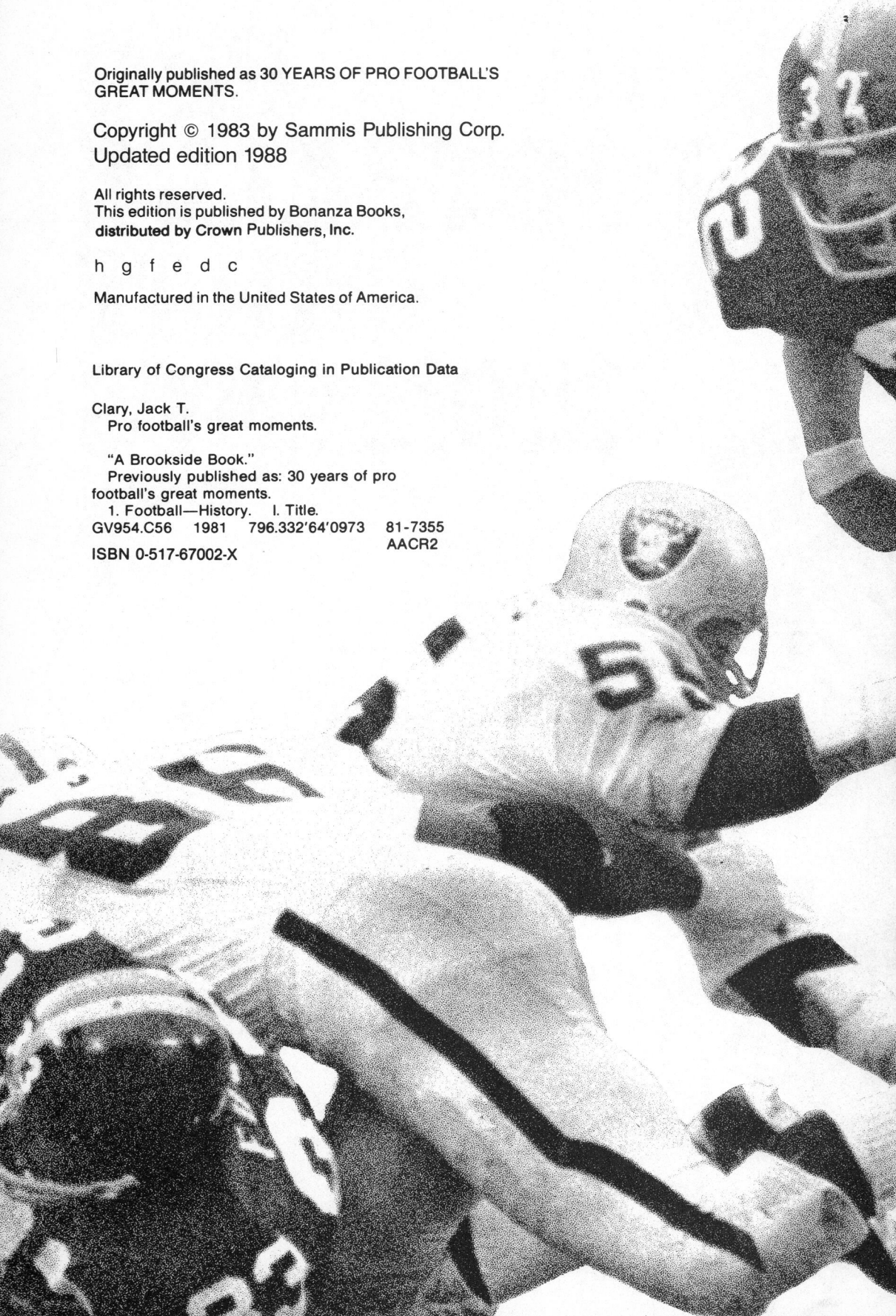

Library of Congress Cataloging in Publication Data

Clary, Jack T.
    Pro football's great moments.

    "A Brookside Book."
    Previously published as: 30 years of pro
football's great moments.
    1. Football—History.   I. Title.
GV954.C56   1981   796.332'64'0973   81-7355
                                        AACR2
ISBN 0-517-67002-X

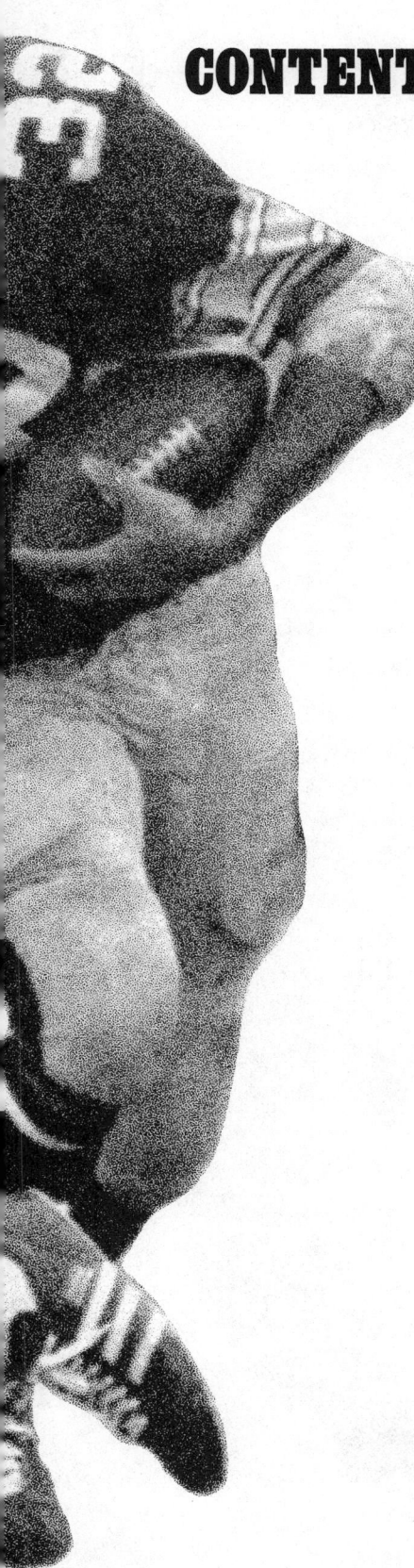

CONTENTS

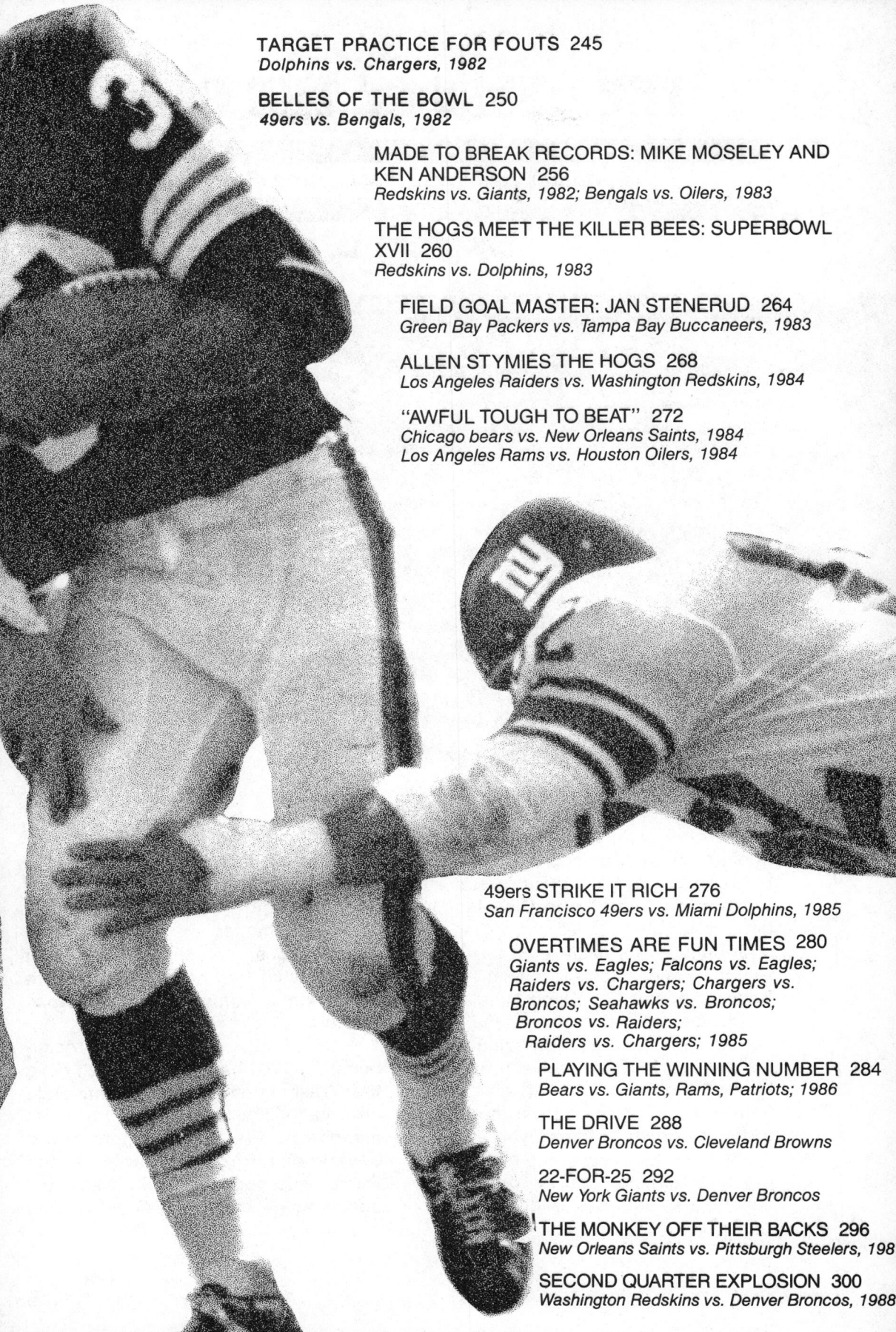

THE RULES OF THE GAME

Cleveland Rams vs. Washington Redskins

DECEMBER 16, 1945

The week before the 1945 National Football League championship game, between the Cleveland Rams and the Washington Redskins in Cleveland, a bitter cold wave roared out of Canada and numbed the eastern Great Lakes region. The Rams' owner, Dan Reeves, spent $7,500 on nine thousand bales of hay to cover the field, hoping to keep it from freezing. Over the hay, Reeves draped a protective tarpaulin, only to watch in dismay as tons of snow dropped from the skies, forming a crushing third layer.

On the morning of the game, with the thermometer barely above the zero mark and the wind whipping about the cavernous Municipal Stadium, some three hundred specially conscripted men shoveled snow from atop the field's protective covering. Then they hauled the tons of hay to the sidelines, revealing the playing area in what had come to look more like a winter farmyard than a football stadium.

Despite the cumbersome precautions, the field had frozen, which gave the Washington team an immediate advantage. The Redskins had brought along sneakers to give them better traction on a frozen field, whereas the Rams had only cleats. Cleveland coach Adam Walsh appealed to Dud

The bitter cold weather in which the 1945 championship game was played may have cost the Redskins (opposite, on the bench) the title and Cleveland its franchise. Above: Steve Bagarus scored the Skins' first touchdown on a pass from Frank Filchock. Right: Cleveland's Jim Gillette got the clincher on a pass from Bob Waterfield.

DeGroot, his counterpart on the Redskins, and DeGroot agreed that his team would play in the conventional football shoes. He refused to rescind the order even after his players found the field hazardous in their pregame warm-up. That decision alone may have decided the game. "There's no doubt we would have won with the better footing," says Washington's Wayne Millner today.

The weather affected more than the outcome of the game. On warmer days in Cleveland, Municipal Stadium had accomodated as many as eighty-two thousand spectators. On this vicious December Sunday, less than

half that number—32,178 to be exact —watched this, Cleveland's first championship game. Had the temperature made it as high as even the freezing mark, the stadium probably would have been filled and the Rams would have had cause to reconsider the decision they had made to move to Los Angeles. Instead, the fans stayed home and the Rams left. When Cleveland would next see Bob Waterfield and his explosive charges they would be the enemy Los Angeles Rams, playing against the new hometown heroes, the Cleveland Browns.

So it is hardly overstatement to claim that the weather that day

helped shape the structure of pro football today. And yet this game is remembered less for its historical importance than for the anachronisms that decided it—a goal post on the goal line, a pass from the end zone that hit the posts, and the rule that such a pass was a safety if it rebounded into the end zone. The next year the rule was changed, and some three decades later the goal posts were moved to the end line. As for the title the Redskins lost before such mischief had been corrected, well, that doesn't rate even an asterisk in the record book.

And to complete this little counterpoint of irony and trivia, remember that the victimized passer was one of pro football's greatest at the height of his prowess—none other than "Slingin' Sammy" Baugh, who in 1945 had completed seventy percent of his passes, still a record.

The fateful play followed what seemed to be a Redskins' highpoint, if not a turning point, early in the game. After driving to a first-and-goal on the Washington 8-yard line, the Rams failed in four tries not only to breach the goal line but even the 5-yard line. So Washington took over in front of its goal posts.

Baugh was hurting, having severely damaged his ribs late in the season, and he was all but encased in tape for this game. DeGroot didn't want him to play, but Sam insisted. On the Skins' first possession he failed to move the club and it was obvious he was not his free wheeling self. Nevertheless, he was calling the plays when the Redskins got the ball after the Rams' fourth-down miss.

On the first play Baugh called for a direct snap in the end zone, lining up as if to punt the ball. Actually, Baugh wanted to pass, but the ball

Washington's Joe Aguirre had a chance to win the game in the fourth quarter with a 31-yard field goal, but his kick, opposite, *was buffetted by the wind and went wide. Steve Bagarus,* right, *ran with distinction but on the frozen field the defenses controlled the game.*

struck his cold hands and dropped to the turf. As the Cleveland linemen began to descend on him, he quickly picked up the ball and heaved it toward the sidelines, far from any Washington receiver or Cleveland defender. The referee's horn tooted (officials did not throw flags in those days), and the Skins were penalized half the distance to the goal line for intentionally grounding the ball.

Even with the ball inside his 3, Baugh put aside any thoughts of punting. He decided he could get his team out of its hole with a quick crossing pattern to either Wayne Millner, an end, or running back Steve Bagarus. And he was right. Millner quickly broke into the secondary and was clear when Baugh straightened to throw. "I had a damn touchdown," Sammy still says of the play. "Wayne was clear out there, but I couldn't get as much on the ball as I usually did.

We were going against the wind in that first quarter, and as soon as that ball left my hand, up came a gust and lifted it right into the crossbar.

"'Damn!' I said as soon as that ball hit that post. I was upset about not completing the pass. I had no idea about a safety until the referee made the signal, but even then I still was more damn mad at missing a touchdown than at Cleveland getting two points."

The play was Baugh's last substantial one of the day. He reinjured his ribs and after the first quarter left the game, having completed just one of six passes for a paltry seven yards. The Redskins sorely missed Baugh not only on offense but on defense. Even in comparison to today's specialists, he was a superb safetyman —a sure tackler and a crafty strategist who read the opposition's offense as though he were operating it.

After the Redskins scored on a 38-yard pass from substitute quarterback Frank Filchock to Bagarus, Waterfield drove the Rams upfield by sending Fred Gehrke and Jim Gillette on runs to the outside. A pass to Jim Benton for 14 yards gained a first down on Washington's 37-yard line, and then Waterfield completed the 70-yard drive with a touchdown pass to the same man. "It was so cold I remember thinking at the time. 'How do these guys hold the ball?'" Waterfield says. "I didn't have any trouble with the ball, but then I didn't have to catch it."

He did, however, have to kick it, and that proved a bit more difficult. The Rams' place-kicker lined up to kick the extra point, but as his toe struck the ball, Washington tackle John Koniszewski grazed it with his hand and left it wobbling toward the goal posts. The ball struck the crossbar and hung there for an instant as if trying to decide what to do. Finally it dropped over for the extra point and a 9–7 Rams' lead.

Clearly, it was not the Redskins' day. Washington's famed marching band formed to begin its Christmas halftime show, only to find that its reeds and brass had frozen.

In the third quarter Waterfield got his offense rolling again, capping a drive by passing to Gillette down the middle and over Ki Aldridge, who had two interceptions this day, for the touchdown. This time Waterfield's extra point was a clear miss, sailing well to the right.

Trying to overcome the 15–7 lead, Filchock passed 50 yards to Bagarus to the Rams' 6-yard line, then scrambled about on the next play, only to be thumped for an 11-yard loss. But Filchock prevailed when on fourth down at the 9-yard line he calmly passed to Jim Seymour standing alone in the end zone. The extra

point of Joe Aguirre, the leading place-kicker that year, brought Washington to within a point, 15–14.

Twice during the last quarter Filchock guided his offense into scoring position. The first time he made it to Cleveland's 31-yard line and in came Aguirre. The wind that had gusted so badly stopped as he lined up the kick, but no sooner had his toe struck the ball than the wind whipped furiously again, gradually pushing the ball to the side until it just missed sailing through the uprights for what would have been the winning points.

A few minutes later Filchock clicked on short passes, moving the ball to Cleveland's 46-yard line, but this time Aguirre's field goal try was far short. So, finally, were the Redskins' efforts for a fourth NFL title in ten years.

In the end it was the weather that doomed the Skins. The cold, for which the Redskins' players had been prepared with their sneakers, might have been an advantage if they had gone ahead and worn the rubber-soled footwear. The wind, which blew Baugh's pass into the goal posts and Aguirre's field-goal attempt wide, punished the Skins more than the Rams. Yet weather, as essentially beyond man's control, somehow escaped the blame. It was the rule on safeties that inflamed the Washington management. It took the Skins' fiery owner, George Preston Marshall, precisely 27 days, until the next rules committee meeting, to have that rule amended. It was, after all, easier than reforming the weather. □

| Washington | 0 | 7 | 7 | 0—14 |
| Cleveland | 2 | 7 | 6 | 0—15 |

Cle—Safety, Baugh pass hit crossbar
Wash—Bagarus 38 pass from Filchock (Aguirre kick)
Cle—Benton 37 pass from Waterfield (Waterfield kick)
Cle—Gillette 44 pass from Waterfield (kick failed)
Wash—Seymour 9 pass from Filchock (Aguirre kick)

Steve Van Buren slogged through the rain and mud for 196 yards in 31 carries, leading his Eagles to a 14–0 victory over the Los Angeles Rams in the 1949 title game. He accounted for more than half his team's total yardage for the day.

STEVE VAN BUREN: RAINY DAY OFFENSE

Philadelphia Eagles vs. Los Angeles Rams

DECEMBER 14, 1949

Along the beaches near Cape May, New Jersey, twice each day during June and July for each of nine summers, the almost squarely built man would run through the white, powder-soft sand. Wearing only shorts and high-top football shoes, he would churn along those beaches at a brisk pace, made even more trying by weights he had strapped to his ankles. This man seemed almost oblivious to the encumbrances, though it was tough enough for anyone even to walk barefoot through that sand. Ob-

viously, Steve Van Buren liked to run.

So it was no wonder that one rainy afternoon at Los Angeles Memorial Coliseum he slogged through ankle-deep mud and water 31 times and never seemed to tire. He assaulted the Los Angeles Rams' defense time after time, single-handedly controlling a championship game as no man would until Larry Csonka and Franco Harris played in then-distant championship games called Super Bowls.

At 6 feet, 208 pounds, Van Buren was not big by the standards of the sixties and seventies, certainly not as big as Jim Brown or O. J. Simpson. But he was the first to combine the power of a fullback and the speed of a halfback. He could run between the tackles or to the outside, where Brown and Simpson amassed so much of their yardage. Either way, Van Buren could bust a play for a touchdown. He fairly exploded into the line of scrimmage and, if he

wasn't stopped, actually accelerated into the secondary. Many a beleaguered safetyman had to sacrifice his body as the last obstacle between Van Buren and the goal line.

He wasn't cute when he ran, yet neither was he all brute force. Instead of using his legs to deceive defenders, as Brown, Simpson, and their ilk did, Van Buren would fake with his head and his shoulders. Maintaining his straight-ahead course, he would shift his head or drop a shoulder as if to turn or veer, and more often than not the defender would be left bewildered, having missed the tackle and perhaps having been simply run over.

Van Buren came from Louisiana State, where he played blocking back for two years while another running back, Alvin Dark (later the famous baseball player and manager), rolled up the yardage. Van Buren became a prime offensive threat only in his se-

While Van Buren ground it out, "the Eagle Defense" controlled the Los Angeles running attack Opposite: *Russ Craft (33) stops Norm Van Brocklin.* Left: *Eagles' captain, Al Wistert (left), who opened up many of the holes for Van Buren, celebrates the victory with coach Earle ("Greasy") Neale.*

nior year, when he performed impressively enough to be a top draft pick of the Eagles after the 1943 season.

Earle ("Greasy") Neale, the coach of the Eagles, once noted, "He made me a great coach"—probably the highest praise Van Buren ever received, and a radical departure for Neale, who rarely credited others for his success. "There never was a player like him," Neale contended. "He was better than Red Grange because Grange needed a blocker; Steve didn't. And he could run away from tacklers like Red or over them like Bronko Nagurski."

Van Buren was the National Football League's best running back in 1949, setting a rushing record of 1,146 yards during the 12-game regular season. When he left football, after nine seasons, he had rushed for a total of 5,860 yards. A quarter century later, after Simpson had nearly doubled Van Buren's single-season total and

Brown had more than doubled the old Eagle's career mark, these figures seemed no longer impressive. Fortunately, the fame of this running back does not rely on his statistics. Van Buren did things on a football field that neither Simpson nor Brown could overshadow. His one-man show in the 1949 championship game ranks as one of pro football's finer exhibitions of running.

As they prepared for their first NFL championship since coming to the West Coast in 1946, the Rams primed themselves to cope with Van Buren most of all by outdoing him. They were a team that incorporated the vast array of coach Clark Shaughnessy's offensive ideas into one of pro football's most brilliant offenses. They thrived on blinding speed from their running backs and wide receivers, proving Shaughnessy's theory that a swift-striking offensive team could bury an average defense in any game.

15

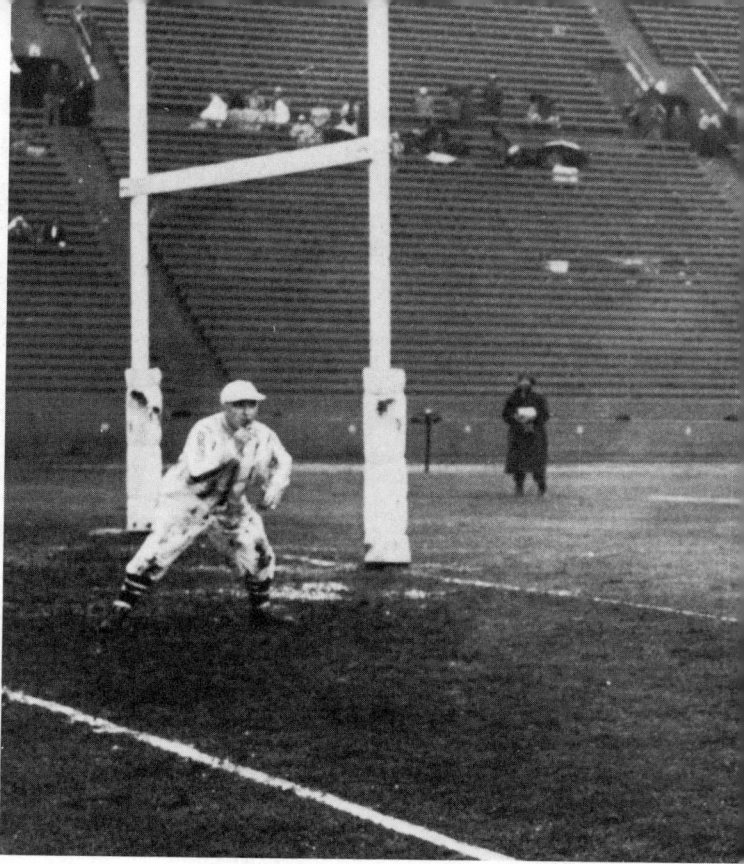

The rain kept the fans away (only thirty-two thousand showed up) and the Los Angeles passing attack mostly under wraps. Frank Reagan intercepted this Rams' pass at his goal line.

Yet the Eagles had whipped the Rams 38–14 earlier in the season and went on to win all but one of their games. Neale's famed "Eagle Defense" seemed the perfect answer to Shaughnessy's offensive theorems, and to all others. Philadelphia allowed the fewest points in the NFL that season. "The Rams will be duck soup," Neale boasted. The bookmakers agreed and made his team nine-point favorites.

When the Eagles arrived by train in Los Angeles the day before the game, the sky was overcast, but forecasters predicted that the famed Pacific Ocean sea breezes would disperse the clouds, leaving blue sky and sunshine for the championship game the next day. Instead, torrential rains were deluging Los Angeles at dawn on the day of the big game.

It wasn't long before the tele-phone in the Philadelphia home of NFL Commissioner Bert Bell was ringing. Back East it was almost noon, and Bell was waiting to watch the first NFL championship ever to be nationally televised. He had signed a contract with the Dumont Network for $30,000 and in addition had arranged a coast-to-coast radio broadcast.

"Could we postpone the game for a day?" the voice calling from Los Angeles asked. "Conditions are impossible. The gate sale will be lost." The Rams had expected approximately sixty thousand persons for the game, maybe more if the weather cooperated. They had sold forty thousand tickets beforehand. As it turned out, more than five thousand ticketholders stayed home.

Nevertheless, Bell refused to allow a postponement. He reminded the caller from Los Angeles that there

were radio and, particularly, TV commitments. "This is a chance to show pro football's championship coast to coast and we're not going to give it up," he said resolutely.

And so pro football's love affair with television began, as love affairs will, in the rain. Granted, neither football nor television is at its prettiest in a downpour, but beauty is in the eye of the beholder and the beauty football and TV beheld in each other had nothing to do with the weather. Besides, even if it was a little embarrassing for televised pro football to debut in the rain in Southern California, where everyone knows it doesn't rain in December, a little embarrassment between sweethearts is part of the mating ritual.

The Rams were most disadvantaged by the weather. Shaughnessy's offense depended on speed, and the saturated field all but eliminated that weapon. It would be up to his defense to stop Van Buren, perhaps causing a turnover or two close to the Eagles' goal line and allowing the Rams to score that way. Tank Younger, V. T. ("Vitamin T") Smith, and Dick Hoerner were good power runners but not as adaptable to the inside running game as Van Buren, Joe Muha, and the Eagles' other backs.

The two teams sparred for the first quarter. As Shaughnessy knew would happen, Van Buren was the Eagles' chief weapon. Time and again he came at the Los Angeles defense, first running behind All-NFL tackle Al Wistert, then going inside behind the blocking of center Vic Lindskog and guards Bucko Kilroy and Cliff Patton. As the pouring rain continued, the Eagles seemed to rely even more heavily on Van Buren, and the Rams became single-minded in their determination to stop him. Soon their safeties were playing closer to the line to try to contain Philadelphia's one-man offense.

The Rams were making the mistake they and many other teams had made in playing the Eagles. Neale's sleek wing-T offense, which Earl Blaik had copied for his great Army teams, could be most flexible when necessary. In the second quarter, the coach told quarterback Tommy Thompson to open his passing game. The ball was slippery and the footing treacherous, but the old quarterback trundled back into the pocket and began throwing. Suddenly, the startled Los Angeles defenders were scurrying backward, trying to cover the Eagles' receivers.

First Thompson hit Jack Ferrante for 11 yards, then again for 16 more. Van Buren teased the loosened up Los Angeles defense, and Thompson could sense that his opponents were vulnerably indecisive. He called a pass play that sent Pete Pihos across the middle after a fake to Van Buren running to the inside. The ball slipped coming off Thompson's fingers as he aimed it at Pihos near the 15-yard line. "Pete made a great catch under any conditions," Kilroy remembers. "He had great hands to begin with and rarely dropped a ball. This one seemed to stick as soon as it hit his fingers, and he came down with it and with no one around him. He just turned and ran into the end zone. The Rams couldn't believe it. We had used a play that was supposed to be a specialty of theirs and had scored against them. All of that work trying to stop Van Buren had netted them zero. . . ."

At the half the Eagles still led 7–0. Thompson had thrown only nine passes, and though he completed five, he had twice been intercepted. Not wanting to risk costly turnovers, Neale shelved the passing part of his game plan.

On the other hand, Van Buren had carried the ball on 13 of the Eagles' 24 rushing plays, and Neale informed the runner that he would have even more work in the second half, as Philadelphia attempted to continue to control the game. Steve already had collected 121 yards, rushing for more than four times as much as Los Angeles' total. Worse still for the Rams, their great passing quarterbacks, Bob Waterfield and Norm Van Brocklin, combined had thrown for only five completions and just 45 yards.

The Rams' attack would get no better in the second half, though the rain finally ceased. The middle of the Eagles' defensive line—Vic Sears, Walt ("Piggy") Barnes, and Mike Jarmoluk —held the Rams to just 21 yards rushing for the day. The Los Angeles passing was stymied as well.

The game's only other touchdown came early in the third quarter when Leo Skladany of Philadelphia blocked Waterfield's punt at the Rams' 2-yard line, scooped it up, and skidded into the end zone. With the score now 14–0, the Eagles made no pretense; it would be Van Buren attempting to waste both the Los Angeles defense and the time remaining in the game. The official play-by-play of the game gives an indication of Van Buren's continued dominance. For one point early in the fourth quarter it reads:

"Van Buren hit center for 5. Van Buren again hit center for 6 and a first down on the 14. Parmer hit RG for 5. Van Buren hit LG for 3. Van Buren ran LE for 16 and a first down at the Eagles' 48. Eagles penalized 5 yards for offside. Parmer ran RE for 1. Van Buren made 5 inside LE. Van Buren again hit inside LE for 6."

And after another exchange of punts: "Van Buren went over center for 6. Van Buren ran LE for 3. Van Buren held for no gain at RG. Van Buren held for no gain at RG."

That was it for the day. Those last two rushing attempts were his thirtieth and thirty-first. Total yards gained: 196 (of the team's total of 342). Total carries: 31 (of the team's total of 61 offensive plays). It would be 25 years until those records for a championship game would fall.

Kilroy, who helped wedge open some of the holes that his teammate used so expertly, puts this great running back in final focus: "Once every ten years a guy like him comes along —Marion Motley, Jim Brown, then O. J. Simpson—all guys with size and speed, all great athletes. But there is just one every decade. Van Buren belonged to the forties."

| Philadelphia | 0 | 7 | 7 | 0—14 |
| Los Angeles | 0 | 0 | 0 | 0— 0 |

Phil—Pihos 31 pass from Thompson (Patton kick)
Phil—Skladany 2 run with blocked punt (Patton kick)

In 1950, the Cleveland Browns dazzled the NFL champion Philadelphia Eagles with a passing attack more sophisticated than any in the NFL. Mac Speedie, above, and the Browns' other receivers consistently beat the Eagles' man-to-man coverage.

THE GREENING OF THE BROWNS

Cleveland Browns vs. Philadelphia Eagles

SEPTEMBER 16, 1950

The Super Bowl of 1950 was played on a September Saturday night in Philadelphia between the National Football League champion Philadelphia Eagles and the Cleveland Browns, a team that had totally dominated the defunct All-America Confer-ence. This was the first game of the season and technically not for any championship, but few games of the sixties or seventies exceeded its stature. It was supposed to demon-strate the absolute supremacy of the NFL, but instead it proved the estab-

19

Cleveland coach Paul Brown, top, found the antidote to "the Eagle Defense," designed by Philadelphia coach Earle Neale, above, and the result was a 35–10 pasting of the Eagles by the Browns.

lished league to be more complacent than supreme, and it made the NFL a better league for having deflated it. It would be some time before the NFL learned all that the upstarts from the rival league had to teach it, but this game marked the beginning. There have been many more exciting contests in professional football but few as significant.

The All-America Conference today is little more than a repository for those antique sports memories on which trivia and nostalgia buffs thrive. While it lived, it had the air of an ambitious sideshow, bursting with empty claims to fame. Two of its teams borrowed the names of the champion baseball teams of the era, the New York Yankees and Brooklyn Dodgers. In the end only three AAC members survived to be admitted to the NFL. One, the Cleveland Browns, who had so dominated the league that they had hastened, if not directly caused, its demise, had become the target for NFL chauvinists not quite content with the economic triumph of their league. In four seasons the Browns had won every AAC title and 51 of their 58 games. They had lost only four times and in their third season not once.

The NFL fans, led first by Commissioner Elmer Layden, did their best to debunk these achievements. When asked if the two leagues ever would play each other, Layden had told the AAC "to go get a ball first." Paul Brown, who had hand-picked a team of superior players and, with his exacting system and philosophy, molded them into a great team, was pictured as a heartless egotist who enjoyed running up the score against woefully outclassed opposition. To be sure, the Browns' competition was less than rigorous, but no doubt the NFL fans regretted harping on this point when their Eagles hardly put up a fight.

The Eagles were led by Steve Van Buren, the league's premier running back, who in three seasons had gained the then-amazing total of 3,091 yards. Against the Rams in the 1949 NFL title game, he had slogged through a mini-monsoon for 196 yards. He was assisted by halfbacks Bosh Pritchard and Clyde ("Smackover") Scott. Quarterback Tommy Thompson threw to a one-eyed end named Jack Ferrante and a powerful young Greek-American, Pete Pihos. Thompson was the top passer in the league in 1948, besting such luminaries as Sammy Baugh, Paul Christman, Sid Luckman, and Bob Waterfield.

Coach Earle ("Greasy") Neale had originated Philadelphia's much-imitated 5–4 defensive alignment called "the Eagle Defense." With its tackles plugging the middle by lining up close to the center and its free-wheeling linebackers foreclosing the sweep, the Eagle Defense seemed to be the ultimate defense against the run. Its weakness, as the Browns were to demonstrate, was the pass, but against the unsophisticated passing attacks of the other NFL teams, it seemed more than adequate.

In all the Eagles were a good team, but Cleveland was more than a match for them in every area. Brown would later call his quarterback, Otto Graham, "the greatest quarterback in the history of pro football," and the record is evidence in favor of the claim. Marion Motley was a fullback of great size, speed, and quickness, and was an equally talented linebacker. Receivers Mac Speedie and Dante Lavelli were perfect targets for Graham in Brown's sophisticated pass offense, which perfected the come-back, or hook, passes, as well as a wide variety of sideline patterns.

Neale called the Browns' attack a "pass-trap" offense because it seemed to depend on mixing trap plays and passes to keep the defense off-balance. However, the Browns used men in motion, the power sweep, and the bulldozing inside running of Motley, as well as their many traps and excellent passing game.

Paul Brown long before had begun to plan for this confrontation. While the All-America Conference struggled along, he kept watch on the NFL teams. In 1949, when the AAC began to fold and Brown learned that the NFL would admit three of its teams, including his own, he launched full-scale preparations. First, he dispatched assistant coaches Fritz Heisler and Blanton Collier to Los Angeles to watch the Rams and Eagles play for the NFL title. Collier was a brilliant football tactician, as thorough as his boss, and with a knack for dissecting offenses. He took his scouting report home and gathered films of the Eagles from every available source. When the Browns reported to training camp that next summer, the master battle plan to beat the Eagles already had been drawn.

Even had they not been strategically outmaneuvered, the Eagles probably were outgunned long before the game began. In their game against the College All-Stars, they lost their number-one backfield of Van Buren and Pritchard. Their best lineman, offensive tackle Al Wistert, also suffered an injury. Brown knew that the revamped Philadelphia offense would be far less of a challenge to his defense, led by the accomplished middle guard, Bill Willis.

Brown had moved to shore up his team, acquiring such former AAC players as defensive ends Len Ford and John Kissell, running back Rex Bumgardner, and offensive linemen Abe Gibron and Hal Herring. When Neale watched the films of the Browns, he never saw those players. "Cleveland was not the same team we studied. We played what amounted to an AAC all-star team," Philadelphia guard and tackle Frank ("Bucko") Kilroy observes. "We were a good team but we weren't capable of beating any all-star team."

The Browns' dress rehearsal for this game came against Detroit in the next-to-last preseason game. Here Brown confirmed that a team using the Eagle Defense could not cover a running back in motion and double-cover wide receivers at the same time. That meant that the Browns could dictate when and where they wanted man-for-man coverage by the vulnerable secondary of the Eagles. "There was no way any defensive back could cover them man-for-man," Brown reported.

Besides having their offense stripped of Van Buren and Pritchard and being put at a further disadvantage by Brown's reinforced personnel, the Eagles found themselves facing a third major obstacle—overconfidence. They had heard everyone, including their coach, demean the Browns, so they truly believed that the NFL brand of football was unbeatable. When early in the game they learned otherwise, the psychic blow was devastating.

On the other hand the Browns had the quiet confidence that comes from thorough preparation, and of course they were primed for the kill. "It was the highest emotional game I ever coached," Brown says. "We had four years of constant ridicule to get us ready."

There was little doubt that the Browns were ready. They stopped the Eagles' offense in three plays and forced a punt. Don Phelps returned the kick for what appeared to be a touchdown, but the officials said that Ford was guilty of clipping. Worse yet, Lou Groza, Cleveland's best offensive tackle and great place-kicker, injured his shoulder and spent the rest of the game stretched out on a rubbing table in the Browns' dressing room.

Graham was in no hurry to unleash his offense. His first three plays were passes, all incomplete but all designed to test Philadelphia's method of coverage. He sent Bumgardner as a man in motion and saw linebacker Joe Muha move to cover him, leaving defensive back Russ Craft alone on either Lavelli or Speedie. The game plan was sound. "We had only the five-four defense," Neale said later. "If they beat that, then we didn't have anything to turn to. We were dead."

Yet it was the Eagles who scored first, when Cliff Patton kicked a 13-yard field goal. Philadelphia had muscled its way to a first down at the Browns' 9-yard line, then moved only one more yard in three plays. With their offense already shorn of its big guns, the Eagles became discouraged when they realized that the Browns' defense would not yield to the makeshift replacement.

Graham was ready now. Dub Jones had been working on Craft's side of the field, running square-out patterns while Otto went elsewhere with his passes. When Graham saw Craft creeping up to cover Jones, he knew it was time to pull the string.

Jones started another square-out pattern, but as Craft moved to crowd him, he broke it off and zoomed toward the end zone. Dub was 10 yards in the clear when he caught Graham's pass and easily finished a 59-yard scoring play. There was almost a minute and a half left to play in the first quarter when Groza's replacement, Chubby Grigg, added the extra point (though he hadn't place-kicked since high school). The Browns led 7-3, and it now remained only for them to show the Eagles, the NFL, and the rest of the country how truly great they were.

First they did it again on defense. When the Eagles reached Cleveland's 6-yard line, Marion Motley moved into the game as a linebacker and made four straight tackles, limiting Philadelphia to just three yards. Moreover, on this series the Eagles lost Clyde Scott with a broken shoulder, all but ending their running game for that night.

On offense Graham turned to Lavelli. Dante shed linebacker Alex Wojciechowicz (something Neale had worked hard in practice to prevent), then sped past safety Frank Reagan by faking a move to the outside and driving toward the goal posts. He easily caught Graham's pass and scampered into the end zone for a 26-yard touchdown play. The Browns had a 14-3 halftime lead.

Cleveland increased that to 21-3 early in the third quarter. Knowing that the Eagles would not cover the fullback if he was used as a man in motion, Brown switched Bumgardner to Motley's fullback position, sent him in motion, and gained thirty yards in three passes from this formation when the Eagles did not notice the switch. When they did adjust, they resumed single coverage on the outside receivers, and Graham promptly passed 32 yards to Lavelli. On the next play, from the Eagles' 12-yard line, Speedie and Graham collaborated for the score.

Brown was now ready to demonstrate another facet of his team's overall power. Following Philadelphia's only touchdown of the night, on Bill Mackride's pass to Pihos, Graham assaulted the Eagles' vaunted defense of the ground game. Otto had called only 10 running plays in the first three quarters, avoiding the jammed middle. Now he attacked the middle by carefully spacing his linemen a little wider on each play. The Philadelphia defensive linemen moved with them and thus inadvertently left good blocking angles for the Browns' linemen.

Into these openings roared Motley, Jones, and Bumgardner. Graham ran seven straight times from the Eagles' 28-yard line and scored the fourth touchdown. "We wanted to show them we could run the ball better than they could," he said later.

It was left to Jones to set up the final touchdown with a spectacular 57-yard run to the Philadelphia 7. Bumgardner carried it over.

The 35-10 final score stood as a monument to one of the most proficient games ever played by a professional football team. It was so clinically perfect that Greasy Neale, among many others, found it hard to accept. Although admitting that the Browns had "a lot of guns," he attributed their success to being proficient only with the forward pass. So the next time the two teams met that season the Browns won 13-7 without throwing a pass.

Not all the Eagles took quite as long to recognize the significance of that first meeting. Bosh Pritchard put it in its proper perspective when he met his wife afterward. She asked, "What happened out there tonight?"

"Honey," he said, "we just met a team from the big leagues."

Cleveland	7	7	7	14—35
Philadelphia	3	0	0	7—10

Phil—FG Patton 15
Cle—Jones 59 pass from Graham (Grigg kick)
Cle—Lavelli 26 pass from Graham (Grigg kick)
Cle—Speedie 12 pass from Graham (Grigg kick)
Phil—Pihos 17 pass from Mackrides (Patton kick)
Cle—Graham 1 run (Grigg kick)
Cle—Bumgardner 1 run (Grigg kick)

THE BEST EVER

Cleveland Browns vs. Los Angeles Rams

DECEMBER 24, 1950

The greatest pro football game? Most would nominate the 1958 championship game, when the Colts beat the Giants in sudden-death overtime. But herewith a by-no-means lone vote for the 1950 championship tussle between the Browns and the Rams. The finest football teams functioned at their most brilliant, seemingly leaving nothing to chance and everything to skill, and neatly resolved the issue in the closing seconds. A perfect fit.

So often the matchups with the greatest potential for excitement become resolute but essentially dull wars of attrition, as if each side fears the other too much to dare risk being great at its expense. Yet when the Browns and Rams battled in their first championship confrontation, every star shone at his brightest. And there were plenty of them—no less than eight who would later be elected to the Pro Football Hall of Fame: Otto Graham, Marion Motley, Bob Waterfield, Norm Van Brocklin, Tom Fears, Elroy Hirsch, Lou Groza, and Dante Lavelli.

How good were these teams? Some statistics: The Rams scored 466 points in 12 regular-season games, an average of nearly 40 points per contest. Their two quarterbacks, Waterfield and Van Brocklin, passed for 3,709 yards, or more than 300 yards per game. One week the Rams piled up 10 touchdowns and 70 points against Baltimore. The next they made 9 touchdowns and 65 points, including 41 points in the third quarter, against Green Bay.

Unlike most teams, which needed to establish a running game before they could pass effectively, the Rams unabashedly came out throwing.

Fears caught 84 passes that season, including 7 for touchdowns. Hirsch grabbed 42. Not that the Rams couldn't run. Indeed they boasted two offensive backfields—the fast-striking unit of Glenn Davis, Verda ("Vitamin T") Smith, and Tom Kalminir, and "the Bull Elephant Backfield" of Paul ("Tank") Younger, Dan Towler, and Ralph Pasquariello.

Against this high-flying team, the Browns pitted the best defense in the league—144 points in 12 games. Their offense had produced points at a less prolific rate than the Rams had, but quarterback Graham did not give away much to the Waterfield-Van Brocklin combination, or Speedie and Lavelli to Hirsch and Fears, or Motley and Rex Bumgardner to the Rams' backfields.

Other than Van Brocklin, who had broken ribs from the Rams' 24–14 playoff victory over Chicago, the arsenals of both clubs were ready for the battle on the frozen turf at Cleveland Stadium. Sure enough, the game began with a series of dazzling offensive explosions. Knowing that the Browns' defense would be concentrating on covering Hirsch and Fears, and that its linebackers would be keying on Smith, L.A. coach Joe Stydahar designed a play in which all three men were used as decoys. On the game's first play from scrimmage, the ends and the fullback started on patterns to the right while Davis stayed momentarily in the backfield as if to block. So conscious were the Browns of the Rams' power that they forgot about Davis. As they moved right to cover Hirsch, Fears, and Smith, Davis streaked down the left sideline, caught Waterfield's pass near mid-

With a 16-yard field goal 28 seconds before time expired, Lou Groza decided perhaps the greatest football game ever played. Clustered in front of the goal posts, the Browns and Rams watched the ball together as it resolved their struggle.

field, and flew past Ken Gorgal and Tommy James of the Cleveland secondary on an 82-yard scoring play. Elapsed time: 27 seconds, and the Rams led 7–0.

It took the Browns six plays to get even. They covered 72 yards, 21 on runs by Graham and 31 on the scoring play—a strike from Graham to Jones. Groza converted and the game was tied.

Then it was the Rams' turn again. Waterfield hit Fears twice, once on a 44-yard pass. From the 19 Smith charged around left end to the 4. Then, on the eighth play of the drive, Hoerner slammed over tackle for the score. The extra point made it Rams 14, Browns 7.

Three series, three touchdowns, on a total of 15 plays from scrimmage. Not many contests can match that for an opening fusillade. And rather than deteriorate into a ragged, high-scoring free-for-all, as some contests do when points come quickly and easily at the outset, this one emulated and eventually surpassed the taut precision of those opening drives.

The Browns returned the Rams' kickoff to the 35. A pass interference call against Woodley Lewis on Speedie and a 17-yard completion to Speedie moved the ball to the Los Angeles 26. From there Graham went to Lavelli for the score with less than four minutes gone in the second quarter.

Just when the carving up of the defenses seemed effortless, an inexplicable lapse on the most routine play in football, the conversion, seemed to change the game's character. A high snap from center Hal Herring caused James to fumble the extra-point placement, and his desperation pass into the end zone was dropped.

Now the defenses gradually reawakened. The Rams reached the Cleveland 7, only to be waylaid by a penalty and thwarted by a pass interception. Then the Rams' defense stiffened and regained the ball on the Cleveland 46. Waterfield marched his men to a first down on the 12, but Cleveland smothered three plays for only four yards, and Waterfield, though the wind was behind him, missed a 15-yard field goal. The of-

In one of the most explosive starts to any title game, the Rams and Browns produced three touchdowns from the first 15 plays from scrimmage. Only a brief lull followed before Dante Lavelli of the Browns continued the scoring parade.

fenses, which minutes before had appeared irresistible, now had strangely subsided, and the defenses assumed control of the game.

For Cleveland Len Ford led the defensive charge. Having missed most of the season with a fractured jaw, and still fifteen pounds under his playing weight, Ford had come in as a replacement for rookie defensive end Jim Martin, whom the Rams had victimized for sizable gains in their opening drives. On three consecutive plays, Ford threw Smith for a 14-yard loss on a reverse, sacked Waterfield for an 11-yard loss, and threw Davis for a 13-yard loss on a sweep. Total: 38 yards in three plays. The Browns' defense seemed to have solidified.

Before the first half ended, Graham sent the Browns ahead 20–14 on a touchdown pass to Lavelli, capping a superbly executed 77-yard drive. The Rams answered midway in the third quarter with two touchdowns within 25 seconds and took a seemingly invincible 28–20 lead. First, Waterfield passed 38 yards to Smith to the Browns' 17-yard line. Hoerner

then ran at Cleveland's defense seven straight times until he scored on fourth down from the 1-yard line. On the Browns' first running play after the kickoff, Motley—swarmed over all this cold day by the aggressive Los Angeles defense—lost the ball. End Larry Brink scooped it up at the 6-yard line and easily scored the second touchdown.

Paul Brown had inured his team to such sudden turnabouts. There was no question of panic or hopelessness. Brown prepared his great players so thoroughly that they could not easily conceive of an insurmountable obstacle. Surely an eight-point deficit with a quarter yet to play did not qualify. Defensive back Warren Lahr began the Browns' third and final comeback of the game. He intercepted Waterfield's pass some five minutes into the fourth quarter and Graham began to peck away at the Rams' defense. Otto had been magnificent most of this afternoon but now he outdid himself. On a fourth-and-four situation he passed for seven yards. On a fourth-and-three he ran for the first down. Finally, on

27

Dick Hoerner scored two touchdowns for the Rams on plunges, the second when carrying the ball for the seventh straight time. On the kickoff after that score, the Rams recovered a fumble and scored, taking a 28–20 lead. Then Cleveland began its dramatic comeback.

the eighth play of this fine drive, he passed to Bumgardner, who, foiling Woodley Lewis' perfect coverage, made a diving catch just inside the end zone. Groza's kick narrowed the Rams' lead to 28–27.

Graham got the ball back four plays later and with three minutes to play marched Cleveland to within field-goal distance. Not content to allow Groza to kick from near the 30-yard line, Graham sprinted for a first down

to keep the drive going. As he tried to dance and dodge for another precious yard or two, Milan Lazetich, the big linebacker, blindsided Graham, caused him to fumble, and then recovered the ball. "I never saw the guy coming," Graham would say later. "I wanted to dig a hole right in the middle of that stadium, crawl into it and bury myself forever. I got to the sidelines and wanted to hide. But Paul came over, put his arm around my shoulder and said, 'Don't worry. We'll get it back. We'll win this thing yet.' He told me later he really meant it, that he wasn't just trying to make me feel good."

The Rams needed but one first down and the game was theirs. But the Browns' defense struck down Hoerner on two straight runs for no gain, then collared Glenn Davis after he make six yards off tackle.

The fans who had begun to stream to the exit portals stopped for one last look, then continued home when Waterfield boomed a 51-yard kick against the wind. Cliff Lewis caught the ball at his 19-yard line and ran out of bounds after progressing to the 32. A minute and 50 seconds remained and the Browns were 68 yards from the Los Angeles end zone.

Graham forgot his despair. This last, desperate drive began when Otto could find no open receivers and ran 14 yards to the Browns' 46-yard line. Then his passing game came alive— 15 yards to Bumgardner in the left flat, 16 yards to Jones in the right flat. There was one minute to play as the ball rested on the Los Angeles 23-yard line.

The imperturbable Graham, confidently in control now, found Bumgardner again, this time for 12 yards to the Los Angeles 11. Graham called timeout and went to the sidelines for Brown's counsel. Upstairs in the coaches' booth, assistant Blanton Collier had been watching each play unfold. As he considered Groza's field-goal kicking, he was bothered by the brisk right-to-left crosswind that swept the open end of the stadium, toward which his team was driving.

"The ball had been marked on the left hashmark when Otto called a timeout, and this left a bit of an angle," Collier still remembers. "Paul came to the phone and said, 'What do you think?'

"I said, 'Let's run Otto on a quar-terback sneak to the right because of that wind, then kick it.' He said, 'Okay.'

"I lived one hundred years for the next few seconds because all of a sudden it dawned on me, 'You crazy nut! You have the ball down there now and you want to take a chance on someone fumbling it on this frozen ground just to move it in a little better position.' That's all we would get, maybe just a little better position. But I had become so intent on that factor I forgot about the danger of handling the football in one more scrimmage situation."

But Graham was not about to fumble again. After he gained even better position than Collier had hoped for, he called timeout again. Now it was up to Groza, who stood near the spot where Waterfield earlier had missed a 15-yard field goal. "The only thing I thought about was my own little checklist for kicking a ball," Groza says. "I didn't hear the crowd, I blotted out the distance, the time left, even the score. All I had to do was to kick the ball."

And he did. Straight and true, sixteen yards into that tricky wind and through the iron pipes. As the ball soared upward, twenty-two players froze in a bizarre tableau. Once they heard the thud of Groza's famed toe against the ball, there was nothing to do but watch.

Only 28 seconds remained to be played. Cleveland could not have cut it much closer. □

Los Angeles	14	0	14	0—28
Cleveland	7	6	7	10—30

LA—Davis 82 pass from Waterfield (Waterfield kick)
Cle—Jones 31 pass from Graham (Groza kick)
LA—Hoerner 3 run (Waterfield kick)
Cle—Lavelli 26 pass from Graham (kick failed)
Cle—Lavelli 39 pass from Graham (Groza kick)
LA—Hoerner 1 run (Waterfield kick)
LA—Brink 6 run with fumble (Waterfield kick)
Cle—Bumgardner 19 pass from Graham (Groza kick)
Cle—FG Groza 16

NORM VAN BROCKLIN: THE PERFECT PASS

Los Angeles Rams vs. Cleveland Browns

DECEMBER 23, 1951

The man who beat the Browns for the 1951 NFL title later went into coaching, where he projected the same determined, if not always successful, will to win.

In more than a quarter century of playing and coaching in the National Football League, Norm Van Brocklin left his mark. His playing skills, his passing particularly, were without peer, and his coaching left equally vivid impressions. Opposing coaches still say he was one of the great offensive innovators during his more than 13 seasons as a coach in Minnesota and Atlanta. There were many who saw arrogance and insensitivity in him, but few disputed his brilliance.

Blanton Collier, a distinguished former assistant and head coach for the Cleveland Browns, nominates one play as the epitome of Van Brocklin's daring genius—a pass he threw that sailed some seventy yards through the warm, late afternoon air in the Los Angeles Coliseum and nestled into the outstretched hands of end Tom Fears. That was a quarter century ago, but the play still reruns in Collier's mind today. It beat the Browns for the 1951 NFL championship, 24–17, and gave the Los Angeles Rams the only title they managed to win through their first two and a half decades in Los Angeles. "It was," Fears says today, "the best thrown pass I ever caught in my life."

Collier remembers learning very quickly that the best way to defense Van Brocklin was not to challenge him. Coaching the defense at the Pro Bowl that same year, Collier instructed his safeties, particularly

Emlen Tunnell, "When Dutch comes into the game, you go back farther than you think he can throw it, then go back another twenty yards because, believe me, he'll throw it that far."

"So," Collier recalls, "Van Brocklin came in the game and beat Emlen for a touchdown. Em came off the field, went to the phone, and said to me, 'So help me, I'll never disbelieve you again in my life.' "

It was vintage Van Brocklin—audacious excellence when the pressure to be less ambitious seemed irresistible. He was a man who thought coup d'etat in the face of a firing squad. And he was at his uncompromising best in the 1951 championship game.

The 1951 Rams were a different team from the one that had come so close to winning the year before. They had lost both their starting and replacement offensive tackles by trade or retirement. Yet line coach Ray Richards had in one season rebuilt his unit so that it functioned with hardly diminished effectiveness. The running and passing games ran as smoothly as ever.

The Rams had shifted from their two running systems—"the Bull Elephant" backfield and the scatback backfield—to a quick-strike, long-pass offense that often stunned an opponent into submission. With quarterbacks Van Brocklin and Bob Waterfield, and receivers Fears, Elroy ("Crazylegs") Hirsch, and Glenn Davis, it was the easiest way to go.

On defense the Rams began 1951 with 14 rookies on a 33-man team, though the nucleus of the supremely talented 1950 defensive unit remained. The newcomers included defensive end Andy Robustelli, defensive back Norb Hecker, center Leon McLaughlin, and tackles Jim Winkler, Tom Dahms, Charley Toogood, Bob Collier, and Don Simensen. Robustelli

was a nineteenth-round draft pick from Connecticut's tiny Arnold College (now the University of Bridgeport). He got his chance to play when veteran defensive end Jack Zilly was injured, and Zilly never got his job back. Robustelli did so well with the Rams and later the New York Giants that he wound up in pro football's Hall of Fame.

Cleveland's defense was essentially the one that had helped win the 1950 title: Len Ford and George Young at the ends, John Kissell and Darrell Palmer at the tackles, Bill Willis the middle guard, and the three deep backs—Warren Lahr, Tommy James, and Cliff Lewis.

The game, everyone agreed, would pivot on the effectiveness of the pass rushes. The Browns knew they would have to stop the Rams' passing to win. The Rams' defense was equally mindful of the importance of disrupting the Cleveland aerial attack. In their 1950 title game defeat and a 38–23 lacing earlier in the 1951 season, the Rams had experienced as much as they cared to of Otto Graham's success in throwing to Mac Speedie, Dante Lavelli, and Dub Jones.

In the key matchups Robustelli was pitted against veteran tackle Lou Groza, and Larry Brink against the Browns' other tackle, Lou Rymkus. When the game ended, the Robustelli-Brink combination would be a lopsided winner, dramatically influencing not only the outcome of this game but the concept of defensive line play. After watching the two Rams disrupt the cool passing game of Graham, coaches began to favor such quick-striking defensive linemen to combat the offenses' increasing stress on passing.

The emotion and tension of this game built slowly, as the men in the pit fought each other. The Browns had a 10–7 lead at halftime on

The Browns led 10–7 at halftime on the strength of this Otto Graham, top, pass to Dub Jones for a 17-yard touchdown. The score marked one of the few times that afternoon that the Rams' defensive ends, Andy Robustelli and Larry Brink (84 and 62 respectively, top), failed to pressure Graham.

Groza's mighty 52-yard field goal and a 17-yard pass from Graham to Jones. Dick Hoerner had given the Rams a 7–0 lead in the second quarter.

Although the Browns led, Graham was already taking a beating. Robustelli was beating Groza with his quick inside moves, and Brink had begun to overpower Rymkus and his substitute, rookie John Sandusky. The Browns' offense, which had clicked off 11 straight victories that season, beginning with its win over Los Angeles, was sputtering.

Unfortunately, the Rams' attack too was unusually quiescent.

Throughout the practice week, coach Joe Stydahar had received reports from a "spy" in Cleveland who had watched the Browns' preparations from a hiding place in a tree at the Browns' practice field. "They're planning a six-man line on defense," the man is said to have told Stydahar. So the Rams studied this alignment and may have been taken aback when the Browns opened with their standard four-man front, with Willis, as always, the roving middle guard.

As the Rams' offense failed to move, the defense did its best to provide momentum of its own. Midway through the third quarter, Brink and Robustelli converged on Graham as he set up to pass. Brink hit him, jarring the ball loose, and Robustelli picked it up on the first bounce at the Browns' 30-yard line. "I never got a really good grip on the ball because I just grabbed it off-balance and began to run," Robustelli says. "I stumbled as soon as I started, and it seemed I kept stumbling all the way down the field, trying to keep that ball in my grasp."

Marion Motley, the Browns' big fullback, finally caught him from behind and leveled him at the 2-yard line. Three plays later, Dan Towler bulled for the touchdown, and Los Angeles was ahead again, 14–10.

Eager to avenge the giveaway, Graham hurled a 52-yard touchdown pass, only to have it called back because Groza had been detected holding Robustelli. Instead of a 17–14 lead, the Browns still trailed and now had to punt, whereupon Van Brocklin trotted into the game for the first time.

Stydahar had said that he picked his quarterbacks on the basis of who he felt "had the hot hand," but more than intuition guided him in this change. "The Dutchman had nearly three-quarters of the game to get an idea of what was working and what

was not, and most importantly, why these things were happening," Stydahar said. "He had a great football mind, almost photogenic when it came to looking at alignments and formulating his own plan of attack to suit them." Moreover, Van Brocklin had a history of being able to produce key plays, and Stydahar wanted some insurance points for his young defense against the Browns' ever-explosive offense.

On his first series Van Brocklin drove the Rams to Cleveland's 1-yard line, mainly on a 48-yard pass to Fears, who had overcome his knee miseries and seemed to be playing in almost perfect physical condition. However, the Browns' defense pushed the Rams back to the 18-yard line, and capped that tremendous stand by smothering Glenn Davis on a reverse springing from a fake field goal attempt by Waterfield.

Back came the Rams on their next possession. The pass rush had forced Graham to hurry a pass, and rookie Marv Johnson intercepted. Again the offense found itself at Cleveland's 1-yard line. But again the Browns' defense proved stronger, pushing the Rams back to the 11-yard line with the help of two penalties. This time Waterfield kicked a field goal, and Los Angeles led 17–10.

The Browns' running game having been effectively contained for most of the game, Stydahar knew that Graham would continue to rely on his passing despite the battering he was taking from the Rams' pass rush. So Los Angeles pulled out its linebackers and inserted seven defensive backs, including Hirsch, who played the deep safety position. However, Graham was not so desperate or impatient early in the fourth quarter that he could not recognize the odds against attacking this alignment only by passing. First, he dropped back to throw but tucked the ball in and ran for 34 yards. Los Angeles had to return to a more standard defense, and Graham began to eat away at its outside, polishing off a 70-yard drive with Ken Carpenter's 5-yard run off tackle. Groza kicked the extra point and the game was tied at 17 with just under eight minutes to play.

Van Brocklin seemed personally offended. He stomped along the sidelines while Graham guided the Browns to the tying score. But once Van Brocklin got another chance to control his offense, and thus the game, his fuming gave way to icy confidence. "Van Brocklin had the uncanny knack of getting a mental picture of an opponent's pass coverage from a given formation and retaining that picture," said Hampton Pool, then an assistant to Stydahar. "Whenever he wanted something, he'd dig that picture out of his mind and use it to his own advantage.

"He had done that very thing when he first went into the game, sending Fears down the sideline and then having him cut to the middle of the field. During the game he had noticed the Browns' two backs, Lewis and James, giving away too much of the middle, and he wanted to see how they reacted when he ran a play in that direction."

Van Brocklin never programmed his surprise attacks. Though only in his third NFL season, he was already a fine strategist. When the first two plays of the series after the Browns' touchdown gained only three yards, Van Brocklin decided it was time to unload.

"We knew he loved to throw long on those third-and-eights, third-and-tens," Collier remembers. "He never changed that style.

"I can see that ball coming off his hands and going through the air. Fears had run down the sidelines and made his cut. It looked like the pass might be overthrown, but Tom reached out and made a great catch as the ball came right down on his fingertips between Lewis and James."

Fears caught the ball in full stride. No one had a chance to catch him as he completed the 73-yard play. Waterfield's extra point sent the Rams ahead 24–17 and left to the defense the job of preserving the lead.

Everyone knew that the Browns, like Van Brocklin, were most dangerous when faced with the greatest challenge. They had come from 71 yards away in less than two minutes the year before to beat the Rams, and now they had more than half a quarter to gain a tie or better. Time and again Graham went to his short passing game, a series of flare or flat passes to Jones and Carpenter so deftly timed that the defense had little or no time to react. But the Rams could anticipate, and on fourth-and-two at the Los Angeles 42, they did. Graham threw short to the swift Jones, but no sooner had he caught the ball than Hecker was on him for a two-yard loss. After that the Rams' defense was all but immovable.

The defense held center stage for the start and end of the drama, but it was Van Brocklin front and center at the climax. He threw only six passes (four of which he completed, for 126 yards), but he directed the game when control of it wavered between two superbly matched teams. The Rams' defense had neutralized the Browns' offense. Van Brocklin was the difference. □

Cleveland	0	10	0	7—17
Los Angeles	0	7	10	7—24

LA—Hoerner 1 run (Waterfield kick)
Cle—FG Groza 52
Cle—Jones 17 pass from Graham (Groza kick)
LA—Towler 2 run (Waterfield kick)
LA—FG Waterfield 17
Cle—Carpenter 5 run (Groza kick)
LA—Fears 73 pass from Van Brocklin (Waterfield kick)

34

THE BATTLE OF LAKE ERIE

Detroit Lions vs. Cleveland Browns

DECEMBER 27, 1953

Detroit first drew blood in the Battle of Lake Erie when Doak Walker scored from one yard out. The drive began when the Lions' Les Bingaman recovered a fumble on the Cleveland 13. Walker reached the end zone six plays later.

In the late forties and fifties, major league baseball thrived on New York's "Subway Series," when the New York Yankees played either the Giants or Brooklyn Dodgers in the World Series. Those pairings posed and answered the universally appeal-ing question, "Who's the toughest guy on the block?"

Out in the midlands professional football cast the question to suit the local topography and came up with, "Who's the toughest guy on the lake?" That would be Lake Erie,

across which the Browns in Cleveland and the Lions in Detroit glared at each other.

In 1953, Detroit had bragging rights. The Browns had mopped up most everybody else during their four seasons in the National Football League, but after winning a preseason game in 1950 against Detroit, in their first crack at NFL competition, the Browns did no better than a tie (24–24 in 1953) in the next three preseason games. And when it counted, Detroit beat Cleveland twice without losing, 17–6 in 1952 and 17–7 for the league championship later that year in Cleveland. Thus, on the eve of their meeting with the Lions for the 1953 NFL championship, before some fifty-five thousand Detroit partisans in Briggs Stadium, the Browns had tussled with the cross-lake competition six times and prevailed only once.

Like most intercity rivalries, this one became a contest of stylistic and personality differences, some real and some fabricated. The coaches were direct contrasts: Paul Brown, the

Jim Doran (right) besting Ken Gorgal, spent the afternoon in an increasingly testy struggle with the Cleveland secondary, particularly Warren Lahr (left). In the end it was the Doran-Lahr matchup that decided the game.

sombre taskmaster of the Browns, against Buddy Parker, the irrepressible keeper of the Lions.

On the surface the teams might have seemed to reflect the contrasting characters of their coaches—the Browns coldly efficient, the Lions more spirited but less convincing. The Browns had rolled to within one game of a perfect season, their only flaw being a loss to Philadelphia (after leading 21–0) in the season's final game. The Lions had not secured the Western Conference title until the season's last game. They had scored fewer points than the Browns and surrendered more.

Yet these teams were more alike than different. They were both accomplished units led by brilliant coaches and great stars. The Browns boasted their splendid quarterback, Otto Graham, who completed more than 62% of his passes in directing the Cleveland offense of superstars: Mac Speedie, Dante Lavelli, Dub Jones, Lou Groza, and, as Marion Motley began slowing down, a big kid from Indiana, Harry Jagade. The Lions answered with Bobby Layne, Doak Walker, Hunchy Hoernschemeyer, and Leon Hart, recognized stars since their college days. And television had brought to prominence a 305-pound middle guard, Les Bingaman. If the Lions were in general not as famous as the Browns, they were far from anonymous or unheralded. They were after all the defending champs.

In short, there wasn't much to choose from between the two teams, despite the fervor of rivalry magnifying every difference. But this bitter struggle demanded a decisive choice between the two teams, even as it resisted one. And so it was perhaps fitting that it fell to two unglorified players to resolve the issue. At the climax, the celebrities on both sides functioned only as supporting cast, and

the principals were a second-string end and a workmanlike, unsung defensive back. This game consumed every resource on both sides, and only then did it reach its wrenching conclusion.

The role of the unlikely hero was foreshadowed on the second play of the game, when Graham dropped back to pass and found himself engulfed by a rookie linebacker, Joe Schmidt. As a first-year man, Schmidt had been ostracized by Layne and some other Detroit veterans who resented a rookie costing one of their friends a spot on the team. No doubt they mellowed when Schmidt cracked into Graham at the Cleveland 15-yard line, the ball dropped from the quarterback's hands, and the huge Bingaman recovered the fumble at the 13. This was the beginning of a very bad afternoon for Graham.

Hoping to confuse the coordinated Cleveland defense, the Lions opened their offense with a single-wing type unbalanced line that attempted to pressure the left side of the Browns' defensive line. Cleveland held off the Lions for six plays before Walker finally scored on a counter play to the weak side. Doak also kicked the extra point.

Schmidt's blitzing of Graham early in the game was part of Parker's plan to upset Cleveland's passing attack. The coach reasoned that if Graham had to guess where the Lions' linebackers would be then he would either keep his backs in with him to protect against a blitz or he would be reluctant to throw his patented flare passes. Parker felt his defensive line could exert enough pressure to aid the blitz and would further help his fine secondary in containing Lavelli, Speedie, and Jones.

The strategy worked to perfection. At one point Graham became so frustrated at his passing problems that he asked Brown to remove him. George Ratterman came in, found the going just as tough, and soon was relegated to the sidelines in favor of Graham.

Cleveland did not penetrate into Detroit territory until late in the first quarter, when Len Ford recovered Hoernschemeyer's fumble at Detroit's 6-yard line. In three plays Cleveland lost a yard and could produce only three points from the opportunity, when Groza kicked a 14-yard field goal early in the second quarter.

Jim David compounded the Browns' problems late in the second quarter by intercepting a pass and returning it 33 yards to Cleveland's 20-yard line. However, at this point, the Lions' momentum was checked. On the next play, Layne lateraled to Walker, who, as the Browns' defenders closed in on him, threw a forward pass back to Layne. Bobby took off, faked defensive back Tom James to the ground at the 15-yard line, and

sped into the end zone. Immediately, Cleveland protested that such a play was illegal—a quarterback taking a direct snap could not receive a forward pass—and the officials agreed. So the Lions had to be satisfied with Walker's 22-yard field goal two plays later and a 10–3 halftime lead.

Primed by this reprieve and some acid comments from Brown during the intermission, the Browns took charge at the start of the second half. Ken Gorgal intercepted Layne's pass on the first series of plays in the third quarter, and the Browns began the march for the tying score. Staying on the ground, Graham hammered away at the edges of the Lions' defense. Then, on the eighth play of the 51-yard drive, he faked a pitchout to halfback Billy Reynolds and, as the middle of the line trapped Bingaman, handed off to Jagade going up the middle. The big fullback rumbled over right guard for nine yards and a

Above: The leaders of the Lions, coach Buddy Parker (right) and quarterback Bobby Layne. Right: After Layne drove the Lions 80 yards in the closing minutes for the tying touchdown, Doak Walker kicked the game-winning extra point.

touchdown. It was one of the most basic plays in the Browns' offense— the classic trap. Groza's extra point tied the score, 10–10, with seven minutes to play in the quarter.

Pressing their advantage, the Browns took the lead after another turnover by Layne, this time a fumble that defensive tackle Don Colo recovered. Jagade led another sustained march as Graham all but forgot his passing attack, and Groza capped the drive with a 15-yard field goal shortly after the last quarter began.

Layne rallied his forces for a drive to the Cleveland 26, but Walker missed a field goal and the Browns retaliated by making one, a 43-yarder by Groza after a time-consuming march. And so it stood 16–10 Cleveland, with only 4:10 to play.

Now this struggle between two magnificent teams boiled down to a stark one-on-one confrontation between two foot soldiers, Detroit's Jim Doran and Cleveland's Warren Lahr. Though an offensive end in college, Doran had played defense for the Lions in 1952 and was chosen the team's most valuable player that season by his teammates. In the middle of the 1953 season, Parker became so dissatisfied with his receivers that he shifted Doran back to offense, but he had played little in the last half of the season. Then Leon Hart was injured in the first half of this game, and Doran found himself at his old position again. His adversary in the Browns' secondary was Lahr, an accomplished veteran among many in the Cleveland defensive unit.

From the start of the game the Detroit receivers had been either blocking or faking a block on their defenders, whether on a passing play or a run. When Doran came into the game, he and Lahr engaged in some lively contact. Gradually the rolling blocks began to annoy the Browns' corner-

back, and he became more aggressive. Before long Doran was returning to the huddle and telling Layne, "I can beat him on an 'up' pattern."

When Groza kicked off into the end zone after his last field goal and the Lions started from their 20-yard line, Layne began throwing to Doran. "Just give me time, boys," he drawled, "and I'll get you into the end zone and back to that College All-Star Game next year. Dammit, just block."

On the first play, the swashbuckling star quarterback passed for 17 yards to the substitute receiver, who was punished by Lahr after he caught the ball. Two incompletions later, on a vital third down Layne hit Doran on a buttonhook in front of Lahr. It gained 18 yards and a first down at the Browns' 45-yard line, keeping the Lions alive. "If we missed that one, the game was over," Layne contends. "Parker had made up his mind he would punt and see what happened."

Now the Lions were charging. Cloyce Box caught a nine-yard pass to the 36-yard line. After Hoernschemeyer was stopped, Layne got the first down on a three-yard quarterback sneak. And then the big play.

Parker wanted Layne to call a screen pass over hard-charging Len Ford, but Doran finally convinced Layne to throw him the bomb. "I can beat him on the up pattern," the end repeated. Layne leaned into the huddle and called the play: "Nine up and go."

Lahr watched Doran break from the line of scrimmage and move toward him. Anticipating another block, he moved to counter the end's move and exact a little punishment of his own. Doran made a move as if to block but, as Lahr charged, quickly cut around him. The instant he had a step lead, Layne let the ball go.

As the ball sailed toward its target, two things happened: Doran opened up another yard on his defender, and the crowd, sensing the play of the game unfolding, roared in anticipation. As the ball settled perfectly into Doran's outstretched hands, a thunderclap of bedlam struck Briggs Stadium. Doran never broke stride running into the end zone, still two yards ahead of Lahr. On the clock: 2:08.

Then, as quickly as the noise erupted, it ceased, because Walker now had to kick the tie-breaking point. He did quite easily, and the great roar shook the old wooden park once more. And again a third time a minute later when rookie defensive back Carl Karilivacz intercepted another Graham pass. The Lions had nailed down a second straight NFL title.

More than two decades later, Layne can still hear Doran begging him to call the "up pattern." That decisive touchdown pass stands not only as a brilliant call and the definitive conclusion to a thrilling game. It was also the most succinct and powerful expression of the rivalry between these two teams, and indeed of any two. One man ran to catch a ball; another man to stop him. The winner of that little game won the bigger game. "It was," concludes Layne, "the right shot for the right moment." □

Cleveland   0   3   7   6—16
Detroit   7   3   0   7—17
Det—Walker 1 run (Walker kick)
Cle—FG Groza 14
Det—FG Walker 22
Cle—Jagada 9 run (Groza kick)
Cle—FG Groza 15
Cle—FG Groza 43
Det—Doran 33 pass from Layne (Walker kick)

BLOWING IT

Detroit Lions vs. San Francisco 49ers

DECEMBER 22, 1957

At first the San Francisco 49ers looked unstoppable in their 1957 Western Conference playoff against the Detroit Lions. R. C. Owens (right) caught this Alley-Oop touchdown pass, helping the 49ers to a 24–7 halftime lead. In the second half, things changed.

Question: What is an insurmountable lead?

Answer: A win.

If you doubt it, consider the case of the San Francisco 49ers in the 1957 playoff for the National Football League's Western Conference cham-pionship. These were the 49ers of Y. A. Tittle, Hugh McElhenny, Joe Perry —Hall of Famers all—R. C. Owens (the high-jumping, "Alley-Oop" re-ceiver), and Gordy Soltau (the reliable field-goal kicker). They were playing at home against the Detroit Lions,

whose most successful and popular coach, Buddy Parker, had quit in a huff before the start of the season and whose star quarterback, Bobby Layne, was sidelined with his leg in a cast. The nearly sixty thousand people who packed Kezar Stadium that sky blue December afternoon can be forgiven for having anticipated a conference title for the home side. Indeed at the start, the 49ers did everything to encourage them.

First, Tittle passed to Owens for a 34-yard touchdown on one of their famous, Alley-Oop passes. This play had been discovered in practice one day when a bored Tittle heaved the ball downfield, and to the astonishment of the 49ers' coaches who were watching, Owens outleaped their defensive backs for the ball. After that spectacular debut, Alley-Oop became a set play, though this was the first time it had clicked since the 49ers used it to beat the Lions in midseason, 35–31.

After the touchdown pass to Owens, Tittle sent McElhenny scurrying out of the backfield on a pass pattern between Detroit defensive backs Jim David and Yale Lary. Tittle tossed

McElhenny the ball, and "Hurryin' Hugh" produced a 47-yard touchdown play complete with a typically scintillating assortment of cutbacks and changes of pace, leaving Lions sprawled across the field in confusion and frustration.

Here the 49ers relented a bit, yielding a touchdown on a 3-yard pass from substitute quarterback Tobin Rote to rookie Steve Junker. But Tittle came right back, capping an 88-yard drive with a 12-yard touchdown toss to Billy Wilson. That made it 21–7. The uptight Lions then fumbled the ball away at their 41-yard line, allowing the 49ers to add a 25-yard Soltau field goal.

And so it stood 24–7 at halftime, and the public address announcer felt safe enough informing the fans that tickets were now on sale for the 49ers' next home date, the NFL title game. Meanwhile, the 49ers were busily celebrating in their dressing room, and the Lions, as they had been for the first half, were the captive audience. The visitors' dressing room was only one thin wall away from the 49ers', so the losers heard every chortle. "All we could do was sit and

Tom ("the Bomb") Tracy led the Lions' resurgence. Right: He races past Dicky Moegele on 58-yard scoring jaunt. Opposite: The Lions had the last laugh— left to right: Tobin Rote, coach George Wilson, Tracy, Buster Ramsay, and captain Joe Schmidt.

listen," quarterback Rote remembers.

The second half began with perhaps the most memorable run of McElhenny's career. Taking the ball at his 20-yard line, "the King" headed upfield and veered to the left sideline. He was trapped there so he charged across to the right sideline, where he advanced some ten yards before being trapped again. For a second time he ran across the field and made another short gain, only to find himself hemmed in again. A third time now he spun on his spikes and took off across the field. This time he found an opening and slashed his way toward the Lions' goal line. He finally was tackled by Lary at the Detroit 9-yard line, having gained 71 yards and traveled about 200.

On this play the Lions looked like anything but a team infuriated at being counted out at halftime. Had Hugh made six points on this run or the 49ers after it, Detroit probably would have caved in. But unaccountably the defense stiffened and allowed only a field goal. The 49ers had peaked.

Lions' coach George Wilson says pointedly, "The 49ers might have scored all those points too quickly.

They became clock watchers and abandoned everything that had worked for them. Their game plan seemed to change in the last two quarters. They would run the ball for three downs and punt it back. A team just asks for trouble doing that with so much time to play. It wasn't a case of a good team getting the jump on a bad one and not having to worry about getting caught. Either team had the capability of scoring a lot of points in a hurry. We got a couple of early breaks in that second half and the momentum clearly swung our way. There seemed to be nothing the 49ers could do to stop it, either."

The next time San Francisco had the ball, Tittle fumbled and the Lions' Bob Long recovered at the 49ers' 28-yard line. Into the backfield at running back came squat Tom ("the Bomb") Tracy, nicknamed as much for his appearance as his running. Nine plays later, with six minutes left in the third quarter, Tracy bowled over from the 1-yard line for a touchdown, cutting the edge to 27–14.

The 49ers were still taking no chances. Tittle ran three plays, and when the Lions held, the 49ers were forced to kick. Suddenly, as if rushing to fill a vacuum, the Lions seized control of the game with a play so daring that it seemed foolhardy. On fourth down with the Lions at their 20-yard line, Wilson ordered a pass instead of a punt. Incredibly, Rote connected, for 14 yards to Howard ("Hopalong") Cassady and a first down. The Lions were on their way.

Two plays later Rote faked a pitchout to Gene Gedman, spun around, and handed the ball to Tracy heading across the block of right guard Harley Sewell on a superb trap play. Sewell obliterated defensive end Ed Henke, and Tracy made like McElhenny. He danced through the secondary, dodging and ducking tackles, reversed his field, and with Gedman screening the last defender, Dicky Moegle, finished a 58-yard touchdown run. Jim Martin's extra point cut San Francisco's lead to 27–21 with 2:20 still to play in the third quarter.

Again the 49ers relinquished the ball to the Lions after only three plays. On the first play of the Lions' counterattack, Junker caught a 36-yard pass, advancing to the 49ers' 15-yard line. Having been caught paying too much attention to Tracy on that play, the San Francisco secondary was now caught paying too little, and Tracy bolted through for 10 yards to the 5. After a fake to Tracy, Gedman slipped off tackle from the 2-yard line for the tying touchdown with 44 seconds gone in the last quarter. Martin added the conversion for a 28–27 lead. In less than one quarter, the Lions had obliterated a three-touchdown lead.

At the urging of Wilson and middle linebacker Joe Schmidt, the Lions' defense now got the ball for the offense without the benefit of a punt. It smashed Perry on the first series of plays after Gedman's touchdown. He fumbled and Gil Mains recovered for the Lions. The next time Tittle had the ball, Carl Karilivacz intercepted a pass, but Tracy's lost fumble at the 49ers' 3-yard line dissipated the drive for the clinching touchdown. Unrelenting, the Lions got the ball back again, this time on an interception by Schmidt, who returned it to the 2-yard line. As desperate now as Detroit had been at the start of the half, San Francisco didn't yield an inch, but Martin kicked a field goal for a 31–27 lead. Now the 49ers needed nothing less than a touchdown, so Soltau's potent place-kicking was negated.

Y. A. attacked the Lions with one last flurry. The 49ers reached Detroit's 49-yard line with 66 seconds to play but none of their timeouts left. Defensive end Darris McCord threw Tittle for an 11-yard loss, and the 49ers' quarterback hurried to get off the next play and stop the clock. But Mains burst through and was on Tittle before he had a chance even to aim the ball. It fluttered impotently toward the sidelines, where right linebacker Roger Zatkoff made the interception, the third in the last ten minutes for Detroit. The amazing Lions' comeback and 49ers' collapse was complete.

When the teams were secured in their dressing rooms again, the walls reverberated with shouts once more, but of course this time it was the Lions who were doing the celebrating. The 49ers had already done theirs. □

Detroit	7	0	14	10—31
San Francisco	14	10	3	0—27

SF—Owens 34 pass from Tittle (Soltau kick)
SF—McElhenny 47 pass from Tittle (Soltau kick)
Det—Junker 3 pass from Rote (Martin kick)
SF—Wilson 12 pass from Tittle (Soltau kick)
SF—FG Soltau 25
SF—FG Soltau 10
Det—Tracy 1 run (Martin kick)
Det—Tracy 58 run (Martin kick)
Det—Gedman 2 run (Martin kick)
Det—FG Martin 10

A FIELD GOAL IN THE SNOW

New York Giants vs. Cleveland Browns

DECEMBER 14, 1958

The Giants had to beat the Browns twice in a row at the end of the season for the 1958 Eastern Conference championship. And to do it, they had to contain the great Jim Brown. They faltered on the first play from scrimmage, when Brown galloped 65 yards for a score.

New York's Pat Summerall, barely able to see the white goal posts, had just kicked an impossible, astonishing 49-yard field goal across snow-swept Yankee Stadium, giving the Giants a crucial 13–10 victory over the division-leading Cleveland Browns. It was as if an entire season had condensed itself into a single, florid moment—a moment that described perfectly the parabolic rise of the Giants' fortunes.

For the 1958 Giants were an enigma. A diehard fan might well have anticipated in early summer

The Giants evened the score at 13–13 when Bob Schnelker (85) beat Junior Wren (42) and Ken Konz (22) on the halfback option pass. Moments before, the Giants had worked the same play to Kyle Rote for 39 yards.

great things from them. But despite a peerless coaching staff, which included Vince Lombardi and Tom Landry, in those days assistants to head coach Jim Lee Howell, and despite a polished veteran roster that included Charlie Conerly, Frank Gifford, Kyle Rote, Emlen Tunnell, Rosey Grier, and Sam Huff, the Giants slogged through a dismal 0–5 preseason. Then the regular season began, and after four contests, the Giants found their record a quailing 2–2, while undefeated Cleveland led the Eastern Division at 4–0.

But the Giants clawed their way into contention. Inspired by Tom Landry's potent defense, New York eked out clutch wins against the Colts and the Lions. By the final Sunday of the regular season, the tenacious Giants needed but a victory over Cleveland to tie in the standings and force a playoff. The schedule maker was a genius. To reach the lofty plateau of a championship game, the Giants needed to conquer coach Paul Brown's formidable Cleveland squad not once but twice—there could be no ties—in a week's span.

The Browns had proved themselves to be a tough, offense-minded team, featuring a heady mixture of slashing dash and drive epitomized by the angry power of fullback Jimmy Brown. The brains of the outfit was coach Brown, widely regarded as best in the business. A taciturn, coolly efficient man, Brown did not take risks. Calling each play from the sidelines, he favored quick thrusts through the middle of the line. To confuse opposing linebackers, he varied these running plays with a devilish assortment of short, high-percentage passes, basic turn-outs, and screens to his running backs. When anxious defensive backfield men dared inch closer to the line of scrimmage, Brown went for the bomb.

There was something predictable about all this. Brown patiently stuck to a rigid game plan. It was a fine plan. But Tom Landry divined a pattern from it. A trained industrial engineer, Landry meticulously documented Cleveland's plays, cross-referencing the down, distance, field position, time in the game, and score. From his analysis Landry predicted that if the Giants smothered the Cleveland running attack, coach Brown could be depended upon to call a prearranged sequence of pass plays. In this way, the Giants' front four could know exactly when the Cleveland quarterback was preparing to throw the ball. Landry had proved his theory in the first Cleveland contest, when the Giants had battled from behind three times and won 21–17.

"He used to tell us that people have habits and can only do certain things," Andy Robustelli recalls. "If a player only can run outside, coaches program him to do just that. If you are facing a good passing quarterback, then you know you will see a lot of passes. 'Trump your aces,' he'd say. He'd always tell us we'd match our defenses against what the other guy does best and not worry about what he won't or can't do."

Thanks to Landry, the Giants' defense perfected a new look, the 4–3 alignment, which was widely copied throughout professional football. Four solid, sturdy linemen fronted the squad: Robustelli, Dick Modzelewski, Rosey Grier, and Jim Katcavage. Three cat-quick linebackers followed: Harland Svare, Sam Huff, and Cliff Livingston. Patrolling the backfield were Hall of Famer Emlen Tunnell, Jim Patton, Lindon Crow, and Carl Karilivacz.

The 4–3 defense depended upon an interlocking arrangement of the four linemen, each controlling his own area. When a lineman's turf was invaded, the linebackers and defensive backs would assist with the tackle. On a pass play, Landry counted on the four linemen's great strength and agility to break down a quarterback's protection and force him to unload the ball before the receivers downfield had wriggled free. Coverage in the backfield was man to man.

Clearly, the disciplined Cleveland offense was the sternest challenge Landry's 4–3 formation had yet faced. On the game's first play, the Browns prevailed mightily. Big Jim Brown bowled over the middle of the Giants' line and chugged 65 yards for a touchdown. But then the Giants' defense stiffened, and Brown gained only 83 more yards that afternoon. Summerall and Lou Groza traded field goals and the score stood 10–3 Cleveland at the half.

During halftime, flanker Kyle Rote told quarterback Charley Conerly that Cleveland defenders Don Paul and Junior Wren were vulnerable to the pass on the halfback option because they were coming up to force the sweep. He said he had only to swivel left instead of right to get free. "We sat on that play waiting for the right time, and when it got to the five-minute mark of the fourth quarter, Charley figured that was the right time," Frank Gifford says.

Moments before, Jimmy Brown had slipped and fumbled, and Robustelli had recovered on the Cleveland 45-yard line. On the first play from scrimmage, Conerly pitched out to Gifford, who veered smartly right, three blockers leading, as if to run a power sweep. The Browns' defense was completely fooled. Rote mimicked a block, then broke downfield as Gifford unloaded. Pumping valiantly on worn-out knees, the receiver was caught from behind at the 6-yard line. Two inside power runs fizzled and on third-and-goal Conerly repeated the option pass. This time Gifford lofted a touchdown to tight end Bob Schnelker. Summerall's extra point made it 10–10.

Since a tie would give them the Eastern Division title, the Browns stalled on their next possession, no doubt hoping that the snowy weather would prevent the Giants from scoring.

47

But after three leisurely running plays, Milt Plum was rushed hard on his punt and the Giants took the ball at midfield. Conerly drove the Giants swiftly to the Cleveland 29, and Pat Summerall was called upon to attempt a 36-yard field goal. Summerall admits he was nervous. His kicking had been erratic over the course of the season and a week before this game he had injured his knee. The instant he kicked the football he knew it was flubbed. He watched it spoon sickeningly to the left. With five minutes to play, he was convinced he had blown the game and the title.

"I wanted to stay on the field and play defense if I had to," Summerall says today. "I thought I'd never get another chance. When I went back and sat down, my head was hanging to my knees. But four or five guys came over and said, 'Forget it.' That's the *nice* thing to say to anyone who misses a kick or drops a touchdown pass. But I didn't really feel anything until Cliff Livingston came over and

said, 'We'll get the ball back. You'll get another shot.' Then I truly believed I would."

Summerall's chance came when Plum muffed another punt near midfield. On third-and-long, Conerly lofted a perfect pass to Alex Webster on the goal line. Webster dropped it. "If I had caught that ball, no one ever would have heard of you," Webster told Summerall later.

It was growing late. The snowfall, which had stopped around game time and then resumed, now covered the darkening stadium like a clean, white lid. The footing was treacherous, the field markings invisible. A bitter, weary gloom engulfed the sixty-three thousand Giants fans. It was fourth-and-long on the Cleveland 42.

Summerall remembers setting up behind Conerly. He thought about missing. Minutes before, he had missed an easier one. This was the second. There would be no third. "Vince Lombardi, our offensive coach, wanted to try a pass for the

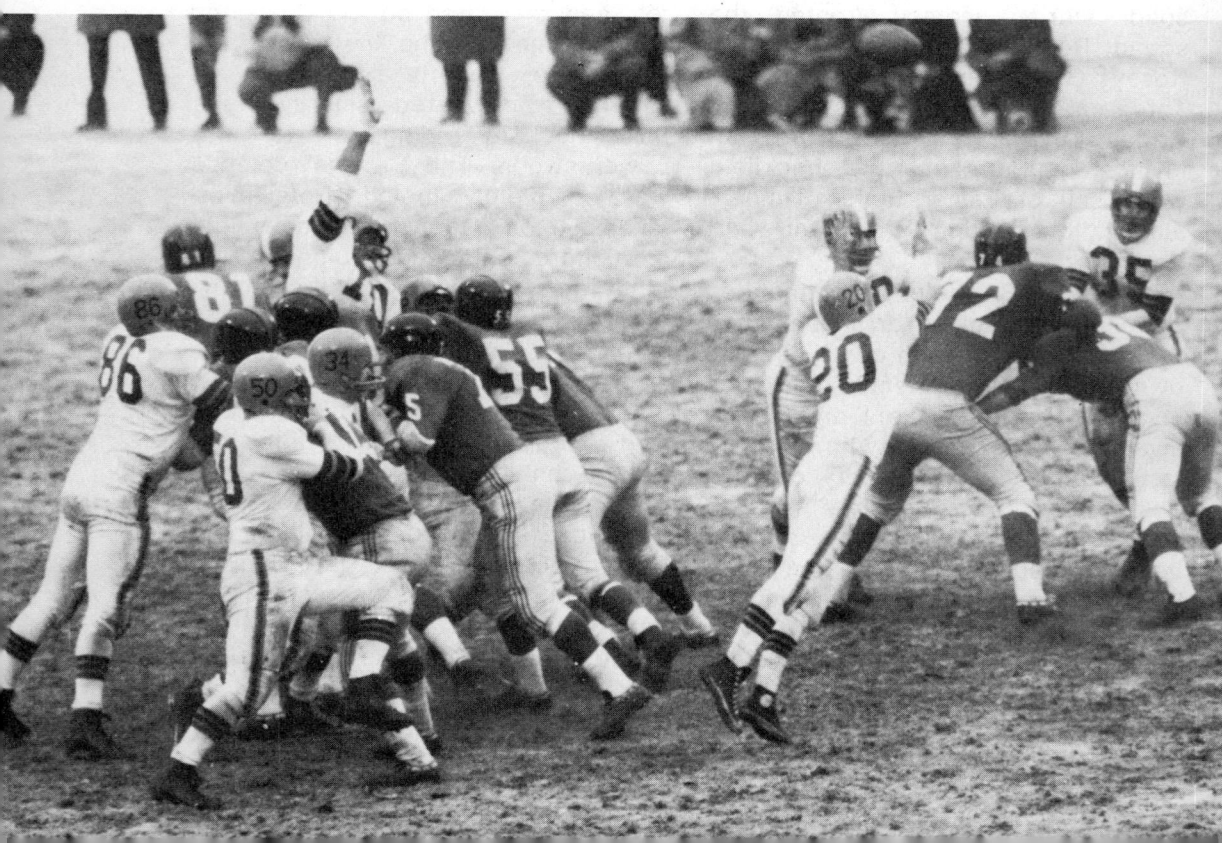

first down and tried to talk Jim Lee out of the field goal. But Jim looked at me, asked me about the leg, then said, 'Go kick it,' " Summerall says.

A kneeling Conerly methodically brushed away the snow from the spot where the ball would rest. The Cleveland defense massed at the line, ready, confident. A linebacker screamed, "Stay on sides! Stay on sides!" The ball spiraled back into Conerly's hands and he spun the laces toward the center of the goal posts, nearly 50 yards away. Summerall presented a vivid picture, poised, helmet down, his quick leg lifted at a ninety-degree angle above the crouched form of holder Conerly. The tiny ball flew toward the end zone, tumbling endlessly through the cold, black air.

"As soon as I hit it, I knew it would be far enough," Summerall says. "But from that distance a ball often has a tendency to float, like a knuckleball. I watched it all the way and as it passed the ten-yard line, I could see that it was inside the left upright. Then it straightened itself out and was okay."

Okay? That ball sailed straight through the uprights and plopped to the ground ten yards back. The New York faithful erupted in a frenzy. Two minutes and seven seconds remained, but the Giants' defense quickly stamped out a feeble Cleveland drive and the game was over. And the following week Summerall and the Giants did it again. He kicked another field goal and they did not allow Cleveland a score, winning 10–0.

Pat still remembers greeting Lombardi at the sidelines after his game-winning 49-yard kick. "He was the first person I saw and he said, 'You know you can't kick a football that far, don't you?' "

Cleveland	7	3	0	0—10
New York	3	0	0	10—13

Cle—Brown 65 run (Groza kick)
NY—FG Summerall 41
Cle—FG Groza 33
NY—Schnelker 6 pass from Gifford (Summerall kick)
NY—FG Summerall 49

The snow had stopped and night had fallen when Pat Summerall, who moments earlier had missed from the 36-yard line, kicked a winning 49-yard field goal.

MASTERPIECE FOR THE MASSES

Baltimore Colts vs. New York Giants

DECEMBER 28, 1958

The 1958 National Football League championship game stands alone. Many consider it the greatest game ever played. That can be argued. But it is beyond dispute that the Baltimore Colts' 23–17 sudden-death victory over the New York Giants captivated a nationwide television audience, creating millions of new fans for NFL football. Henceforth, the NFL championship would rival the World Series as a national event.

A growing interest in the NFL coincided with the rising fortunes of the New York Giants. The Giants were the first of a host of memorable, innovative defensive teams. And it was defense—the bone-jarring tackles and goal-line stands—that the fans cheered the loudest. Since winning

the 1956 NFL title, the Giants had become extremely popular in the New York area, and their fame soon spread throughout the land, borne by the New York wire services, networks, and magazines. This was the "big blue team of destiny," a miracle team that won dramatically, as two clutch late-season victories over Cleveland seemed to prove. Who could resist miracles?

Surely not the Baltimore Colts, who had lost to the Giants earlier in the season. True, the powerful Baltimore offense, featuring Lenny Moore, Alan Ameche, L. G. Dupre, and Raymond Berry, led the league in scoring. But 25-year-old quarterback Johnny Unitas, a cast-off from the Pittsburgh Steelers in 1955, was not yet considered a superstar. And Baltimore on the whole wasn't considered as

strong as the Cleveland Browns, a team the Giants had beaten three times.

Though the Giants were a tired and bruised team (their two clutch wins over Cleveland had badly hobbled defensive tackle Rosey Grier, who would play only sporadically against Baltimore), still they were the favorites, and it was somewhat of a surprise when the underdog Colts easily surged to a 14–3 halftime lead. Pat Summerall's field goal had put the Giants ahead. But the Colts capitalized on a pair of fumbles by Frank Gifford, scoring touchdowns after each. The second score came on a brilliant 88-yard drive by Unitas, capped by a 15-yard pass to Berry.

Unitas was just as sharp at the start of the second half, marching the Colts to New York's 3-yard line. But the

The 1958 NFL title game featured the Baltimore Colts' comeback in the last quarter and win in overtime. But first the New York Giants overcame a 14–3 Colts' halftime lead. Opposite: Mel Triplett squeezes through for the first of two touchdowns that gave New York the lead. Above: Steve Myrha's 20-yard field goal with 7 seconds left necessitated sudden death.

Giants dug in and with an inspired goal-line stand stopped the Colts on three straight plays. Facing fourth-and-goal, Unitas called timeout and conferred with head coach Weeb Ewbank. "We talked about going for a field goal, but I wanted to bury them right there with a touchdown," Ewbank says.

The plan was for Ameche to fake a pass and run into the end zone, but the Giants weren't fooled. Linebacker Cliff Livingston burst through the Colts' line and nailed Ameche for a four-yard loss. Livingston's timely play seemed to ignite the listless New York offense. Frank Gifford and Alex Webster hurried the ball to the 13-yard line. On third-and-two, quarterback Charley Conerly hit Kyle Rote at the Baltimore 40-yard line. Dashing upfield, Rote was tackled hard and the ball popped loose. But Webster, trailing the play, retrieved the ball and carried it to the 1-yard line. Fullback Mel Triplett powered in for the score. Suddenly, momentum seemed to swing the Giants' way.

Starting from the New York 19-yard line on the next series, Conerly

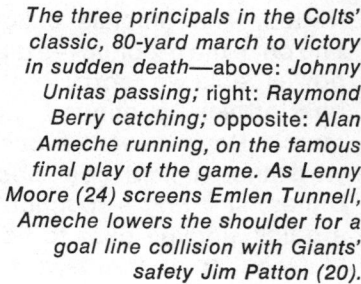

The three principals in the Colts' classic, 80-yard march to victory in sudden death—above: Johnny Unitas passing; right: Raymond Berry catching; opposite: Alan Ameche running, on the famous final play of the game. As Lenny Moore (24) screens Emlen Tunnell, Ameche lowers the shoulder for a goal line collision with Giants' safety Jim Patton (20).

threw a 17-yard pass to Bob Schnelker. He then faked a handoff to Webster and lofted the ball to Schnelker again, who carried it up to the Colts' 15-yard line. When the Baltimore defense rolled right, Gifford peeled left, beating the linebacker on a touchdown pass. Fifty-three seconds into the last quarter, the Giants led 17–14.

While time slipped away, the New Yorkers smothered two Baltimore drives. With less than three minutes left in the game, Conerly faced a third-and-four at New York's 40-yard line. A first down would all but ensure

victory, so Conerly called New York's best power play, an off-tackle run to the right by Gifford, following the blocks of Roosevelt Brown and Schnelker against Gino Marchetti and Art Donovan. But Marchetti, though he fractured his leg on this play, fought off Schnelker's block and, with the help of 300-pound Gene ("Big Daddy") Lipscomb, dragged Gifford down. Gifford had bounced past the first-down marker, but head linesman Charley Berry, ignoring the moans of the Giants' fans, moved the ball back. On fourth-and-inches, head coach Jim

Lee Howell ordered a punt. To this day Gifford insists he made the first down.

Many have second-guessed his decision because it proved to be the pivotal moment in the game. Assistant coach Vince Lombardi, for one, defended Howell. "I would have done the same thing every time," Lombardi said. "Don Chandler's kick was a beauty. The Colts had to fair catch it at their fourteen-yard line and I was sure then it was all over."

So were the more than 64,000 spectators jamming Yankee Stadium, who settled back to watch the Colts try to negotiate the seemingly non-negotiable New York defense. The Giants' defense had been superb in the second half. The Colts had floundered under New York's pressure. Unitas' passes had been off-target.

But now, suddenly, the talented young quarterback rallied his forces for a pressure-defying march downfield. "We were so damned disgusted with ourselves that when we got the ball for that last series, we struck back at the Giants in a sort of blind fury," Unitas says.

On third-and-10 Unitas hit Lenny Moore on the 25-yard line, a key play because the Giants then double-teamed Moore, freeing Berry to run his patterns. On the next play Berry slanted through the middle for a 25-yard completion. Then he made a diving catch at New York's 35-yard line in front of Carl Karilivacz. Next, Berry hooked in front of Karilivacz and caught the ball at the 13-yard line. With 30 seconds to play, the Colts' field-goal unit quickly assembled. Kicker Steve Myhra sent the ball spinning through the uprights. When time expired, the score stood 17–17.

The Giants' fans were stunned by the sudden turnabout. An overtime period, the first in NFL history, would be needed to decide the championship. The Giants won the coin toss, received the ball, and missed a first down by a yard. Chandler's long punt backed up the Colts to their 20-yard line.

Once again, the young field marshal went to work. "I wanted to move the ball on the ground to minimize any chances of losing the ball," Unitas says.

He called on Dupre, who rumbled 11 yards on a power sweep. On third-and-eight Ameche caught a flare pass for a first down. Facing yet another third down, Unitas fired 21 yards to Berry. With the Giants' defense anticipating a pass, Ameche charged through the middle for 23 yards.

As the nation edged closer to its television sets, captivated by the brilliant play-calling and execution by Unitas, suddenly a technical flaw blacked out the picture. For two and a half minutes football fans everywhere fretted. The officials called timeout, and once the problem—a disconnected power cable was corrected—the Colts' quarterback continued his historic march. Berry caught a pass at the 8-yard line. A field goal beckoned but Unitas, smelling a touchdown, tossed a quick sideline pass to tight end Jim Mutscheller at the 1-yard line. Then he called a power play.

"When I slapped the ball into Ameche's belly and saw him take off, I knew nobody was going to stop him," Unitas says. Nobody did. Eight minutes and 15 seconds into the overtime period, Ameche burst into the end zone.

Said Raymond Berry, "It's the greatest thing that's ever happened."

□

Baltimore	0	14	0	3	6—23
New York	3	0	7	7	0—17

NY—FG Summerall 36
Bal—Ameche 2 run (Myhra kick)
Bal—Berry 15 pass from Unitas (Myhra kick)
NY—Triplett 1 run (Summerall kick)
NY—Gifford 15 pass from Conerly (Summerall kick)
Bal—FG Myhra 20
Bal—Ameche 1 run (no kick)

In 1959, playing the defending NFL champion Baltimore Colts, Jim Brown had the most productive day of his career. He scored five touchdowns, and the Browns needed every one, winning 38–31. Here he plunges over from the 1-yard line for his fifth score.

GOLDEN BROWN

Cleveland Browns vs. Baltimore Colts

NOVEMBER 1, 1959

Jim Brown was the kingpin running back of his era. Built like a black Adonis, he was quick, strong, agile, and durable, never missing a game during his nine-year career with the Cleveland Browns. He was also dangerous. Few runners could hurt an opponent so badly in so many ways.

Unlike most fullbacks, Brown was a constant threat to break away. Up close, wedged between linemen, he'd twist and shimmy and punch his way into the clear. Oftentimes, seized by a tackler, he'd play possum, sagging

supinely from head to foot only to wrestle free when the startled tackler eased his grip. Though a solid 225 pounds, Brown was among the swiftest and trickiest open-field runners ever. Paul Brown, his coach, adopted option blocking to accommodate his fluid, improvisational style. A phalanx of blockers would precede him across the field while Brown took advantage of the openings.

Brown quit pro football at his peak to become a movie star. Even so, his abbreviated totals set standards that still elude National Football League running backs. His one-season rushing mark of 1,863 yards in 1963 was bested a decade later by O. J. Simpson. But his career totals of 2,359 carries, 12,312 yards, and 5.22 average, remain all-time highs.

In the days when stopping Brown was something of an obsession throughout the league, no other team enjoyed the success against him that the New York Giants did, thanks mainly to the efforts of defensive coach Tom Landry. Landry's celebrated 4–3 wasn't much different from what the Dallas Cowboys employ today. Each of the four linemen was expected to control a specific area until the point of attack was determined. Then the linebackers and defensive backs would move up and assist with the tackle. The key man was the middle linebacker, usually the first to see and react to the unfolding play.

Sam Huff probably wasn't New York's best defensive man or the NFL's finest middle linebacker. But he was fast and smart and a hard-hitter. As the public became increasingly interested in defense, he attracted plenty of media attention, particularly after appearing in a network television special, "The Violent World of Sam Huff" in which his gear was wired for

56

Never one to lose his cool, Brown endured the assaults of such combative defenders as Sam Huff, (70) opposite, with such equanimity that he seemed more placid in the game than on the sidelines, above.

sound. Soon after, flattering articles and books appeared, and coupled with the glamour of Jim Brown, confrontations between the two took on the drama of a mano-a-mano.

Though the two faced one another in college, their rivalry didn't really catch fire until after the Giants beat the Browns out of an Eastern Division title in 1958, and again in 1959. There were also insinuations of bad blood between the pair. This was never true, though. Gentleness was not among Huff's outstanding virtues.

"We didn't get paid to look fancy," Huff says. "The idea was to stop the runner the best way you could. Sometimes I twisted their heads a little, but most of them didn't seem to mind. I always felt I played clean. Football is a man's game, and any guy who doesn't want to hit hard doesn't belong in it. The football field is no place for a crybaby."

Brown acknowledged Huff's on-field peccadillos. Indeed, he considered Huff's aggressive style a backhanded compliment. "If I were a middle linebacker playing against a back who received the ballyhoo I did, I'd make the same special effort," Brown says. "I got it all, from the guys who would hit and let it go at that, to the ones who'd hit and then keep at it until the whistle blew. The Giants' coaches keyed Huff on me quite a bit. He played hard but not dirty. I think there was only one game where he got out of line and twisted my head at the bottom of a pile. 'That's not like you, Huff,' I told him. But that was it. Normally, I wouldn't even tell an opponent he was overdoing it. But in Sam's case, I figured he might appreciate my opinion because we'd been slamming each other since college."

Sam was very fond of the Cleveland star. Once, after a bitterly fought

New York victory over the Browns, a reporter asked Huff if he resented Brown because he was black. Sam was a West Virginian and the inference was obvious. The reporter was ordered from the locker room.

"Jim Brown was a phenomenal running back, the greatest who ever played," Huff says. "I am proud to have played on the same field with him. No matter how hard you hit him, he never said a harsh word. If you tackled him or gave him a good lick, he'd pat you on the fanny and say, 'Nice tackle, big Sam.' Pretty soon you'd think, 'Boy, what a great guy!' He'd lull you to sleep that way. The next thing you'd know, he would come running through like a freight train. When you hit him, it was like hitting an oak tree."

Another defensive nemesis during Jim Brown's heyday was the legendary Gene ("Big Daddy") Lipscomb of the champion Baltimore Colts. A human mountain at 6 feet 6 inches, 300 pounds, Lipscomb acquired the nasty habit of squashing star running backs like so many empty beer cans.

"Big Daddy was the only defensive player I ever tried to psych," Brown says. "I didn't taunt him or try to intimidate him. Only a fool would have tried that. I didn't want him mad at me. The thing that inspired him most was the chance to make mincemeat out of a star."

A week before the Browns were scheduled to meet the Colts in 1959, Lipscomb told the press that he'd been "waiting a long time to get my hands on that Cleveland cat." There was no special grudge between the two, but then, Big Daddy's challenges, like his silent moods, tended to be implacable. Jim Ray Smith, the all-pro guard charged with blocking Lipscomb, wasn't worried a bit. He did a superb job. Time and time again, Brown ran right over the huge tackle, or he'd slide off to the side, leaving Big Daddy in the dust. Early in the second quarter, Brown took a pitchout from quarterback Milt Plum and

Opposite: *Brought down by Don Shinnick (66). ("Big Daddy" Lipscomb, 76, is at the far left.)* Above: *Assisted by Lou Groza, in sidestepping Ordell Brasse (81) and Milt Davis (20).*

58

stormed 70 yards for a touchdown. Minutes later, he scored another.

At halftime, as the players straggled off the field, Big Daddy collared Brown.

"Look Jimmy," he said, "you were laughing at me out there. I don't like that."

"Daddy, I didn't say a thing," Brown replied. "What are you talking about?"

"You were making fun of me, boy," Lipscomb shot back. "I'm gonna get you in the second half. You look out. I'm gonna get you. I thought you were my friend."

But nothing came of it. Lipscomb had to spend much of the second half pursuing halfback Bobby Mitchell. And when the Colts began to look for the halfback, Brown galloped forward with the ball. At times poor Big Daddy nearly overturned the entire Cleveland bench. Meanwhile, Brown scored three more touchdowns and Cleveland won 38–31, negating a remarkable, four-touchdown, 397-yard

passing performance by Baltimore quarterback John Unitas. On the day, Jim Brown gained all but 19 of his team's 197-yard rushing total. Even the highly partisan Baltimore rooters could not begrudge him a standing ovation. Paul Brown called his performance "one of the greatest ever," and Big Daddy Lipscomb moaned to the reporters surrounding his locker, "I'm still waiting to get my hands on that cat." He wasn't the first or the last whom the big cat eluded. □

Cleveland	3	14	14	7—38
Baltimore	3	7	7	14—31

Balt—FG Myhra 23
Cle—FG Groza 16
Cle—Brown 70 run (Groza kick)
Balt—Moore 5 pass from Unitas (Myhra kick)
Cle—Brown 17 run (Groza kick)
Cle—Brown 3 run (Groza kick)
Balt—Richardson 7 pass from Unitas (Myhra kick)
Cle—Brown 1 run (Groza kick)
Balt—Berry 11 pass from Unitas (Myhra kick)
Cle—Brown 1 run (Groza kick)
Balt—Mutscheller 5 pass from Unitas (Myhra kick)

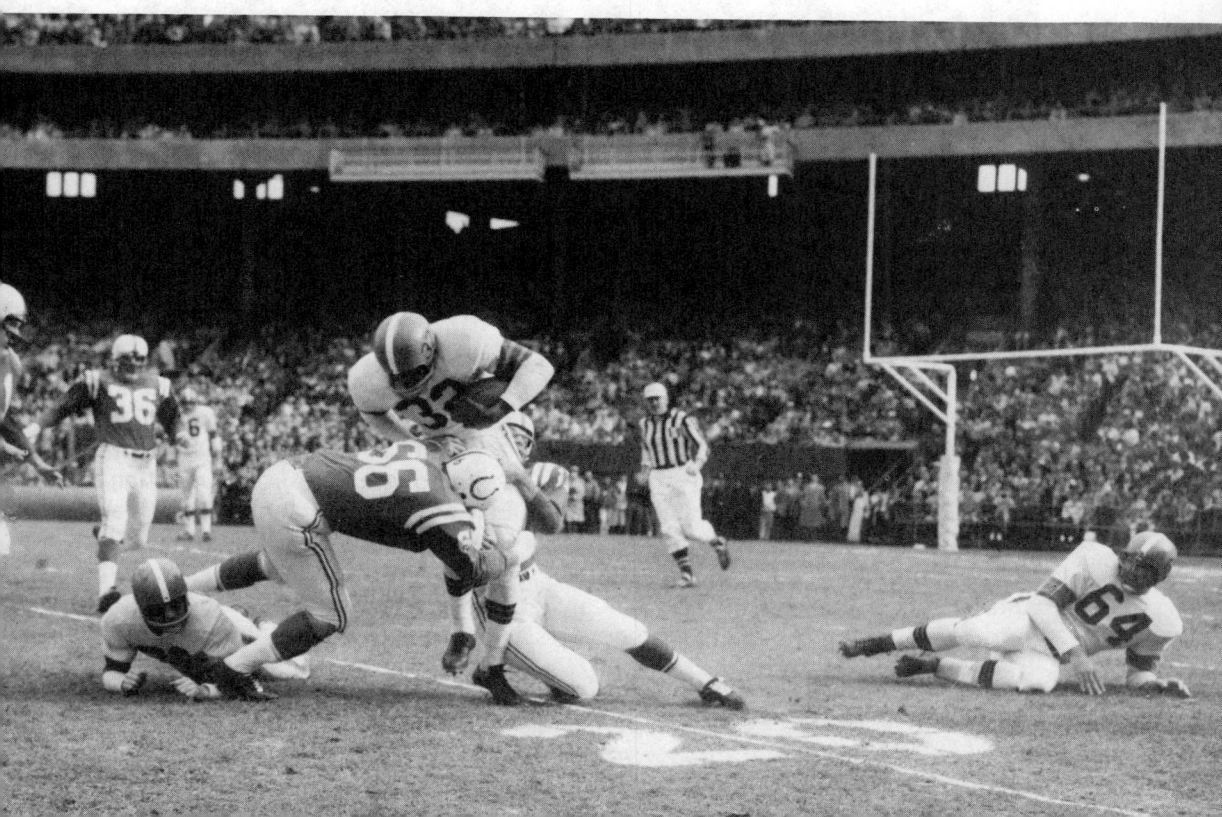

WELCOME TO THE AFL

Denver vs. Boston, Houston vs. Los Angeles

1960

They called themselves the American Football League and played in such exotic places as Buffalo, Denver, and Oakland and the ancient Polo Grounds, already slated for the wrecking ball. Some of them, in that first season of 1960, were simply National Football League castoffs—lame and grizzled has-beens. But many more were talented players who never quite cut it in the established league, men who craved a second chance to prove they could play pro ball.

The AFL was the brainchild of Texas oil millionaires Bud Adams and Lamar Hunt, who had been rebuffed in their attempts to buy new NFL franchises. In a few months they enlisted backers to sponsor AFL franchises in Houston, Dallas, Oakland, Los Ange-

The championship game between the Houston Oilers and the Los Angeles Chargers closed the American Football League's first season. George Blanda (16), one of the refugees from the National Football League to the new league, guided the Oilers to a 24–16 victory.

les, New York, Boston, Denver, and Buffalo.

By July 1960, less than a year after the league had been founded, the AFL had signed players and coaches, opened training camps, and even had a five-year television contract with ABC worth nearly $9 million. Some of the players were familiar already to NFL fans: George Blanda, Cotton Davidson, Frank Tripucka, Frank Gatski, Tommy O'Connell, Maurice Bassett, Cookie Gilchrist. But others, the vast majority, were like the shadowy three hundred who flocked to the University of Massachusetts in hopes of making the roster of the newly formed Boston Patriots, only to slip back forever into obscurity.

Despite the jeers of comfortable

The pioneers of the American Football League included (seated, left to right) Bud Adams, Commissioner Joe Foss, and Harry Wismer. Lamar Hunt (standing third from left) was the original moving force.

NFL owners who controlled all the best talent and cities, the AFL was no joke. Some of the teams, notably those owned by Adams and Hunt, signed some fine college talent, including Heisman trophy winner Billy Cannon of LSU. Cannon signed with Houston for a lucrative bonus following LSU's victory in the Sugar Bowl. The league also attracted a flock of out-of-work coaches and former NFL greats, among them Eddie Erdelatz of Navy, Sid Gillman, who had been fired by the Rams the season before, Sammy Baugh, Lou Rymkus, Frank Filchock, and Lou Saban.

Ignoring predictions of imminent financial disaster, the AFL staged its first regular season game on September 9, 1960, in Boston. For a while, there was a problem finding a field for the opener. The Boston Patriots did not have a permanent home field. Harvard University and Boston Col-

lege said no. The Boston Red Sox wouldn't tolerate football at Fenway Park. The Patriots' choice finally fell to dowdy old Braves Field, erstwhile home of baseball's Boston Braves and a one-time pro football team called the Boston Yanks, which had failed for lack of fan support.

Many predicted the same fate for the Patriots. In that first season their offices opened in a basement, causing certain fans to snicker predictably, "They can't go any lower." Feuds between management and the coaches were as common as fumbles. For more than a decade the team lacked a home field. Once, they were even forced to schedule a home game in Birmingham, Alabama. The Patriots' prospects on the field weren't much brighter. Their quarterback was Butch Songin, a 36-year-old NFL and Canadian Football League player. Songin earned $9,000 for the season, a step up from the $50 per game he earned on the sandlots. The Patriots' top draft pick was Gerhard Schwedes, a highly touted Syracuse halfback who signed a multi-year, no-cut contract. In his three years with Boston, Schwedes almost never played.

But the Patriots' problems seemed minor when compared with those of their first-game opponents, the Denver Broncos. The Broncos had lost all five of their preseason games (including a crushing 43-6 loss to Boston), surrendering more than 200 points in the process. It surprised no one that Denver trotted onto the field a 16-point underdog. The fans packing Braves Field didn't seem to care, as long as the advertised product was pro football. They listened to Howard Keel sing the national anthem, then watched a 6-foot 5-inch lineman named Tony Discenzo execute the first official AFL kickoff.

Surprisingly, the game was a close one. The Broncos had strengthened their defense, and the Patriots didn't score until late in the first quarter when Gino Cappelletti, an ex-bartender from Minnesota, kicked a 35-yard field goal. Denver fought back. Quarterback Frank Tripucka lofted a swing pass to halfback Al Carmichael, who raced 59 yards for a touchdown. Denver's Gene Mingo later returned a punt 76 yards for a score, though he then missed the extra point. The final score came late in the third quarter when Boston's Jim Colclough caught a 10-yard touchdown pass. Denver held on, defeating the overconfident Patriots 13–10.

The AFL had come to stay. But for the remainder of that first season, most of the teams struggled at the gate. Hardest hit were the league's flagship teams, New York and Los Angeles. In New York, the Titans' flamboyant owner, broadcaster Harry Wismer, ran a budget-conscious operation from his Park Avenue apartment. Titans' fans sometimes selected their seats from among tickets strewn across Harry's bed. On the field the Titans were an embarrassment. When the fans stayed away, preferring instead the highly successful New York Giants of the NFL, an unfazed Wismer simply inflated the attendance figures he gave the press. As one reporter put it after scanning the vast, vacant Polo Grounds, "People showed up disguised as empty seats."

In Los Angeles the Chargers, winners of the Western Division title, drew sparse crowds also. The Chargers took the hint and moved to San Diego the next season.

The Houston Oilers were one of the new league's few early successes at the gate. More than 32,000 of their fans jammed Jeppesen Stadium for the nationally televised AFL championship game. It was quite a finale to the season. Leading 17–16 late in the game, Houston quarterback George Blanda threw an 88-yard touchdown bomb to Billy Cannon, and Houston won 24–16. Cannon accumulated 250 yards rushing, receiving, and returning punts, and was named the game's most valuable player. He had had a good rookie season, and so, on balance, had his new league. □

Denver   0 7 6 0—13
Boston   3 0 7 0—10
Bos—FG Cappelletti 35
Den—Carmichael 59 pass from Tripucka (Mingo kick)
Den—Mingo 76 punt return (kick failed)
Bos—Colclough 10 pass from Songin (Capelletti kick)

Los Angeles 6 3 7 0—16
Houston   0 10 7 7—24
LA—FG Agajanian 33
LA—FG Agajanian 32
Hou—Smith 17 pass from Blanda (Blanda kick)
Hou—FG Blanda 18
LA—FG Agajanian 27
Hou—Groman 7 pass from Blanda (Blanda kick)
LA—Lowe 2 run (Agajanian kick)
Hou—Cannon 88 pass from Blanda (Blanda kick)

CHUCK BEDNARIK:
LAST OF THE TWO-WAY TERRORS

Philadelphia Eagles vs. Green Bay Packers

DECEMBER 26, 1960

Before his last and perhaps his greatest pro game, the 1960 NFL championship, Chuck Bednarik (right) of the Philadelphia Eagles, greeted a fellow center, the Green Bay Packers' Jim Ringo.

Chuck Bednarik was the last of a durable breed—the two-way football player. Both as an outside linebacker and an offensive center for the Philadelphia Eagles, Bednarik played 58 minutes against the Green Bay Packers in the 1960 National Football League championship game. It was the fourth time during the season that he covered two positions in a single game. Each of these was an important Philadelphia victory, including a last-second triumph over Cleveland, back-to-back wins over the Giants, and finally the league championship. An impressive physical feat for a young man, a startling one for a veteran who was 35 years old.

"It amazes me today when I think about it," Bednarik says. "But then, it was mind over matter. We were winning and that's what was important."

Philadelphia coach Buck Shaw never planned to use Bednarik as a two-way player when the season began. The Eagles and all the other teams had converted to the platoon system a decade earlier, using specialists on offense and defense. Bednarik was the regular Philly center. He had converted to center two years before when a knee injury seemed to end his career as an outstanding linebacker. But late in the 1960 season, during a game against Cleveland, Philadelphia linebackers Bob Pellegrini and John Nocera were injured, and Bednarik was the only reserve left to play the position.

"I never expected it," Bednarik says. "I was sitting on the bench and Buck called me over. 'You're the only guy left,' he told me. 'Get in there, but don't pull any hero stuff.' I played the rest of the game."

Bednarik was perfect for his two-way role. Aging linebackers are considered fair game in pro football, but few dared tussle with Bednarik. In a game against the Giants, for example, the Eagles' starting center, rookie Bill Latham, was simply overwhelmed by the veteran Giants' defense. Bednarik replaced him in the second half and the Eagles' offense began to roll smoothly. In the same game Bednarik terminated Frank Gifford's season and very nearly his career with a devastating, though clean, tackle that caused a fumble Bednarik recovered. Gifford was carted off to the hospital with a severe concussion. He remained out of action until 1962. The New Yorkers cried "cheap shot," but Bednarik only smiled and savored the victory.

Bednarik played linebacker for the rest of the season, doubling at center for the two Giants games. In the second game he played nearly 53 minutes, and the Eagles came from behind, wrapping up the Eastern Division title.

"There was no question that I would play both ways against Green Bay," he recalls. "Pellegrini was out and there just wasn't anyone else with any experience, so that settled the matter."

The championship game fell on a Monday in 1960, the day after Christmas. The Eagles trotted onto Philadelphia's Franklin Field seven point underdogs to the Western Division champs, the Packers. In its second season under Vince Lombardi, Green Bay was a superb young team, with star backs Bart Starr, Paul Hornung, and Jim Taylor, all just entering their prime. Lombardi stressed running plays and a tight, error-free, ball-control offense. It was a sturdy game plan that would win him many games in the future, but on this afternoon it may have cost him the championship. In this, the first and only playoff game Lombardi was ever to lose, he may have underestimated the stubborn Philadelphia defense. Twice he declined easy field goals in favor of running plays.

Lombardi's first mistake followed the Packers' interception of a pass on the game's opening play. Faced with fourth-and-two at the Philly 6-yard line, Lombardi sent Taylor up the middle. He smacked against Bednarik and fell a yard short. "We didn't do anything too fancy on defense," Bednarik says. "We played a straight four-three, but we executed like hell. The Packers were a good team, but we just swarmed all over them."

The Eagles' defense was severely

Right: Ted Dean scores the game's decisive touchdown, aided by Eagle Billy Barnes's clutch on the leg of defensive end Bill Quinlan (83). Above: Flanked by his two sprightly veterans, Bednarik (60) and Norm Van Brocklin (11), coach Buck Shaw cradles the game ball.

tested only three plays later when the Packers' Bill Forrester recovered a fumble by Ted Dean at the Philadelphia 22-yard line. The Packers plunged ahead for 9 yards, wasted two passes, then settled for a 20-yard field goal by Hornung and a 3–0 lead. When a Green Bay drive sputtered later in the second quarter, Hornung had to kick another field goal. "We lost the game right there," Lombardi said later. "Instead of being ahead fourteen-nothing, we were ahead only six-nothing."

Minutes before halftime, yet another well-executed Green Bay drive died, this one at the 7-yard line. So that Hornung could aim with a slightly better angle for a field goal, the Packers declined a fourth-down penalty that would have moved the ball a bit closer to the goal line. But the kick missed anyway.

Meanwhile, the Eagles' offense had begun to perk up under the able guidance of veteran quarterback Norm Van Brocklin. This was the Dutchman's last game, but he played with the brash energy and enthusiasm of a youngster. Van Brocklin hit for a touchdown on a simple slant pattern to little Tommy McDonald, an All-American halfback from Oklahoma, giving the Eagles the lead. Philadelphia's Bobby Walston increased it to 10–6 with a field goal just before the half.

Late in the third quarter, a Van Brocklin pass toward the end zone was intercepted by John Symank. Green Bay then drove upfield to a score in 12 plays, a drive built predominantly around a faked punt and a 35-yard gallop by Max McGee. The touchdown came on Bart Starr's 7-yard toss to McGee, giving the Packers a 13–10 lead with about 13 minutes left in the game.

On the ensuing kickoff, Eagles' assistant coach Charlie Gauer had a surprise in store for the Packers. Gauer had noticed in the game films a weakness in the Green Bay kickoff team's front line: there were two fast men on the right side but alternating fast and slow men in the center and on the left. Gauer told his blockers to clear a path along the slower left side.

66

This they did, paving the way for Ted Dean, who sped to the Green Bay 38-yard line before he was collared from behind by Willie Wood. Then Van Brocklin took command. After the Packers suffered a holding penalty, he flipped quickly to Billy Barnes for 13 yards. Barnes next scampered to the 9-yard line. Two plays later, Dean swept left for the score. With nine minutes to go, it was Eagles 17–10.

"We would have held them," Lombardi moaned. "That kickoff return gave the Eagles a big lift and we couldn't stop them."

Green Bay's last chance for victory came with 70 seconds left in the game. Starr marched the Packers brilliantly from their 35-yard line to the Eagles' 22. But with no timeouts remaining, he had to pass. Eight pass defenders clamped the receivers, so Starr tossed the ball short to Taylor over the middle. The desperate fullback broke one tackle, another, and another. He was still blasting forward at the 10-yard line. The Eagles fans were choleric. Then Bednarik hit, high and hard, slamming Taylor to the turf.

It was a sight Philly fans still cherish: Bednarik, the huge, angry man they affectionately called "Mister Eagle," sitting on Taylor while the clock ran out.

"I could see the clock at one corner of Franklin Field," Bednarik says. "I wasn't about to move until it ran out, but he started squirming and shouting at me, 'C'mon, you bleepety-bleep, get off me.' But I didn't move until that clock hit the zero mark. Then I said, 'Okay, you bleepety-bleep, I'll get up now. You just lost.'"

For Hall of Famers Bednarik and Van Brocklin and for coach Shaw, all headed into retirement, it was a satisfying conclusion to long and memorable careers. For Lombardi and the Packers, it was time to lick wounds and plan for the future. □

Green Bay	3	3	0	7—13
Philadelphia	0	10	0	7—17

GB—FG Hornung 20
GB—FG Hornung 23
Phil—McDonald 22 pass from Van Brocklin (Walston kick)
Phil—FG Walston 15
GB—McGee 7 pass from Starr (Hornung kick)
Phil—Dean 5 run (Walston kick)

THANKSGIVING DAY MASSACRE

**Detroit Lions vs.
Green Bay Packers**

NOVEMBER 22, 1962

One of the more revealing truths in professional football is that a talented, awesomely smooth team can on one or two days at the pinnacle of its power be totally destroyed. There is no explanation in films, charts, or other technical data. The answer lies in the emotions of the men who play the game.

In 1962, the Green Bay Packers were defending their first NFL title under Vince Lombardi. They were unbeaten through the first ten games, though in one of their wins, the season opener against Detroit, they had barely survived, 9–7. It was a lucky win, and therein lay the seeds of the Packers' momentary but devastating lapse in 1962.

Detroit had gone into the final two minutes of that game with the ball and a 7–6 lead. On third down the Lions' quarterback, Milt Plum, could and

Bart Starr was the Detroit Lions' turkey on Thanksgiving Day, 1962. The Lions feasted on the quarterback 11 times, for a total of 110 yards in losses. Roger Brown (76) led this charge.

68

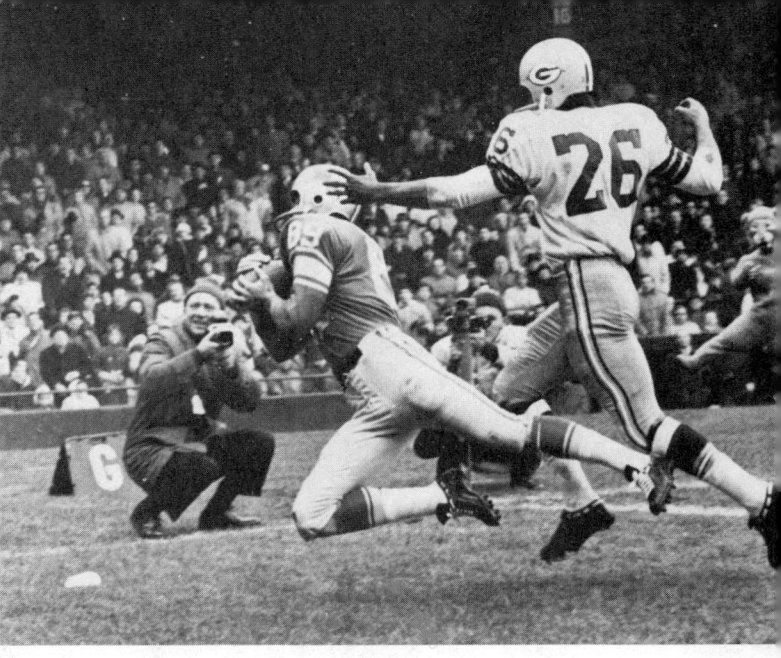

The Lions' quarterback, Milt Plum, who had thrown away an earlier game against the Packers with an ill-advised pass, atoned for his sins with two touchdown strikes to Gail Cogdill, the second over Herb Adderley (right).

should have run the ball to eat up more precious seconds. Then, if the play had failed to gain a first down, Yale Lary, the league's best punter, would have kicked out of danger. The Packers had not moved the ball all afternoon, and the Lions' defense more than likely would have held them for a last time.

However, Plum chose to risk a pass in trying for the first down, and the result was disaster. He threw toward wide receiver Terry Barr, but Barr had slipped while running his pattern and the ball settled easily into the hands of Green Bay cornerback Herb Adderley, who ran back the interception deep into Detroit territory. From there the Packers inched closer, and eventually Paul Hornung kicked the winning field goal.

The bitterness and anger that gripped the Lions after that defeat threatened to tear apart the team. At the center of the storm was Plum, disliked in general by his defensive mates for undoing their triumph over the powerful Green Bay offense. Yet the Lions' rage turned outward as well. The Packers became a hate ob-

ject for every Detroit player. It was ten weeks until the teams met again, but the Lions' craving for revenge grew only more obsessive in that time.

When the clubs did play again, on Thanksgiving Day at Detroit, the NFL's Western Conference race promised to tilt in favor of the winner. Having lost a second game, to the New York Giants by a touchdown, the Lions trailed Green Bay by two games. But the Lions were confident that a win over Green Bay would turn the season around. "I told my players that if we won that game we would win the title," Detroit coach George Wilson remembers. "All it took was for someone to show the other teams that the Packers could be beaten. We were sure they could be beaten at least one more time, and if there was a playoff, we knew we could beat them again."

To win, the Lions faced the formidable task of again putting a crimp in Green Bay's offense and this time mobilizing more of their own. It would require breaking down the well-ordered and highly disciplined Packers, whom Lombardi had insulated against such

70

The voracious Detroit defense produced a touchdown of its own when Roger Brown caused Starr to fumble. Sam Williams (88) picked up the loose ball and lumbered into the end zone, right. Two minutes later the Lions' defensive unit added a safety.

human frailty with his driving, bullying practices. After withstanding him, it seemed they could withstand anyone.

The key, Wilson decided, was to shackle Bart Starr. Detroit could handle the Packers' running game, but on such occasions Starr always seemed capable of turning successfuly to his passing game. "You must keep Starr from throwing," Wilson warned his defense. "Don't give him any time. It's up to you. If you get him, we can win."

It would be a contest of force: defensive tackle Alex Karras against All-Pro guard Jerry Kramer, three-hundred-pound defensive tackle Roger Brown against the veteran Fuzzy Thurston, ends Sam Williams and Darris McCord against perhaps the two best offensive tackles in professional football, Forrest Gregg and Bob Skoronski.

Wilson decided to allow his free-wheeling defense to attack the Packers from every direction. This meant middle linebacker Joe Schmidt pounding ahead at All-Pro center Jim Ringo and more stunting and blitzing by the outside linebackers, Carl

Brettschneider and Wayne Walker. The Lions planned to pressure Starr into worrying when the blitz was coming and from where. In sum the Lions intended to bludgeon the Packers.

To do so the Lions had to harness every bit of the fervor that had built up in them over the last two and a half months. They knew Green Bay would be well prepared technically, but they were betting, correctly as it turned out, that no team could cope with their fury.

"This became one of the most emotional games I ever coached," Wilson recalls. "You could feel the tension in the dressing room the moment the players arrived. There was dead silence. No one said a word to anyone because they had pitched themselves so high. Usually I would say something before a game, but that day I knew there was nothing to say. All I did was open the door and say, 'Let's go.' I think if I hadn't opened that door they would have run right through it. It was a day when the Lions could have beaten any team they played."

The Packers, the NFL's highest

In the second half Green Bay recovered somewhat, scoring two touchdowns, but by then it was too late. Here Ray Nitschke (66) and Willie Davis (87) pile on Detroit's Rick Nyder (34).

scoring team, learned quickly how difficult it would be to tame the Lions' defense this afternoon. On Green Bay's first pass play, the third play of the game, Starr was literally run over for a 15-yard loss. The Tiger Stadium crowd of 57,598, some of whom had stood in line through the cold night to purchase the few remaining bleacher tickets, rocked the old wooden ball park. The fans grew even more exuberant as the Lions' defense began to swarm over the Packers' great line. Before the first quarter had ended, the Lions' ferocious charge had gained control of the game. Physically intimidated, the Packers looked like anything but the invincible machine they were purported to be. Across the nation, while turkeys roasted and families gathered, TV fans sensed the impending violent resolution of this grudge match and resolved to stay tuned.

The Lions jammed the Packers' trap plays and aborted their famed power sweeps. In the first half Green Bay fullback Jim Taylor, the leading rusher in the NFL with more than 1,100 yards, found himself with minus 3 yards. Whenever Starr went back to pass, his protective pocket collapsed before it fully formed. He was thrown for 93 yards in losses in the first half. "We had a great defensive unit as it was," Wilson says. "But on that day our front four got to Starr like no one was blocking it. Karras and Brown just destroyed the middle of what was supposed to be the best offensive line in the NFL.

"We were a pretty good blitzing team and the Packers knew it. When we tore apart their line, they couldn't stop our linebackers."

The Detroit offense was dominant from the start. Fullback Nick Pietrosante pounded through the inside, and the Packers' secondary was forced to make most of the tackles on him.

Midway in the first quarter, the Lions harried punter Boyd Dowler so badly that he shanked a punt just 15 yards, to the Packers' 41-yard line. On third-and-two, with the Packers fearful of the run and therefore overly protective against it, Plum appropriated one of Starr's favorite ploys. He froze the secondary with a play-action fake (to Pietrosante), stepped back, and spotted his wide receiver, Gail Cogdill, with a perfect pass on a post pattern. Knifing between two Green Bay defensive backs, cornerback Jesse Whittenton and free safety Willie Wood, Cogdill snatched the ball and raced untouched to the end zone. Walker's extra point gave the Lions a 7–0 lead.

The Lions' defense now turned loose its full fury on the reeling Packers. Running back Tom Moore, playing for the injured Hornung, fumbled, and Brettschneider recovered at the Lions' 47-yard line. A minute later Cogdill again split between two defenders, this time Adderley and Wood, and caught his second touchdown pass. It was now 14–0.

On the Packers' first series after this score, Brown ran over Thurston and buried Starr as he attempted to pass. Bart lost the ball and it bounced into the hands of Williams, who easily romped for the touchdown. Two minutes after that, Starr was trying to pass from his end zone when Brown came crashing past Thurston and over Taylor and tackled the Packers' quarterback for a safety. The Lions led 23–0, having scored 16 points in two and a half minutes.

As if to assure the Detroit fans that there would be no turnabout this time, Dick ("Night Train") Lane intercepted Starr's first pass of the second half. Plum kicked a field goal, and the count rose to 26–0. Green Bay scored a pair of touchdowns in the last five minutes, but they were inconsequential both to the outcome and the import of the game. Never had the nation seen the mighty Packers so devastatingly dismantled; few could remember any defense so dominating a team so good.

"They were past us before we could find them," Gregg remembers of the Lions' front four and linebackers. "I never saw anyone get off so fast with the snap of the ball. They came out stunting and seemed to blitz us on every play. We never recovered from the first series of the game, when they sacked Starr."

When the day ended, Starr had been caught behind the line of scrimmage 11 times for a total of 110 yards in losses. Taylor finished the day with just 47 rushing yards, and Green Bay's vaunted offense limped off the field with only 132 net yards to its credit. Thanks to the pass rush, Starr's passing netted only 59 yards. Meanwhile, the Lions rolled through the Packers for more than 300 yards.

But for all their fury and power, the Lions had to content themselves with just one cold afternoon of glory. Wilson's prediction that the Lions would show someone else "how to beat the Packers" never came true. Green Bay did not meet another team that season that unleashed such pent-up anger and frustration. Indeed the Thanksgiving Day massacre marked the only time in the illustrious Lombardi years that the Packers lost their poise and failed to match the emotional pitch of an opponent.

Curiously this devastating defeat came when the Packers were at their best, winning more games and scoring more points than they ever would again in a season. Even the greatest football teams, it seems, can be undone by the passions of this most emotional sport. □

| Green Bay | 0 | 0 | 0 | 14—14 |
| Detroit | 7 | 16 | 3 | 0—26 |

Det—Cogdill 33 pass from Plum (Plum kick)
Det—Cogdill 27 pass from Plum (Plum kick)
Det—Williams 6 run with fumble recovery (Plum kick)
Det—R. Brown safety, tackled Starr in end zone (Plum kick)
Det—FG Plum 47
GB—Quinlan 4 pass interception (Kramer kick)
GB—Taylor 4 run (Kramer kick)

Much to the chagrin of the fledgling American Football League, the coin toss became one of the most memorable moments of the 1962 title game's sudden-death overtime, when Dallas' Abner Haynes (28) blew the call, above. Fortunately, the Texans won.

An unwritten football axiom: any team having a chance to receive the ball first in sudden-death overtime does so, because all it takes is one score of any kind to win.

Coach Hank Stram was about to break that rule. It was the 1962 American Football League championship game and Stram's Dallas Texans were tied with the Houston Oilers 17–17 at the end of regulation play. The Texans had won the toss and faced a

ABNER'S BONER

Dallas Texans vs. Houston Oilers

DECEMBER 23, 1962

*Dallas quarterback Len Dawson,
scrambling above, helped
the Texans overcome the blunder.*

choice of either receiving the ball, kicking off, or choosing a goal line to defend. A team has only one choice. If, for example, Stram decided to receive, the other team would pick the field position. If Stram chose a field position, the other team would elect to receive or to kick.

Though many questioned his judgment, Stram felt that in this situation there were compelling reasons for choosing field position instead of the ball. One was the gusty, late-afternoon wind whipping across the field in the direction of the clock atop Houston's Jeppesen Stadium. Having the wind at one's back was an obvious advantage for a field-goal kicker, and Stram's adversaries, the Houston Oilers, owned one of the best in George Blanda. With the strong wind to his back, Blanda was fully capable of ending the game anywhere inside the 50-yard line.

Had Stram elected to receive, his team faced the prospect of struggling forward deep in its own territory against a tenacious Houston defense. Should the Texans then have failed to make a first down, their punter, Eddie Wilson, awful that day, would have been forced to kick into the wind from close to his end zone. Stram reasoned that a short punt would virtually ensure a winning Blanda field goal. On the other hand, Stram's defense was

excellent. Even if he gave Houston first crack at a score, he was confident that his defense could stop the Oilers, giving the Texans the ball, good field position, the wind advantage, and the best possible chance to win.

Confident that he had found the soundest strategy, Stram carefully instructed his offensive captain, Abner Haynes, to take the wind advantage if Dallas won the toss. He did not count on Haynes mistaking his instructions.

Haynes stood in the middle of the field while referee Harold Bourne flipped the coin. As visiting captain, he made the call. "Heads."

"Heads it is," Bourne announced after stooping to look at the coin on the ground.

"We'll kick to the clock," Haynes told the official.

It was a terrible mistake. By uttering the words "we'll kick," he had

surrendered not only his team's right of possession, but the critical wind advantage as well.

Bourne was astonished, but under the rules he could not correct him. "Captain Haynes, you made the choice and said you'll kick," the referee said. He made a swift, kicking motion. The delighted Oilers immediately chose the wind advantage for themselves.

Stram's face appeared stricken as he watched from the sidelines. "Abner just said it wrong," Stram said later. "He should have said, 'We'll take this end of the field, facing the clock.' Forget the 'kick off' bit. Then Houston would have chosen to receive and we would have had what we wanted. Once he said the word 'kick,' that gave away our option to get the wind."

It probably was the first time, certainly in sudden-death overtime, that a player who won a coin toss chose to give the advantage to his opponents. It was foolish and inexcusable, and in the eyes of many pro football fans, completely in character with the AFL. NFL purists still regarded the AFL as a bush league, a kind of backwoods leper colony reserved for unraveling, undistinguished football talents. In its three years of existence, the new league had staggered from crisis to crisis. The New York Titans were bankrupt. Oakland and Houston played in high school stadiums before plenty of empty seats. The NFL's new Dallas Cowboys were about to run the fledgling Texans all the way to Kansas City. The Los Angeles Chargers already had fled to San Diego with negligible gains at the gate.

Only four years earlier, the New York Giants and Baltimore Colts had drawn national attention to the NFL with Johnny Unitas' sudden-death fire-

The Oilers were led by their star running back, Billy Cannon, (20) above, and by their quarterback, George Blanda, passing, left, a mere 13-year, 35-year-old veteran.

77

Dallas coach Hank Stram, pacing the sideline, below, wanted the wind at his team's back at the start of sudden-death overtime. He didn't get it until the second overtime period (thanks to Haynes), but then the Texans' Tommy Brooker kicked the winning field goal, right.

works in the 1958 championship game. Now an embarrassing mistake had tarnished what the AFL had hoped would be a similarly prestigious national showcase for itself.

Apart from Haynes's blunder, it was a tense, well-played game. Dallas dominated the first half, rolling to a 17–0 lead. Tommy Brooker kicked a 16-yard field goal and Haynes himself scored two touchdowns, one on a pass from quarterback Len Dawson, one on a run. For the remainder of the half, the ball stayed in the hands of Dallas running backs Jack Spikes and Curtis McClinton, who smoothly pounded out yards and ran out the clock. Dawson threw only seven passes, and at half-time it appeared that Stram's Texans had the game well in hand.

But in the second half, Houston roared back. Quarterback George Blanda, in those days a mere 13-year veteran, put on a one-man show. He

passed for one score and booted a field goal for another. With six minutes left, Houston tied the score. However, a second Blanda field goal, which would have broken the tie and given Houston the title, was blocked by Sherrill Headrick as time expired.

Then Haynes blundered and for a while things looked bleak for Dallas. Blanda, intent on moving in range for the winning field goal, came out throwing. But the initiative slipped away from him when the Texans' Johnny Robinson intercepted one of his passes and sped with the ball to the Houston 37-yard line. It looked like a certain Dallas field goal, but the Texans were smothered by Houston's blitzing linebackers and had to punt. The Oilers regained possession on their 12-yard line.

Blanda took command again, this time working the ball to the Dallas 35-yard line on a string of short,

swing passes. On second-and-10, he called a down-and-out pattern to Charley Hennigan. But 6-foot 7-inch defensive end Bill Hull read the play well, snatched the ball out of the air, and rumbled to midfield with the interception. Once again Blanda had been thwarted despite the wind at his back, and this time Abner Haynes was off the hook for good.

McClinton struggled for two yards, and the first overtime period ended. Now, as the tired players shifted field positions, Stram at last had the wind advantage. Spikes darted to the 38-yard line for a first down. Then divining a strong-side blitz, Dawson handed the ball to Spikes, who spun around the weak side for a 19-yard gain.

With the ball on the 19-yard line and a field goal beckoning, Dawson fired a sneaky pass that fell incomplete. He didn't risk it again. Two

short, safe runs positioned the ball squarely before the goal posts. Tom Brooker, the now-friendly breeze to his back, set up for the field goal. While Houston coach Frank ("Pop") Ivy ordered an 11-man rush, the huddled Texans tried to relax their rookie kicker. "Don't worry about it," Brooker told his teammates. "It's all over now."

And it was. Brooker sailed the ball ten feet over the crossbar. Eighteen minutes into the overtime period, the AFL's longest day had ended, much to the relief of the Dallas Texans and a long-faced flanker named Abner Haynes. □

Dallas	3	14	0	0	0	3—20
Houston	0	0	7	10	0	0—17

Dal—FG Brooker 16
Dal—Haynes 28 pass from Dawson (Brooker kick)
Dal—Haynes 2 run (Brooker kick)
Hou—Dewveall 15 pass from Blanda (Blanda kick)
Hou—FG Blanda 31
Hou—Tolar 1 run (Blanda kick)
Dal—FG Brooker 25

RIEGELS RIDES AGAIN

Minnesota Vikings vs. San Francisco 49ers

OCTOBER 25, 1964

Remember "Wrong Way Riegels?" He was the unfortunate University of California center who recovered a Georgia Tech fumble during the second quarter of the 1929 Rose Bowl classic. A bit giddily, the big Californian gamboled about, elbowing tacklers aside till suddenly and inexplicably he reversed himself, fleeing for the goal line, the *wrong* goal line, 60 yards distant. While seventy thousand spectators watched aghast, Riegels arrived at the Cal end zone, where a frantic teammate, Benny Lom, spun him around. Starting back in the proper direction, he was overwhelmed by Tech defenders at the 1. Tech blocked a Cal kick on the next play for a two-point safety and went on to win the game 8–7.

Hence, the sobriquet and singular notoriety of Cal's Roy ("Wrong

Way") Riegels. That is, until the Minnesota Vikings' Jim Marshall topped his feat in a pro football game in 1964. Marshall's blunder was even worse. He was credited with scoring two points for the opposing team, the San Francisco 49ers. But the Vikings pulled it out, winning 27–22.

Jim Marshall is an unlikely candidate for such a dubious distinction. He is intelligent and durable, having played in a record 223 consecutive National Football League games through the 1975 season. He is a mainstay of the Vikings' front four, one of the finest in NFL history, and the cutting edge of "the Purple Gang" defense, of which Marshall is captain. In 1963, he had gobbled up a 49ers' fumble and traveled with it the "right way" for a touchdown.

Marshall's nightmare started in-

The wrong-way run in 1964 gave opponents one of their few chances to enjoy Jim Marshall. More often they were ducking for cover, as Len Dawson did here.

nocently enough, with a lob pass from Mira to Billy Kilmer, then a halfback. A conflux of Vikings leveled Kilmer, the ball bounded free, and Marshall, scrambling back from the rush, put it away. He says he can't recall exactly how he turned himself around. "I lost my sense of direction," Marshall says.

"I had to jump over one of the 49ers' linemen to get to the ball, and after that, I didn't remember anything until I got to the end zone."

A speedy runner for a big man, Marshall completed his 60-yard jaunt in near record time. All along the way were the vague shapes of open-mouthed teammates. "I thought they were cheering me on," he says. "Somehow, when I crossed the goal line the whole thing hit me. I didn't know what to do with the ball, so I tossed it away. Later, Fran Tarkenton told me it was a good thing I didn't try to spike it. It could have been a touchdown for the 49ers, enough points for them to win the game."

Bruce Bosley, San Francisco's center, trailed the play warily. When Marshall started out, Bosley expected him to circle back and prepared to make the tackle. "Then I got kind of mixed up and thought, 'Maybe he's right,' " Bosley says. "After that I was just interested in his getting there. I didn't want him to realize he'd run the wrong way until he'd crossed the goal line."

Bosley was the first player to greet Marshall, who stared intently at his shoelaces. "Thanks a lot," Bosley said. "We can use more like that."

"He looked at me like I was off my rocker," Bosley recalls. "All the could say was, 'Huh?' He looked up in the stands with a very strange look in his eyes. I don't think it was until he had walked fifteen or twenty yards that he really understood what had happened."

Quickly, Fran Tarkenton ran over to Marshall and said, "Jim, you just ran the wrong way, the wrong way."

"Huh?" Marshall replied.

"He headed to the bench and put his head between his knees," Tarkenton says. "The unfortunate thing was that Jim didn't get credit for his great play at the start. It was an exercise in total hustle and that's how Jim always played the game."

Later, Tarkenton suggested that Marshall prepare a little ten-minute soliloquy about his flub. "You'll get enough speaking engagements to make five hundred dollars a week off that run," Fran told him.

On the sidelines coach Norm Van Brocklin's thoughts were less sanguine. Jim was the team's goof-off and at first Van Brocklin thought he was clowning around. He had to suppress an urge to kill. For a few lonely minutes, Marshall wanted to crawl into the water bucket and expire. It was hell. But Van Brocklin told him to buck up and forget it, and Marshall played the rest of the game.

An hour or so later, Roy Riegels strolled into the clubhouse of a San Diego golf course and heard about the incident. "Oh no, not another one!" Riegels thought at the time. "I knew that it would take him a long time to live it down. People were going to kid him about it the rest of his life. He'd just have to learn to take it and laugh with the crowd."

A couple of days later, Riegels wrote Marshall a letter. "Welcome to the club!" it began. It was one of more than one thousand letters and calls Marshall received in the wake of his boner.

In the off-season, Jim was scheduled to fly to Dallas to accept a "Bonehead of the Year" award. Naturally, he missed his plane and wound up in Chicago. Everyone suspected that the promoters put him up to that, but they didn't. Marshall reached the ceremony on time. As it turned out, he earned several thousand dollars from speaking tours, television appearances, and advertisements. But no one ever calls him "Wrong Way Marshall." The alliteration isn't the same.

□

Minnesota	3	7	3	14—27
San Francisco	7	10	0	5—22

SF—Brodie 2 run (Davis kick)
Minn—FG Cox 41
SF—Parks 80 pass from Brodie (Davis kick)
Minn—Mason 7 run (Cox kick)
SF—FG Davis 37
Minn—FG Cox 36
Minn—Tarkenton 8 run (Cox kick)
Minn—Eller 45 fumble recovery (Cox kick)
SF—Safety, Marshall 60-yard run
SF—FG Davis 48

BLANTON COLLIER: A QUIET MAN ROARS

Cleveland Browns vs. Baltimore Colts

DECEMBER 27, 1964

The experts agreed that the Baltimore Colts would manhandle the Cleveland Browns when the teams met for the NFL championship on the final Sunday of 1964. They said the Colts were great, the Browns ordinary. And the record seemed to support them. The Colts had been first during the season in total offense, the Browns last in total defense. The Baltimore defense had allowed the few-

Gary Collins caught three touchdown passes (number one below) in the Browns' 27-0 upset of Baltimore for the 1964 NFL title. Unassuming Blanton Collier, opposite, *planned the coup.*

For the most part the Colts stifled the running efforts of Jim Brown. But two big plays—a circle pass to establish field position and a 46-yard sweep that set up a score—were all the Browns needed from their big man.

est points and touchdowns, and had led the league in quarterback sacks. As soon as it stopped the Browns' great runner, Jim Brown, it would shut off Cleveland's passing and the rout would be on, according to the approved scenario. The sophisticates sneered at the betting line, which listed the Colts as merely seven-point favorites.

The experts and the bettors all but ignored the kindly looking, bespectacled coach of the Browns, Blanton Collier, though Don Shula, his opposite number in this championship game, recognized him as one of the most astute and incisive coaches in the league. Shula should have known. As a player for the Browns, he had worked under then-assistant coach Collier; as an assistant coach at Kentucky, he had worked under then-head coach Collier. Now Shula took great pains to eschew any talk of a one-sided football game, but he couldn't prevent it, and he fretted over how it might affect his players. He knew exactly what it would do for the Browns.

"We had all the psychological edges going for us," Collier admits. "We were put down. . . . Johnny Unitas was going to eat us alive.

"Now I hated to be told I couldn't do something, and I didn't like being told my team couldn't win the game. The more we prepared for the Colts in those two weeks before the game, the stronger the feeling got. We never said much then, but afterward every one of us admitted that we felt they couldn't beat us. It wasn't false bravado, but it was a feeling of being absolutely sure we would win."

It was not the first time Collier would lead his team to success in the face of a skeptical football world. He had become the Browns' head coach

The Browns harassed Johnny Unitas, the Colts' great quarterback,
into total ineffectiveness. Here Dick Modzelewski
(74), Jim Kanicki (69), and Bill Glass (80) make the tackle.

as successor to Paul Brown, who left bitterness and turmoil in the wake of his brilliant but increasingly controversial reign. Collier soothed the antagonisms and harnessed the energy into a championship. He was a master planner who had the unique ability to isolate and exploit an opponent's most telling weakness. This game would be his finest demonstration of that talent.

"With Baltimore, we felt the only

chance we had to stop Unitas was to shut off his first or primary receiver," Collier remembers. "That was the only chance we had for our pass rush to get to him because in looking for the second receiver he'd use up the valuable half second more our rush needed to penetrate."

In his film study of Unitas and the Colts, Collier had noticed the quarterback's tendency to hit the pocket and then to shuffle in the direction he would throw. The coach told his defense that on the erratic footing of Cleveland Stadium's frozen field Unitas would be making extra sure he had targeted his primary receiver. If the Browns could cover that man, their defensive line's rush would reach Unitas before he could shift his sights.

"As soon as he looks at that first receiver, clamp that guy," Collier told his defense. "We'll gamble on John operating that way, and I'll take any consequences. If we make him look for a second receiver, then that'll give us a chance to get him. He'll kill us if you let him throw to his first receiver."

The man with the greatest responsibility in this plan was Walter Beach because he would most often be aligned against Unitas' favorite target, the great Raymond Berry. Collier and his defensive coordinator, Howard Brinker, wanted Beach to play not only as close as possible to Berry but between him and Unitas, never giving the quarterback a clear passing lane.

With the exception of Beach, the Browns' secondary was not fast. Therefore, Collier and Brinker decided they would play man-for-man coverage only on the short side of the field, and a zone defense on the wide side. Even in the zones, however, the defensive backs were instructed to tighten up immediately on the Baltimore receivers.

It worked. The secondary gave the line the split second more it needed, and Unitas was in trouble. At times he had to keep tight end John Mackey on the line to help his blockers cope with defensive end Bill Glass, and in not using Mackey as a receiver, he lost a potential gamebreaker. Jim Kanicki, a second-year tackle, won the battle with Baltimore guard Jim Parker, one of the best pass blockers ever to play professional football. "Kanicki played his greatest game," Collier remembers.

At one point Unitas found himself abandoning the pocket and scrambling on four consecutive passing attempts. He tried different formations, desperately trying to break the Browns' stranglehold on his passing game. Yet Berry and the other receivers, Jimmy Orr and Lenny Moore, never got free.

The Browns enlisted all in the stop-Unitas drive. "They played the wind," John recalls. "When it was at my back, they played deeper; when it was in my face they shortened up."

Not uncommon for Cleveland, the day had come up cold and blustery, with a wind of twenty miles per hour blowing through the open end of the massive stadium. As the Browns deferred to it on defense, they overcame it on offense. "We won the toss," Collier remembers, "and I really wanted to kick off and get the wind advantage right away. But I couldn't. This was professional football, and since we had a chance to receive we had to do it."

Collier well knew that he thus risked bottling up his team in its end of the field for the entire first quarter, giving Unitas excellent field position and the chance to strike for an early, insurmountable lead. "The one play that really stands out in my mind,"

Collier says, "was in our first possession. We came out with third-and-long yardage and Frank Ryan passed to Jim Brown over the middle, something the Colts knew we did very rarely. But with our other options, this was about all we could do. Jim made a great one-handed catch and that kept us going until we reached midfield. We got them in their territory and were able to fight them off until we got the wind in the second quarter."

Baltimore made it to the Browns' 12-yard line, but on fourth down the threat died when holder Bobby Boyd dropped the snap for a field goal by Lou Michaels. That drive would be the Colts' deepest penetration throughout this long, cold afternoon, and their only scoring threat.

Neither team scored in the first half. On their first series of the third quarter, the Colts had to punt against that tricky wind, and Tom Gilburg's kick traveled only 25 yards, to near midfield. After Ryan got one first down and moved his team to the Colts' 36-yard line, the Baltimore defense held firm.

Out trotted 40-year-old Lou Groza, the oldest man ever to play in an NFL title game and now in the eighth such game of his illustrious pro career. His famed toe struck the ball and sent it spinning into the jet stream that blew at his back. He and the eighty thousand fans watched the wind carry the ball majestically through the uprights for a 43-yard field goal. The Browns led 3–0. The defense had held long enough for the

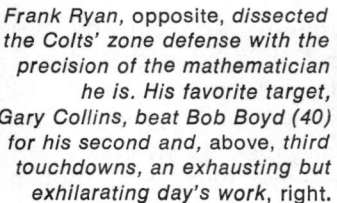

Frank Ryan, opposite, *dissected the Colts' zone defense with the precision of the mathematician he is. His favorite target, Gary Collins, beat Bob Boyd (40) for his second and,* above, *third touchdowns, an exhausting but exhilarating day's work,* right.

offense to begin to assert itself; now it was about to take control.

Collier knew that the Colts' defense, particularly captain and middle linebacker Bill Pellington, had become overly conscious of its middle. After he had been burned by Brown's catch in the first quarter, Pellington had spent most of the rest of the half plugging the inside against the great fullback.

Ryan had refrained from sending Brown to the outside until he felt the Colts' defense was vulnerable. When a second Gilburg punt lost its battle with the wind and carried only to the Cleveland 36-yard line, Ryan knew there would be no better time. First, he teased Baltimore's middle with another Brown plunge. Then he called for a sweep to the right side of Balti-

more's defense. Still protecting the middle, Pellington relied on help from the outside, but defensive back Bobby Boyd missed an audible call and was out of position. When outside linebacker Don Shinnick was caught inside and Ernie Green, the Browns' halfback, sealed him off, Brown had an open highway.

In his classic, fluid running style, Brown sailed around the corner and down the sideline. As the Colts pursued him, he cut back and weaved through the flow of the defense until he was finally cornered and collared 46 yards from the line of scrimmage, at the Colts' 18.

Ryan surveyed a shaken Baltimore defense and, with the wind at his back, now unleashed his passing game. He called a pattern that sent flanker Gary Collins hooking to the inside on Boyd, near the 5-yard line, with tight end John Brewer clearing out the other safety. Paul Warfield, the wide receiver who was being double-covered on every play, was sent away from Collins' area, leaving Gary man-for-man with Boyd. "I hadn't taken four strides off the line of scrimmage," Collins remembers, "when I saw Boyd in the hook area. So instead of hooking, I broke off the pattern and headed further toward the middle and into the end zone."

It was heady thinking but it also made the throw difficult for Ryan, who had little room to get the ball to Collins, what with Boyd, the goal posts, and the other coverage to avoid. As soon as Gary broke past Boyd, Ryan released the ball, high and hard. It just missed the goal posts, and Collins clutched it for a touchdown.

Now the momentum had clearly swung to the Browns, and they had yet to capitalize on all their pregame plans. Offensive coach Dub Jones had noticed that it was possible for a Cleveland receiver to split the Colts' double coverage—between the left cornerback, taking the outside, and Boyd, the safety, taking the inside. Thus the Browns planned a play in which Collins would run his pattern down and across the middle and, as soon as Boyd committed himself, would break straight upfield toward the end zone. Ryan called the play and as it turned out Collins didn't even have to worry about Boyd. As the Browns came to the line of scrimmage the safety misread their offensive formation and moved away from the area where Collins would run his pass route. Gary had plenty of room to clear the Baltimore defenders and Ryan's pass floated easily into his hands.

That made it 17–0; the Colts' defense was unravelling. The Browns were threatening again, at Baltimore's 14-yard line, when the quarter ended. A tricky wind notwithstanding, Groza polished off that drive with another field goal, for a 20–0 lead in the early moments of the fourth quarter.

It remained only for Cleveland's defense to reclaim the spotlight, dogging Unitas to the end and preserving the shutout. Ryan threw another touchdown pass to Collins, who caught five passes for 130 yards in all this day, but by that time it was the defense's show. The Browns allowed the great John Unitas only 45 plays, only 95 yards passing, and 171 yards total offense.

"The Browns' secondary forced us to play conservatively and that wasn't our style," Unitas reflected later. "We wanted to go out and gun 'em down but they took that away. They shut off our bombs. . . .

"They gave their pass rush a lot of help. I remember Galen Fiss, their outside linebacker, blitzing through a couple of times, and even Larry Benz, a safety, came through once. The Browns never played that style of defense before."

Unitas was not the only one who failed to understand the adjustments the Browns had made. The experts too reeled in uncomprehending shock at the sudden and decisive fall of the mighty Colts. Meanwhile, the architect of the victory, quiet, unassuming Blanton Collier, explained it all only with grins and a gracious winner's clichés. Not one to trumpet his triumphs, he seemed unimpressed when his deflated critics now glorified him. After all, the game itself did that.
□

Baltimore   0   0   0   0— 0
Cleveland   0   0   17   10—27
Cle—FG Groza 43
Cle—Collins 18 pass from Ryan (Groza kick)
Cle—Collins 42 pass from Ryan (Groza kick)
Cle—FG Groza 9
Cle—Collins 51 pass from Ryan (Groza kick)

THE SAYERS SCORING MACHINE

Chicago Bears vs. San Francisco 49ers

DECEMBER 12, 1965

Halas and Sayers: an old man who had seen them all and a young man who had just surpassed them.

Seventy-one year old George Halas had perused the talents of Bronko Nagurski, Red Grange, Cliff Battles, George McAfee, Jim Brown, Steve Van Buren, Hugh McElhenny, and Marion Motley during his forty-year tenure as a National Football League coach. And yet he was unequivocal about which single-game performance he considered best. Of Gale Sayers' efforts on a gray, rainy Sunday at Chicago's Wrigley Field, Halas said flatly, "That was the greatest performance I've ever seen on the football field by one man."

Sayers had amassed six touchdowns and 336 total yards in a 61–20 Chicago Bears' rout of the San Francisco 49ers. The six TDs tied the record for touchdowns scored in a single game, held by Ernie Nevers, 1929, and Dub Jones, 1950.

This was Sayers' rookie season as a pro. In summer training camp a lot of people had predicted that he wouldn't make it. Reports from the College All-Stars' camp disparaged his blocking and his mental and physical stamina. He was said to get discouraged by rough going. When he reported to the Bears' training camp, veteran players grumbled about his flashy, free-flowing running style.

But Halas wasn't fooled. He had kept a close eye on Sayers since his freshman year at Kansas, when a Chicago scout had first seen him. After watching the young runner scrimmage against the Jayhawks' varsity, the scout labeled him a "number one," which meant that he had the potential to be a starter in his first pro season. The decision was made then and there in the Bears' office to draft the youngster from Omaha on the first round. The chance came in the 1964 college draft, when Chicago picked third, behind the New York Giants, who took Tucker Fredrickson, and the 49ers, who chose Ken Willard. Chicago selected Sayers and managed to woo him away from the Kansas City Chiefs of the rival American Football League.

Halfway into the 1965 season Halas and the Bears were more than pleased with their rookie. Halas noted that Sayers had a unique ability to reverse direction instantly at top speed, the mark of a true superstar. Defense-minded George Allen, then a Chicago assistant coach, went so far as to call Sayers "the one offensive player who can dictate the defense."

"We felt he'd be a superstar all along," Halas says. "He had the six qualities we used to determine a superstar running back—speed, shiftiness, balance, strength, size, and the most important, the instinct to make

Right: *Touchdown number five: Sayers soared over San Francisco linebacker Dave Wilcox (64) and the goal line on a one-yard plunge in the third quarter.*

Touchdown number two: Sayers eluded San Francisco cornerback Kermit Alexander on a 21-yard dash around end in the second quarter, left.

the right move at the right time, do it automatically, even without thinking."

There was a timeless, exuberant quality to Sayers when he was running at his best. He put it on brilliant display against Baltimore, a week before the 49ers' game. Slick defensive back Bobby Boyd had Sayers trapped for a seemingly certain 3-yard loss. Gale spun, Boyd froze, and Gale sailed 62 yards for a score.

It might have seemed that such a gifted runner would have had difficulty coordinating his moves with his blockers, but Sayers proved to be all but a natural in working with his front line. Mike Rabold, a guard on those Chicago teams, describes the teamwork: "He stayed right with us so that we knew when we made the block, he would take advantage of it. He had a great way of using his moves to set up the defensive backs. First, he'd make them commit themselves. Then he'd slap one of us lightly on the back and

we'd take the guy out. And he didn't slow down when he made his moves. He might have lost a half step. But a half step lost going that fast still meant he was going pretty fast."

The soggy Wrigley Field turf on the Sunday of the game with the 49ers was an unlikely stage for Sayers' all-time rushing record. Before the game, Halas made his players change to shoes with longer nylon cleats for better traction.

Having previously crushed the Bears 52–24, in the season's opening game, the 49ers provoked a new wrinkle in the Bears' attack for this encounter—a triple-wing formation with three receivers on one side of the field. Chicago planned to work to the left side of the 49ers' defense, manned by linebacker Dave Wilcox, cornerback Jim Johnson, and safety El Kimbrough. The Bears drove left the first time they had the ball. On second-and-ten quarterback Rudy

Bukich tossed a screen pass to Sayers. While Bob Wetoska, Mike Pyle, and Jim Cadile threw the blocks, Gale threaded his way through what seemed like the 49ers' entire squad until, with a sharp cut to his left, he flew downfield 80 yards and scored.

Just before halftime, the Bears ahead 13–7, Gale's timely blocking helped Chicago's Jon Arnett run back a kickoff 77 yards to the 49ers' 21-yard line. His next run was a shorter version of his first touchdown. Jim Johnson tried to stop him at the 3-yard line but Gale leaped over him and, when he landed, slid through the mud into the end zone. Quarterback John Brodie's touchdown pass to John David Crow quickly closed the gap to 21–13. But Sayers wasn't finished. He caught a nine-yard pass. Then he swept left yet again, on a seven-yard touchdown stroll.

Early in the third quarter, Chicago was near midfield when Sayers grabbed a pass on the left side. Led by the blocks of flanker Johnny Morris, tight end Mike Ditka, and guard Bob Wetoska, Sayers rambled 51 yards without being touched.

The man seemed unstoppable. Bukich called for a plunge from the one-foot line and Sayers obliged, rocketing over the pile-up and descending headfirst into the end zone. Toward the finish of the game, which had long since become Sayers' one-man variety show, Gale took a punt by Tommy Davis (whose record consecutive string of extra point conversions had been snapped at 234 earlier in the afternoon) and proceeded to treat the 46,278 paying spectators to a free dance lesson. He cha-cha-cha-ed past the 49ers' last, luckless defender in flying 85 yards downfield for his final score and grand exit of the day. As one witness put it, "The only thing chasing him across the goal line were cheers."

Sayers was aware of having tied the record for touchdowns scored. Assistant coach Sid Luckman had told him as much the moment he came off the field. But there would be no curtain calls for Gale Sayers. The 49ers would have been furious and Halas wouldn't risk an injury to his prize rookie. "I never would have forgiven myself if he had gotten hurt," Halas says.

So despite the steady chant from the Bears' aroused fans—"We want Sayers! We want Sayers!"—Gale's touchdown total remained no better than equal to the record of six.

"It wouldn't have done any good for me to have gone back in," Gale says today. "The 49ers would have been ready for me because they would have known why I was there. When you're a rookie, you always think that there will be other games on other days. Records didn't mean that much to me then. My whole outlook was to score any time I had the ball. That's all I thought about when I ran."

It showed. Sayers gained 113 yards in nine carries, 89 yards in two pass receptions, and 134 yards in punt returns. Pretty good, even without six touchdowns. And some observers suggested that the Bears' wonder man could have done even better. Said Mike Ditka, the Bears' tight end, when asked if the weather had restrained Gale's mass production of touchdowns, "If it had been dry, he'd have scored ten." □

San Francisco   0   13   0   7—20
Chicago   13   14 13   21—61
Chi— Sayers 80 pass from Bukich (pass failed)
Chi—Ditka 29 pass from Bukich (Leclerc kick)
SF—Parks 9 pass from Brodie (Davis kick)
Chi—Sayers 21 run (Leclerc kick)
SF—Crow 15 pass from Brodie (kick failed)
Chi—Sayers 7 run (Leclerc kick)
Chi—Sayers 50 run (Leclerc kick)
Chi—Sayers 1 run (run failed)
SF—Kopay 2 run (Davis kick)
Chi—Jones 8 pass from Bukich (Leclerc kick)
Chi—Sayers 85 punt return (Leclerc kick)
Chi—Arnett 2 run (Leclerc kick)

Tom Matte, plays taped to his wrist, needed all the help he could get, including the advice of Don Shula (hatless), in trying to overcome the Green Bay Packers. He almost made it.

TOM MATTE: INSTANT QUARTERBACK

Green Bay Packers vs. Baltimore Colts

DECEMBER 26, 1965

In pro football more often than not the quarterback determines whether his team will win or lose. And yet for three weeks at the end of the 1965 National Football League season, a team without any true quarterback, the Baltimore Colts, battled its way into an intraconference playoff and then, in what could have been an astounding upset, almost to a conference title. Unfortunately, the gods, in the person of an all too humanly flawed official, ceased to favor the heroic effort, and the Colts succumbed to Vince Lombardi's Green Bay Packers by the margin of one phantom field goal.

The "instant quarterback" on this occasion was a part-time Baltimore running back named Tom Matte. Matte's rapid rise to quarterback came late in the season when Baltimore's first- and second-line signal callers, John Unitas and Gary Cuozzo, were injured. Unitas fractured a kneecap in the Colts' ninth game and was out for the rest of the year. Cuozzo remained a viable replacement until the next-to-last game of the season, a crucial contest against the Packers, the Colts' principal Western Conference rivals. The Packers, led by Paul Hornung's five touchdowns, buried the Colts, knocking them out of first place. What was even worse, Cuozzo separated his shoulder in this game and, like Unitas, was lost for the rest of the season. Thus, for the regular season finale, a must-win game with the Los Angeles Rams, coach Don Shula was forced to start Matte at quarterback.

Matte was not completely inexperienced; he had played quarterback in college for coach Woody Hayes at Ohio State. But like most Hayes-trained quarterbacks, Matte spent his apprenticeship doing little more than handing off the ball and rushing it himself. At Baltimore Matte had thrown only 29 passes in regular-season games over five seasons. All of these were halfback option passes, for which he had to practice by throwing no more than five passes a week. Clearly, his arm was not ready for more strenuous work. Despite daily massages, he quickly developed a sore arm, which further limited his already woefully insufficient practice time.

There were more problems. While working with Unitas over the years, receivers such as Raymond Berry, Jimmy Orr, and John Mackey had developed a delicate timing and coordination. They had fine-tuned their pass patterns down to fractions of seconds and precise numbers of steps. In the week or two he had, Matte could hardly become thoroughly familiar with these patterns or with the varieties of moves each receiver used against opposing defenders. He faced an equally Herculean task with play-calling. Through countless repetitions, a quarterback remembers every play in a particular game plan as well as the best sequences for different situations. Shula

The Colts' regular quarterback, John Unitas, opposite with Pete Rozelle (left), was lost to the team in the ninth game; his replacement, Gary Cuozzo, right, a few weeks later.

had ordered some of the plays typed on a card, sealed in plastic, and taped to Matte's left wrist. The coach himself called many key plays from the sidelines. He also rearranged his offense to de-emphasize the pass and to take advantage of Matte's running ability. He installed quarterback draws and run-pass option plays. He taught Matte the shorter pass patterns: the screens, the flares, and the quick turn-ins and turn-outs.

Miraculously, in his first important test, Matte led the Colts to a 20–17 victory over the Rams. He completed only one of seven passes for nine yards, but his running more than compensated. The next day, 350 miles up the California coast in San Francisco, the Packers could do no better than a tie against the 49ers, so the Packers and the Colts finished with identical 10–3–1 records and faced a playoff for the Western Conference championship.

Shula perfectly understood his team's plight. Baltimore's defense had failed to stop the Packers twice already during the regular season. It absolutely had to do so now, for there was very little chance that Matte would solve the Green Bay defense. Tom had hurt the Rams with his roll-outs—faking passes, then slicing upfield with the ball. Lombardi told his defensive ends to pinch off Matte's routes to the outside. And knowing that Matte couldn't throw long, he moved his defensive backs closer to the line of scrimmage in order to fend off short passes to running backs Lenny Moore and Jerry Hill.

At the start of the game, it looked like luck might bring the Colts another upset victory. On the first play Bart Starr threw a quick 10-yard pass to tight end Bill Anderson at the Packers' 25-yard line. Cornerback Lenny Lyles hit him hard and jarred the ball loose. Linebacker Don Shinnick, who had trailed the play, scooped up the ball and headed for the end zone. Starr, the last man able to stop Shinnick, seemed to have him cornered near the 5-yard line, but Baltimore defensive back Jim Welch sped to the assistance of the ball-carrying linebacker. As Starr lunged at Shinnick, the three men collided in a tangle of arms and legs. Shinnick emerged from the melée still on his feet and scored the touchdown.

Starr was clutching his ribs as he slowly rose and limped to the sidelines. He was replaced for the remainder of the afternoon by his backup,

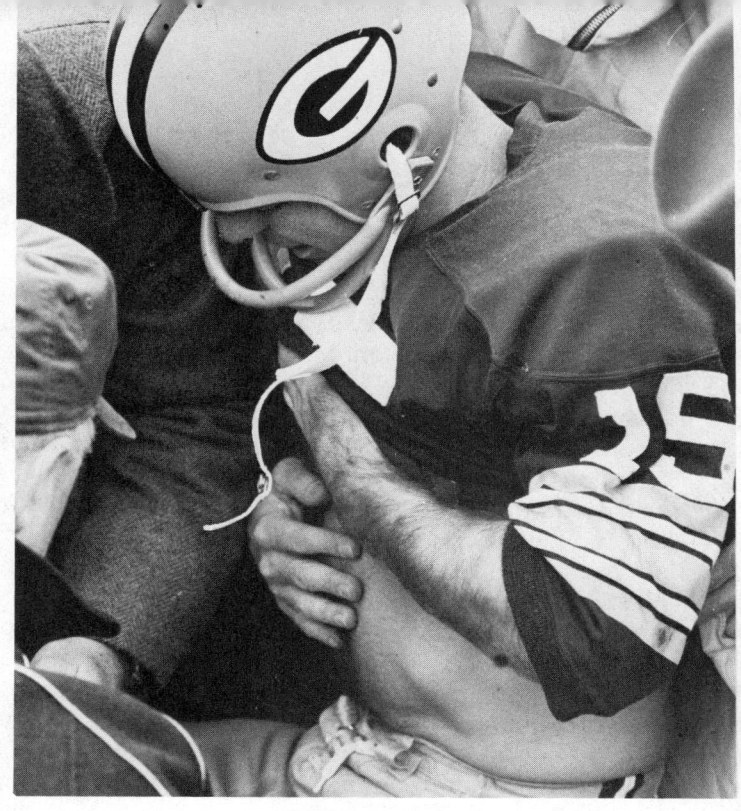

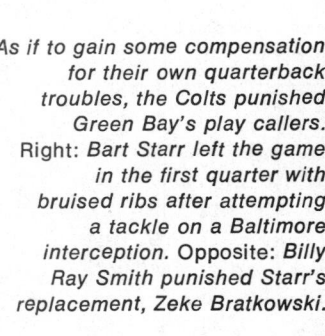

Zeke Bratkowski. Further downfield, a groggy Bill Anderson lay on the ground. Although he recovered and played the rest of the game, catching eight passes for 78 yards, he says he cannot remember it.

Even without Starr, Green Bay had the edge at quarterback. Bratkowski was pro football's foremost reserve that season, saving four games for the Packers, including an earlier 20–17 victory over Baltimore. And if Zeke were to be hurt, Lombardi still had another substitute quarterback in Dennis Claridge. Nevertheless, even with an accomplished quarterback at the helm, the Green Bay offense looked flat midway through the first quarter. The Packers failed on their only scoring chance, a field goal attempt from the Colts' 47-yard line by Don Chandler.

Both defenses controlled the game until three minutes before the half, when Matte got the ball at his 25-yard line. Matte had no tricks planned. Green Bay defensive ends Willie Davis and Lionel Aldridge had succeeded in disrupting his scrambling option plays. He decided to charge straight ahead. "We knew it couldn't be fancy," he says. "So it had to be hard and steady."

And it was. Hill gained four. Matte ran a quarterback draw for another four, and a late hit on the play cost Green Bay fifteen yards. When Matte faced third-and-eight at the Green Bay 48, the Packers anticipated a pass to Mackey. Instead, Matte called a screen pass to Moore, who sped to the Green Bay 39-yard line. The Colts plowed forward to the 8-yard line, where on third-and-two Tony Lorick was stopped a yard short of a first down. Lou Michaels kicked the easy field goal, giving the Colts a 10–0 lead.

The Packers struck right back, helped by a pass interference call that placed the ball on the Baltimore 9-yard line. An eight-yard pass to Anderson gave the Packers three chances to score from the 1-yard line. They failed. First Jim Taylor tried, then Hornung, then Taylor again on fourth down. Baltimore's stubborn 5–1 defense stopped them all cold. Taylor bobbled the ball as he was hit by linebacker Dennis Gaubatz. It caromed crazily back into his hands, but he was still inches shy of the goal line.

The first half ended with the Colts still leading 10–0 and the Packers and their fifty thousand fans at Lambeau Field according the Colts' ad hoc quarterback grudging respect. Matte had done better than anyone could have expected, and his teammates had played nearly perfect football. Unfortunately, they didn't keep up the good work in the second half.

Early in the third quarter, kicker Tom Gilburg juggled a high snap from center Buzz Nutter, dropped the ball, and tried to run. He was smothered at the Baltimore 35-yard line. Bratkowski lofted a pass to Carroll Dale, moving the Packers to the Baltimore 2. Then Hornung followed Jerry Kramer's block into the end zone, and the Colts' lead was cut to 10–7.

Interceptions by Bobby Boyd and Jerry Logan killed Green Bay drives in the third and fourth quarters, but Bratkowski was beginning methodically to pick apart the Baltimore zone defense. A toss to Hornung gave the Packers a third-and-one at the 48-yard line, which Taylor converted into a first down. After Bratkowski fired downfield on the next play, defensive tackle Billy Ray Smith charged into him, drawing a 15-yard penalty for roughing the passer. Nine plays later,

Chandler set up for a field goal from the Baltimore 22-yard line.

Although not a long one, the kick was difficult because it would approach the uprights from a severe angle. Starr held the ball in place. Chandler swung his leg, then glared downfield, shaking his head in disgust. Ordelle Braase, the Colts' right end, swears he saw the ball swing wide the goal posts. The Packers had been stopped again. Or had they? Field judge Jim Tunney paused for a second after observing the kick, then raised his arms: "Good!" Back judge Frank Luzar and referee Norm Schachter agreed with him. The clock read 1:58, and the score was 10–10.

The Colts bitterly protested the decision on Chandler's kick. The *Baltimore News-American* published photos showing that the kick had missed. The paper also cited game films that showed the kick sailing high and to the left of the uprights. The rules committee later ordered that the uprights be extended to 20 feet above the crossbar. Nevertheless, Baltimore's protest failed.

The overtime period was the NFL's first since the Colts had beaten the New York Giants seven years before at Yankee Stadium. Unitas was in charge then, and he got the winning points the first time Baltimore got the ball. On this day there was no such dominant character, and the Colts and Packers would trade the ball four times before the Packers finally scored.

The Colts had the first chance to win. On their second possession, Matte called three consecutive quarterback draws and gained 22 yards to the Green Bay 37-yard line. Baltimore was moving to within range for field-goal specialist Lou Michaels when, on a key third down play, Green Bay threw the Colts back. In came Michaels to try a field goal anyway. On

the Packers' bench, Starr and his teammates seemed to have lost hope. Bobby Boyd knelt to receive Nutter's snap. The ball flew back low and skipped in front of him. Boyd stretched to set the ball in place, but Michaels' timing had been disrupted and he could not muster enough power for his kick to reach the goal posts.

That was the Colts' last chance. With seven minutes to go in overtime, Bratkowski began the winning drive. He passed 18 yards to Anderson. Then Dale caught a pass for another 18 yards at the Baltimore 26. Elijah Pitts and Jim Taylor rushed the ball to the Baltimore 18. Chandler came in and kicked the clinching field goal— no doubt about this one. Thirteen minutes and 33 seconds into overtime, the longest game ever played in the NFL to that time ended with a Green Bay victory, 13–10.

But even in defeat the remarkable Matte could claim at least part of the day's glory. He completed 5 of 12 passes for 40 yards. He also tied the Colts' top rusher with 57 yards. But unmeasured was his courage and unselfish performance. The plastic crib sheet he wore on his wrist was sent to pro football's Hall of Fame. The following week the Colts went to Miami to meet Dallas in the Playoff Bowl. Shula told his team to "have some fun and let Tom throw the ball around." Matte fired three touchdowns in the Colts' 35–3 romp. Not bad for a sore-armed substitute. □

Baltimore   7   3   0   0   0—10
Green Bay   0   0   7   3   3—13
Balt—Shinnick 25 run with fumble (Michaels kick)
Balt—FG Michaels 15
GB—Hornung 1 run (Chandler kick)
GB—FG Chandler 22
GB—FG Chandler 25

After tying the game with a 22-yard field goal that most
observers agreed was wide, Don Chandler won it in
overtime with this 25-yarder, about which there was no doubt.

MEREDITH VS. JURGENSEN: ACES WILD

Dallas Cowboys vs. Washington Redskins

**NOVEMBER 28, 1965; NOVEMBER 13, 1966;
DECEMBER 11, 1966; OCTOBER 8, 1967**

Don Meredith (left) seems to be offering condolences to his counterpart, Sonny Jurgensen, after the Cowboys beat Washington 17–14 on October 8, 1967, the last of four epic Jurgensen-Meredith confrontations.

Sonny Jurgensen and Don Meredith were two of pro football's most colorful quarterbacks during the sixties. Each had his own carefree, light-hearted style. Though his stomach bulged over his belt, Jurgensen was a ruggedly handsome Swede with a potent passing arm. Dandy Don affected the manner of a shy country rube with a wildly uninhibited sense of humor. Part of the image was genuine, part of it an act to enliven the image of the Dallas Cowboys during those early, awkward seasons, when victories were few.

Of the two, without question Jurgensen was the better quarterback. In his prime Sonny was the finest passer in the league. He consistently threw the ball farther, straighter, and with greater accuracy than Johnny Unitas, Bart Starr, Fran Tarkenton, or Len Dawson ever did. Unfortunately, Sonny labored for a losing team, the Washington Redskins, during most of his career, so his stats were less impressive than they might have been. Injuries curbed Jurgensen's career at the very time the Redskins reached respectability, under coach George Allen.

At first Meredith too played for a loser. But he then benefited from the steady improvement of the Cowboys and had the pleasure of playing in three playoffs before he retired.

Both players achieved distinction though they were often hurt. Don

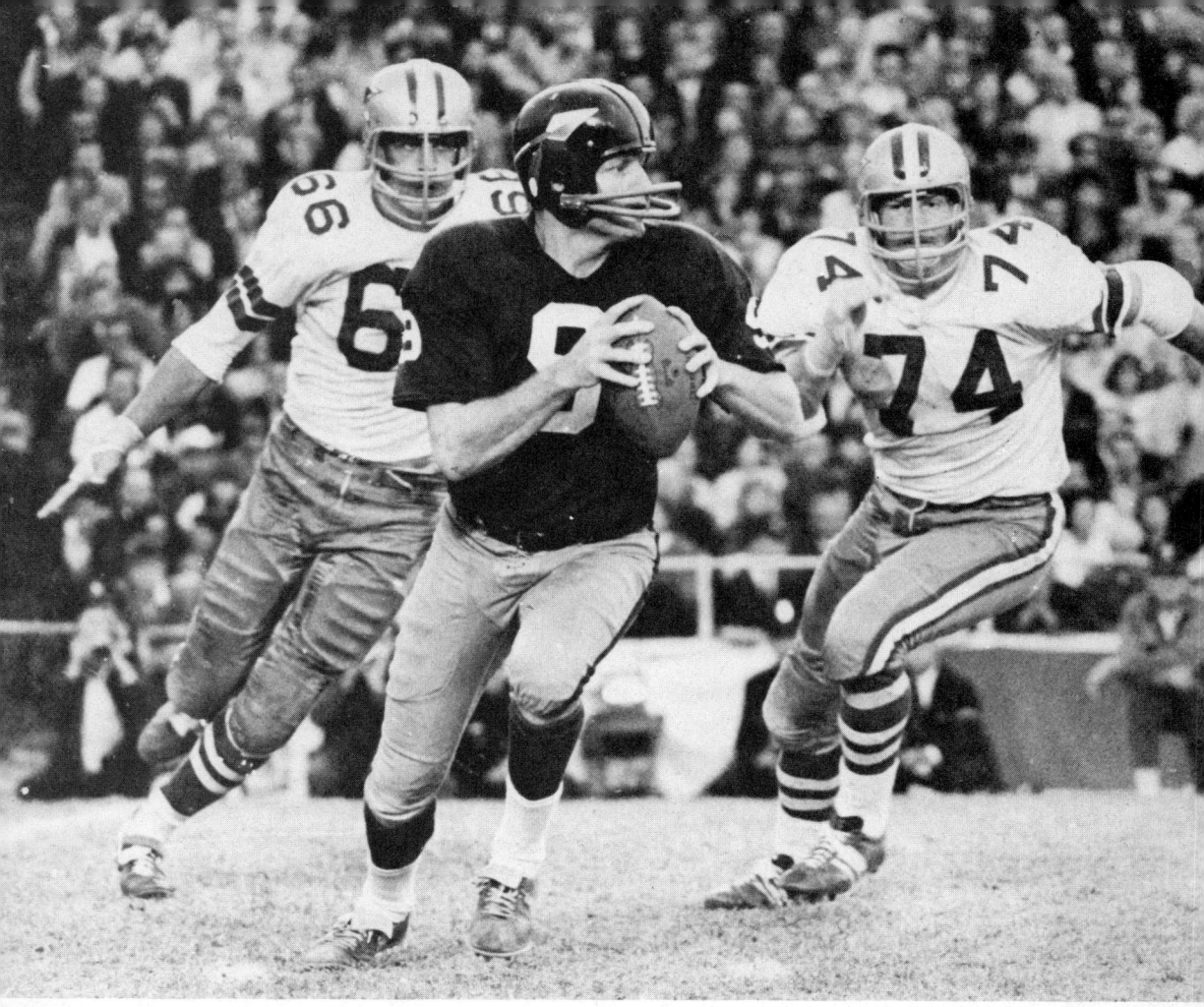

On December 11, 1966, against the Cowboys at Dallas, the Skins held the lead four times before Jurgensen drove them to a clinching last-second field goal. The year before in Washington, he threw for 411 yards in another 34–31 win.

often played while severely injured, for which he earns high praise from coach Tom Landry. Jurgensen underwent a half dozen major operations, including one for a torn Achilles tendon, about the worst injury an athlete can suffer. He played most of the 1968 season with his rib cage encased in a removable plaster cast to protect damaged ribs.

When matched against each other in their primes, these two remarkable leaders produced some of the more thrilling football of the sixties, particu-

larly in four consecutive games in 1965–67. Jurgensen and Meredith led their teams to a combined total of 222 points in those games. Yet the overall difference between the clubs was just 10 points. Dallas won two of the games, and Washington won two. In each game the quarterback brought his team from behind and won with less than two minutes to play.

Late in a close game quarterbacks use what is called "the two-minute drill." It is a series of plays designed to move a team downfield as quickly as possible. For the first minute a quarterback will throw to any open receiver but particularly those near enough to the sidelines to dash out of bounds and stop the clock. Defenders try to combat these tactics by forcing the quarterback to throw into the middle, where there is more of a chance for an interception, and, at worst, a completion keeps the clock running. By calling a sequence of plays, quarterbacks dispense with the need for a huddle after each play. Thus, they can conserve their timeouts for when they are likely to need them most, in the final seconds.

Unitas was the first to master the two-minute drill, most brilliantly of all in the 1958 National Football League title game against the Giants. In their mid-sixties shootouts, Meredith and Jurgensen made the two-minute drill a ritual. No matter how impressive they were until the closing minutes, at the finish they always seemed to produce feats greater still. At times it seemed as if this high-scoring duo had somehow picked the wrong sports—that instead of slingers in football they should have been gunners in basketball, where last-minute surges are standard.

On November 28, 1965, at Washington's D.C. Stadium, Jurgensen brought his team back from a 21–0 deficit in the first half, despite the angry fans' thunderous chant of "We Want Shiner!" meaning Dick Shiner, the Redskins' other quarterback. "It got so loud I couldn't call signals and almost raised my hands for quiet," Jurgensen remembers. "Imagine what would have happened if I had asked them to quit yelling for Shiner?"

Jurgensen silenced the crowd by driving Washington to a touchdown, cutting the Cowboys' lead to 24–13. On his next series he scored again. Meredith's 53-yard pass to Frank Clarke padded the Dallas lead. But Jurgensen quickly threw a 10-yard touchdown pass to Bobby Mitchell, closing the gap to 31–27. With less than two minutes to play, Jurgensen took possession again at the Redskins' 20-yard line.

First-and-ten, Redskins' 20: Jurgensen fumbled and recovered. As the Cowboys overran him, he scampered nine yards, then called his first timeout with 1:41 to play.

Second-and-one, Redskins' 29: His pass to Jerry Smith fell incomplete, but Chuck Howley was called for pass interference.

First-and-ten, Redskins' 38: Sonny threw a 22-yard pass to Smith, then used his second timeout with 1:28 to play.

First-and-ten, Cowboys' 40: Jurgensen hit Mitchell on the Dallas 5-yard line. He called his last timeout with 1:20 to play.

First-and-goal, Cowboys' 5: Sonny passed to Angelo Coia for the touchdown. The drive consumed 37 seconds and gave Washington a 34–31 lead.

Dallas was not finished. Meredith moved Dallas to the Redskins' 37 with seven seconds to play, but Lonnie Sanders blocked Danny Villaneuva's 44-yard field-goal attempt as the clock expired. On the afternoon Jurgensen completed 26 of 42 passes for 411 yards while the Washington running backs gained 51 yards, not exactly a balanced attack.

On November 13, 1966, at D.C. Stadium, Meredith's two touchdown bombs to speedy Bob Hayes propelled Dallas to a 21–6 lead. But late in the game Jurgensen's pass to Charley Taylor put the Redskins on top 30–28. As Meredith took the ball with no timeouts left, Washington resorted to a three-man pass rush, sending everyone else downfield to guard against a pass.

Don Meredith pulled out a game against Washington on November 13, 1966, by guiding his team virtually the length of the field in the final minute, without the benefit of a timeout. A year later he won one with another last-minute drive.

First-and-ten, Cowboys' 3: Meredith threw a 26-yard pass to Pete Gent.

First-and-ten, Cowboys' 29: Meredith rolled to his right for 12 yards before skipping out of bounds. There were 59 seconds to play.

First-and-ten, Cowboys' 41: Meredith's pass to running back Walt Garrison fell incomplete.

Second-and-ten: Cowboys' 41: Meredith passed one yard to Garrison, who ran out of bounds. The clock stopped with 48 seconds to play.

Third-and-nine, Cowboys' 42: Meredith fired a 25-yard pass to Gent.

First-and-ten, Redskins' 33: Scrambling away from a strong pass rush, Meredith fled out of bounds. The officials said linebacker John Reger hit him as he crossed the sideline, so the Skins were penalized 15 yards.

First-and-ten, Redskins' 12: Danny Villanueva booted a 20-yard field goal and the Cowboys won 31–30.

On this day, Meredith raked the Redskins for 21 completions in 28 attempts for 406 yards; Jurgensen completed 26 of 35 for 347.

On December 11, 1966, at the Cotton Bowl in Dallas, Jurgensen tied the score 31–31 when Taylor caught a 65-yard pass between two defenders for a touchdown. This was a wild game. The lead changed hands three times and Taylor's touchdown marked the fourth time the score had been tied. With two minutes to go Washington took the ball.

First-and-ten, Redskins' 46: A. D. Whitfield scooted right, gaining 30 yards.

First-and-ten, Cowboys' 24: Tom Barrington dived over left tackle for one yard.

Second-and-nine, Cowboys' 23: Whitfield ran for one yard. With 32 seconds to play, Jurgensen decided to call a timeout but not before running down the clock a bit further.

As the clock ran out, Charley Gogolak kicked a 29-yard field goal, giving Washington a 34–31 win.

On October 8, 1967, at D.C. Stadium, Washington led 14–10 after Jurgensen's eight-yard pass to Taylor. With 70 seconds to play, the Cowboys' Craig Baynham returned the kickoff to the Dallas 29-yard line.

First-and-ten, Cowboys' 29: Meredith threw a 17-yard pass to Baynham, who danced out of bounds.

First-and-ten, Cowboys' 46: A pass to Lance Rentzel fell incomplete. There were 50 seconds to play.

Second-and-ten, Cowboys' 46: Meredith passed 12 yards to Rentzel. Dallas called timeout.

First-and-ten, Redskins' 42: Rentzel caught a six-yard pass. Dallas called its second timeout.

Second-and-four, Redskins' 36: Meredith's pass fell incomplete.

Third-and-four, Redskins' 36: Dan Reeves dropped a pass. There were 23 seconds left.

Fourth-and-four, Redskins' 36: Washington linebacker Chris Hanburger failed to pick up Reeves circling out of the backfield. Meredith hit him with a touchdown, giving Dallas a 17–14 lead.

Interestingly, after coach Landry sent in the play and Meredith called it in the huddle, Reeves wanted to modify it. "I tried to tell Meredith to run it to the other side," Reeves says. "I wasn't so sure I'd be open going to the left against Hanburger. He told me

that when coach Landry sends in a play and says run it to the left, we run it to the left."

The Dallas drive covered 71 yards in seven plays, using just 43 seconds. That left some seven seconds to go after Washington took control on the kickoff. Jurgensen lofted a bomb to Taylor, and it clicked. But as time expired Taylor was wrestled down at the Dallas 20, needing but a step to break free and score. As usual, a Jurgensen-Meredith duel had consumed every second. □

November 28, 1965
Dallas   14   7   3   7—31
Washington   0   6   7   21—34
Dall—Dunn 6 pass from Meredith (Villanueva kick)
Dall—Green 5 run with fumble (Villanueva kick)
Dall—Gaechter 60 run with fumble (Villanueva kick)
Wash—Taylor 26 pass from Jurgensen (kick failed)
Dall—FG Villanueva 30
Wash—Jurgensen 1 run (Jencks kick)
Wash—Lewis 2 run (Jencks kick)
Dall—Clarke 53 pass from Meredith (Villanueva kick)
Wash—Mitchell 10 pass from Jurgensen (Jencks kick)
Wash—Coia 5 pass from Jurgensen (Jencks kick)

November 13, 1966
Dallas   7   7   7   10—31
Washington   6   0   17   7—30
Wash—FG Gogolak 35
Dall—Meredith 1 run (Villanueva kick)
Wash—FG Gogolak 33
Dall—Hayes 52 pass from Meredith (Villanueva kick)
Dall—Hayes 95 pass from Meredith (Villanueva kick)
Wash—Smith 4 pass from Jurgensen (Gogolak kick)
Wash—Taylor 78 pass from Jurgensen (Gogolak kick)
Wash—FG Gogolak 11
Dall—Reeves 1 run (Villanueva kick)
Wash—Taylor 18 pass from Jurgensen (Gogolak kick)
Dall—FG Villanueva 20

December 11, 1966
Washington   0   10   7   17—34
Dallas   7   0   10   14—31
Dall—Perkins 20 run (Villanueva kick)
Wash—FG Gogolak 42
Wash—Reger recovered blocked punt (Gogolak kick)
Dall—FG Villanueva 26
Dall—Hayes 23 pass from Morton (Villanueva kick)
Wash—Mitchell 11 pass from Jurgensen (Gogolak kick)
Dall—Reeves 67 run (Villanueva kick)
Wash—Smith 11 pass from Jurgensen (Gogolak kick)
Dall—Perkins 6 run (Villanueva kick)
Wash—Taylor 65 pass from Jurgensen (Gogolak kick)
Wash—FG Gogolak 29

October 8, 1967
Dallas   0   0   10   7—17
Washington   0   7   0   7—14
Wash—McDonald 1 run (Love kick)
Dall—Rentzel 25 pass from Meredith (Villanueva kick)
Dall—FG Villanueva 27
Wash—Taylor 8 pass from Jurgensen (Love kick)
Dall—Reeves 36 pass from Meredith (Villanueva kick)

DALLAS FRAZZLE

Green Bay Packers vs. Dallas Cowboys

JANUARY 1, 1967

Vince Lombardi's Green Bay Packers were the National Football League's blue-chip stock. They were never expected to lose. When it was announced in the summer of 1966 that the champions of both the NFL and the American Football League would meet the following January in the first Super Bowl to determine at last who was really "number one," the Packers were the logical choice of many NFL rooters to defend the honor and reputation of the older league. For the Packers completely dominated pro football in the sixties, capturing five NFL championships.

Green Bay excelled in every phase of the game. On offense there was splendid veteran quarterback Bart Starr backed by a talented and experienced squad, including Carroll Dale, Boyd Dowler, Max McGee, Marv Fleming, Jerry Kramer, Jim Taylor, Paul Hornung, Elijah Pitts, and Jim Grabowski. The Packers' defense was simply superb, the best in the NFL. Green Bay had surrendered a meager total of 13 points in the combined first quarters of 14 games. By the second quarter, the Green Bay offense usually had things under control. The Packers easily won a second straight Western Conference crown and were

heavily favored to beat the young Dallas Cowboys in the NFL title game at the Cotton Bowl on New Year's Day.

Lombardi expected some trouble from Dallas, a seven-year-old expansion franchise in its first winning season. The Cowboys' swift-striking multiple offense was said to be the NFL's best, led by quarterback Don Meredith, speedy receiver Bob Hayes, and the small but deceptively powerful runner, Don Perkins. Less than confident that his Packers could contain the explosive Dallas offense, Lombardi planned to win by exploiting the weaknesses he had isolated in the Dallas defense. His basic game plan called for double-teaming big defensive end Bob Lilly and isolating receiver Carroll Dale on defensive back Cornell Green. It was a plan that clicked flawlessly as the Packers rambled 76 yards for a touchdown the first time they had the ball. Dallas' Mel Renfro fumbled the ensuing kickoff and Jim Grabowski recovered and ran across for another score. With four minutes and 21 seconds gone, the game looked like a sure rout. It wasn't.

Ten minutes later the score stood 14–14. The famous Green Bay defense had been shredded by the Cow-

Dan Reeves put the Cowboys on the scoreboard with a three-yard run, opposite. *Then the Cowboys' Don Perkins tied the score, but Bart Starr found Carroll Dale on a scoring play over Cornell Green,* above, *sending the Packers ahead again.*

boys, who rolled up 124 yards on two quick touchdown drives, the latter ending on a 23-yard bolt up the middle by Perkins. Nearing halftime, the game became a scoring spree. Starr lofted a high pass that fell, tipped by the fingers of a Dallas defender, into the hands of Carroll Dale. He sped past Green for a 51-yard score. Dallas marched right back on a 72-yard drive that netted Danny Villanueva's field goal. A countering Green Bay threat was foiled when lineman Ralph Neely batted aside Don Chandler's field-goal attempt. The half ended with Green Bay on top 21–17 and with every indication that the offenses would continue to dominate the rest of the way.

The second half proved to be just as furious as the first, though in the end there was less scoring to show for all the fireworks. Elijah Pitts fumbled and the Cowboys recovered at their 21. This time they moved 79 yards in 13 plays, barely missing a touchdown when a lunging Willie Wood knocked down a pass to Dan Reeves in the end zone. Villanueva kicked another field goal and Dallas trailed 21–20.

The unruffled Packers scored again almost immediately. Starr threw a 43-yard pass to Dale, and four plays later Boyd Dowler vaulted into the end zone for the touchdown. The Pack now led 28–20 in the seemingly never-ending spiral of scoring.

Here the young Cowboys seemed to crack a bit under the pressure of staying close to the relentless Packers. Ignoring the warning cries of fel-

low safetyman Mel Renfro, the Cowboys' Bob Hayes fielded a Green Bay punt on his 1-yard line instead of allowing the ball to roll into the end zone for a touchback. Hayes reeled backward into the end zone after catching the ball, started to run, froze, and was overwhelmed by onrushing Packers at the 1-yard line. "I heard Renfro," Hayes admits, "but all I kept thinking was that we needed better field position and I thought I could get it with a return."

Too close to their goal line to operate freely, the Cowboys couldn't advance. Villanueva's punt reached only the Dallas 48-yard line, and the Packers returned to the attack. After a sack by George Andrie, Starr tossed a 24-yard pass to Marv Fleming. On third-and-12 he passed to Jim Taylor.

Jim Colvin and Willie Townes answered with another sack, but the irrepressible Starr promptly fired a 28-yard touchdown pass to Max McGee.

Although down by two touchdowns now, the Cowboys refused to fold. Lilly burst through and blocked the extra point try, keeping the count at 34–20. With five minutes and 20 seconds left, Dallas needed two fast touchdowns to tie. The Cowboys had already manhandled the Packers' defense for more than 300 total yards. They felt confident they could score.

On third-and-20, Meredith sent tight end Frank Clarke man-for-man against strong safety Tom Brown. Brown slipped as Clarke broke into the clear, and the receiver had only to catch the ball for the score. Villanue-

Boyd Dowler (86) sliced past Mel Renfro (20) and Cornell Green (34) for this third-quarter score, then did a half-somersault in the end zone thanks to Mike Gaechter (27).

Tom Brown (40) ended the hectic game by clutching Don Meredith's shaky pass into the end zone, left. The Cowboys had a first down on the Green Bay 2 on their final drive but couldn't produce the score that would have tied the game.

va's extra point cut the lead to 34–27 with four minutes and nine seconds to play. Attempting to waste the clock, the Green Bay offense sputtered, and Chandler, disconcerted by a mammoth Dallas rush, punted only to the Green Bay 47-yard line.

Smelling the tying score, Meredith came out throwing. He tossed up the middle to Clarke for 21 yards. After Perkins pounded through the middle for a couple, Meredith sent Clarke deep downfield. Brown, clearly beaten, grabbed Clarke by the waist at the 2-yard line, and the official made the obvious pass-interference call. Suddenly, Dallas had an excellent opportunity to tie the game.

Meredith trotted to the sidelines at the mandatory timeout with two minutes to play. The play sequence he received from head coach Tom Landry consisted of an off-tackle play, a quarterback roll-out, and, if those missed, two wedge plays. However, the strategy was foiled when in the excitement of the moment, the Cow-

boys failed to make a critically important lineup change. On offensive plays inside an opponent's 10-yard line, Hayes always was replaced by Clarke at flanker, and Pettis Norman came in to block. But this time when Norman entered, Clarke left, leaving Hayes still in the game at flanker. Landry, Meredith, and Hayes all shared the blame—Landry for not ordering the move, Hayes for not taking himself out, and Meredith for not checking the lineup. It was one of a remarkable series of oversights that cost Dallas the title in those final, fatal moments.

On first down Dan Reeves followed Neely's block for a 1-yard gain. Next, Meredith rolled right, tossing accurately to Norman in the end zone. The young tight end dropped the ball, but in any case a yellow flag had fallen at the goal line, denoting an offside penalty that pushed the Cowboys back to the 6-yard line.

Now it was second-and-goal, and the Cowboys' original play sequence was obviously outmoded. It was a

115

good time for coach and quarterback to huddle again, but they did not. Landry still blames himself for not calling timeout and discussing the new situation with his quarterback. Meredith called the play in the huddle—a pass to Reeves, not knowing that a stray finger had nicked Reeves's eyeball on the previous play and given him double vision. Reeves had neglected to inform the quarterback. Now, the ball fluttered through the receiver's hands, incomplete.

On third down Meredith called a crossing pattern and looked for Norman again. The play was designed to draw linebacker Dave Robinson away from Norman as he moved left to right. However, Meredith felt unsure that the tight end could in fact shed the linebacker, and when Norman broke free at the 2-yard line, Meredith rushed his pass. Norman had to stretch to catch it and was immediately wrestled to the ground by defensive back Tom Brown. Photos later showed Brown tugging on Norman's face mask.

"The pass was a little too low," Meredith says. "If it's chest-high, we score."

On fourth-and-two, 45 seconds to go, the Packers' defense huddled. "We've come too far to let this happen," Robinson told his mates. "The offense did their share. We can't let them down."

They didn't. Meredith called a roll-out option pass. Perkins was to fake a run, freezing the linebacker Robinson. If the cornerback rushed at Meredith, he'd toss a pass. If the cornerback hesitated, Meredith would run into the end zone with guard Leon Donohue as an escort. The receiver downfield was supposed to block the linebacker. It was a good call, but Meredith forgot that Bob Hayes, not Frank Clarke, was the receiver. To put it mildly, blocking was not Hayes's forte. In any case Robinson guessed there would be no pass, particularly not to Hayes, who had been rattled by the Packers' double-coverage, so at the snap of the ball Robinson moved quickly to seal off the outside. He moved too quickly for Donohue to stop him. Robinson slapped away Hayes, and suddenly Meredith was in deep trouble.

"I saw Robinson make a good strong move to the outside," Meredith recalls. "I knew I couldn't outrun him. I had to throw. He grabbed my left arm, so I didn't get much on it."

"I almost got sick to my stomach when he got the ball away," Robinson says. "I knew the game was up in the air."

Tom Brown was supposed to cover Reeves but he lost him, so he dropped back to play the ball. He saw Robinson yanking on Meredith and the ball wobbling his way. The one-time first baseman for the Washington Senators never made a bigger catch.

Two of pro football's more orderly units had produced a finish, like the game itself, of thrilling chaos. Through a multitude of mistakes, the Cowboys had squandered a magnificent opportunity to extend the game into sudden-death overtime. The Packers had contributed to the wild finish with errors of their own. But somehow they had covered theirs. In the war of wits that is pro football as much as the clash of bodies, the Packers, had, as usual, prevailed. □

Green Bay	14	7	7	6—34
Dallas	14	3	3	7—27

GB—Pitts 17 pass from Starr (Chandler kick)
GB—Grabowski 18 run with fumble (Chandler kick)
Dall—Reeves 3 run (Villanueva kick)
Dall—Perkins 23 run (Villanueva kick)
GB—Dale 51 pass from Starr (Chandler kick)
Dall—FG Villanueva 11
Dall—FG Villanueva 32
GB—Dowler 16 pass from Starr (Chandler kick)
GB—McGee 28 pass from Starr (kick failed)
Dall—Clarke 68 pass from Meredith (Villanueva kick)

THE SUPER BOWL IS GREEN AND GOLD

Green Bay Packers vs. Kansas City Chiefs

JANUARY 15, 1967

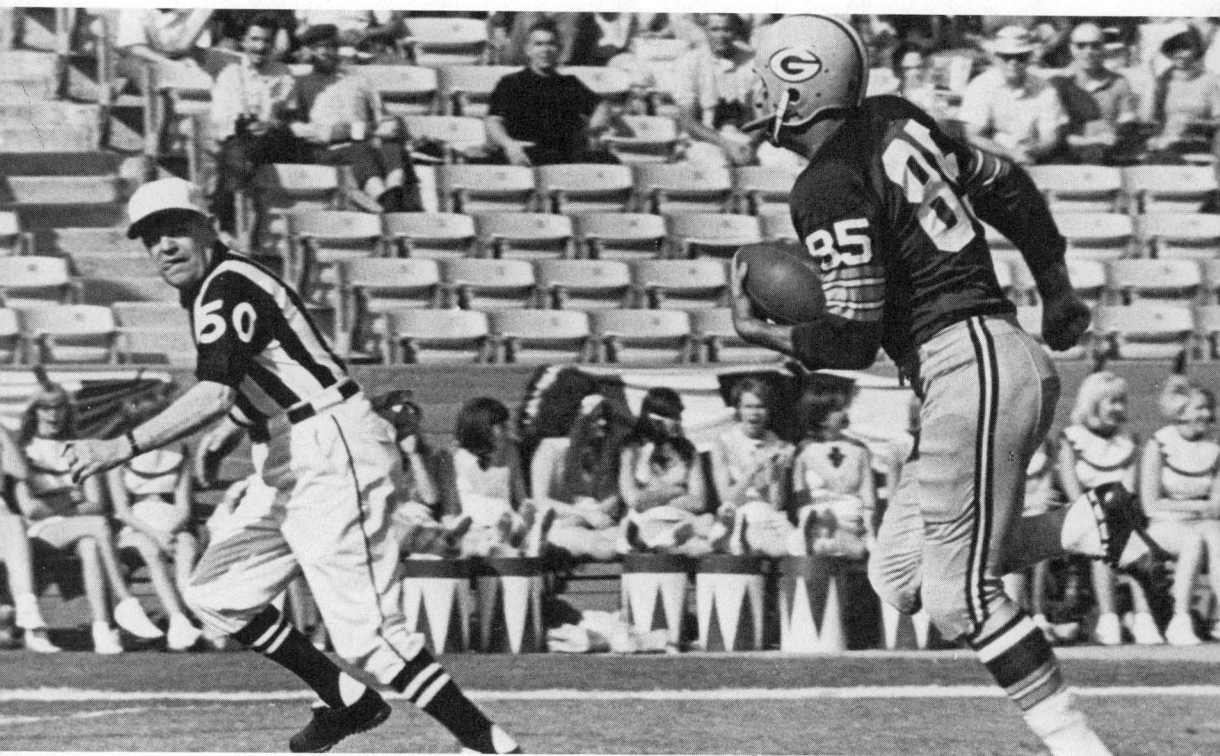

The first Super Bowl was supposed to be a Green Bay romp. Eventually, it was, but for the first half the Packers had to struggle. Max McGee broke the ice in the first quarter with this 37-yard scoring pass from Bart Starr.

To the surprise of no one, except possibly Chiefs' owner Lamar Hunt, the National Football League's Green Bay Packers beat the American Football League's Kansas City Chiefs 35–10 in the first Super Bowl game.

The win proved only the obvious— that the finest NFL team was better than the best the AFL could produce. Yet given a sufficiently unsettling state of tension, even the obvious resolution can resound with a thunder-

The Chiefs' high point came in the second quarter when Len Dawson hit Otis Taylor with a pass that set up the Chiefs' only score of the day. Dawson confused the Packers with his play-action passes until Green Bay blitzed in the second half.

clap of significance. However predictable, the official certification of the NFL as the superior league and the AFL as the inferior one, seemed to be of historic importance. Six years of squabbling between the NFL and AFL over fans and players, and a crushing barrage of publicity had made the Super Bowl equal in stature, as far as Americans were concerned, to baseball's World Series, the major college bowl games, even the Olympics.

At best the game was less than suspenseful. Under the enormous pressure that both teams felt in rep-

resenting their leagues, the Packers' orthodox style and precise execution proved the more durable. During the first half, the Chiefs surprised many NFL diehards with their crisp blocking and tackling and steady play. But in the end the mighty Packers— strong, disciplined, relentless, in a word, pressure-proof—disposed of the Chiefs and their "floating pocket," "stack defense," and brash cornerback, Fred Williamson, nicknamed "the Hammer," like so many frivolous trimmings.

Green Bay revered the basics,

and in a test as big as this one, it could be relied on to adhere to its philosophy. There would be power sweeps left and right, crunching off-tackle plays, fullback draws, and a modest array of pass patterns. The defense was a straight 4–3, with line-backers and defensive backs helping the linemen foreclose the run. On pass plays there were few stunts and blitzes. Lombardi called them "signs of weakness."

No game could have lived up to the media flackery and public expec-tations focused on the first Super Bowl. The game was held in the vast Los Angeles Coliseum, which, despite a local television blackout, was not filled for this match. The extravagant extras included three vast bands, three choruses, a drill team, four thousand swirling pigeons in the sky, forty thousand red, white, and blue balloons, and a pair of jet-propelled space cadets circling overhead. Not one but two major television networks covered the proceedings, a two-week orgy of promotional overkill. For many it was a relief to see the game played just to be rid of the television ads.

Lombardi's game plan was a basic blend of running and passing plays. His intention was first to run, then to throw long against Kansas City cornerbacks Willie Mitchell and Fred Williamson. The Chiefs' "stack defense" made running difficult. The linebackers stood closely behind the tackles to help them fend off blockers and pull down the ball carrier quickly —a defense similar to that of the De-troit Lions, with which Green Bay quarterback Bart Starr had become familiar.

Though well-suited to stopping the rush, the stack defense limited the Chiefs' pass rush. Kansas City was often forced to blitz with linebackers and defensive backs, which in turn weakened the pass protection and opened the middle. It was almost as if Kansas City was daring the Packers to throw. Starr needed no prodding.

Correctly guessing a blitz on Green Bay's second possession, Starr sent veteran Max McGee streaking across the middle on a post pattern. The ball was slightly underthrown, but McGee reached back and gathered it in with one hand as he slipped past Kansas City defensive backs Willie Mitchell and Bobby Hunt. It was an easy 37-yard touchdown. "The post pattern was an automatic call when-ever the Chiefs tried a weak-side blitz," McGee says. "For thirteen years I never got away with it in the NFL, but the Chiefs didn't cover the inside like NFL teams did. That's one reason we were able to beat their cor-nerbacks all day. We planned to throw a lot to our split end."

McGee had played little that year. He caught only four passes in the regular season. But after Boyd Dowler injured his neck, McGee scored the winning touchdown in Green Bay's NFL title game victory over Dallas. When Dowler reinjured himself early in the Super Bowl, the 34-year-old McGee had to go it alone. He substituted splendidly—138 yards on five catches with two touchdowns.

The Chiefs were not bashful on offense. They favored a variety of play-action passes and a flashy roll-out maneuver that coach Hank Stram called "the moving pocket." The idea was to make the defense guess the spot where quarterback Len Dawson would set himself to throw. It was supposed to confuse the Packers' pass rush. Stram planned to throw in front of the Green Bay defensive backs, who sometimes dropped too deep. If they moved closer to the line, Dawson would counter with bombs to Otis Taylor and Chris Burford.

All this tended to inhibit the Packers. They had difficulty coping

*Unspectacular but powerful and reliable,
Jim Taylor put the Packers ahead
to stay by scoring on a 14-yard sally around
left end in the second quarter.*

120

with Dawson's "moving pocket." They hesitated, and they froze when he called a play-action pass. Though trailing 7–0, the Chiefs' offense proved more than a match for Green Bay's defense. Early in the second quarter, Dawson tossed a 17-yard pass to Mike Garrett. Four plays later he hit Otis Taylor at Green Bay's 7-yard line. Still confused, the Packers failed to cover two receivers in the end zone, and on the next play Dawson hit Curtis McClinton for the touchdown. With nearly 20 minutes gone, the score was tied.

But the Packers refused to be rattled. While the defense repaired to the sidelines for adjustments, the third-down heroics of Bart Starr regained the lead. On third-and-six Starr passed 10 yards to McGee for a first down. Three plays later, third-and-ten, he hit Dale for 15 yards. On third-and-five he found Marv Fleming for an 11-yard gain. On third-and-seven Elijah Pitts rolled out of the backfield to catch a 10-yard pass on the Chiefs' 14-yard line. Jim Taylor followed guards Jerry Kramer and Fuzzy Thurston around left end for the touchdown.

Dawson returned with his tantalizing play-action fakes and roll-outs, which the Packers still had trouble containing. Four straight completions moved Kansas City to Green Bay's 24-yard line. With 54 seconds left in the half, Mike Mercer kicked a field goal. When the teams left the field, the upstart Chiefs, behind 14–10, had outplayed the Packers, having outgained them (181–164) and seemingly outsmarted them. Some pretty anxious discussions ensued in the Green Bay dressing room. "We were almost getting desperate," Willie Wood remembers. "The defense was just standing around out there and we had to do something. We finally decided to blitz the linebacker who was opposite the flow of the play. It was a gamble, but we had to take it."

The Packers hadn't blitzed at all in the first half. During the regular season, they had seldom blitzed more than three times a game. Their decision to abandon precedent in the second half turned the game around. On third-and-five at the Chiefs' 49-yard line, Dawson called a delay pass to tight end Fred Arbanas. The play was designed to lure pass defenders to one side of the field by flooding the area with receivers, then to capitalize on the drift by sending the tight end a few yards past the line of scrimmage. The Pack blitzed on the play, shooting outside linebackers Leroy Caffey and Dave Robinson straight at Dawson. Robinson was knocked down, but Caffey burst through and tipped the ball as it left Dawson's hand. Wood, guarding Arbanas, stepped in front of the Chiefs' tight end, caught the wobbly pass, and raced toward the end zone. Garrett finally caught him from behind at the 5-yard line, but the damage had been done. Pitts followed Bob Skoronski's block for a touchdown on the next play. Suddenly, the Packers were in complete command.

The added threat of the blitz forced Dawson to use his running backs as blockers. This cost him the play-action maneuvers that had confused the Green Bay defense. Moreover, Wood's timely interception charged up the Packers' offense, which put the game away with a minute to play in the third quarter on Starr's second touchdown toss to McGee.

With the game in hand, there remained just one small order of business for the Packers. Throughout the week, Fred Williamson, who had nicknamed himself "the Hammer," had predicted dire consequences for Green Bay's wide receivers. In a Muhammad Ali-style routine, Williamson

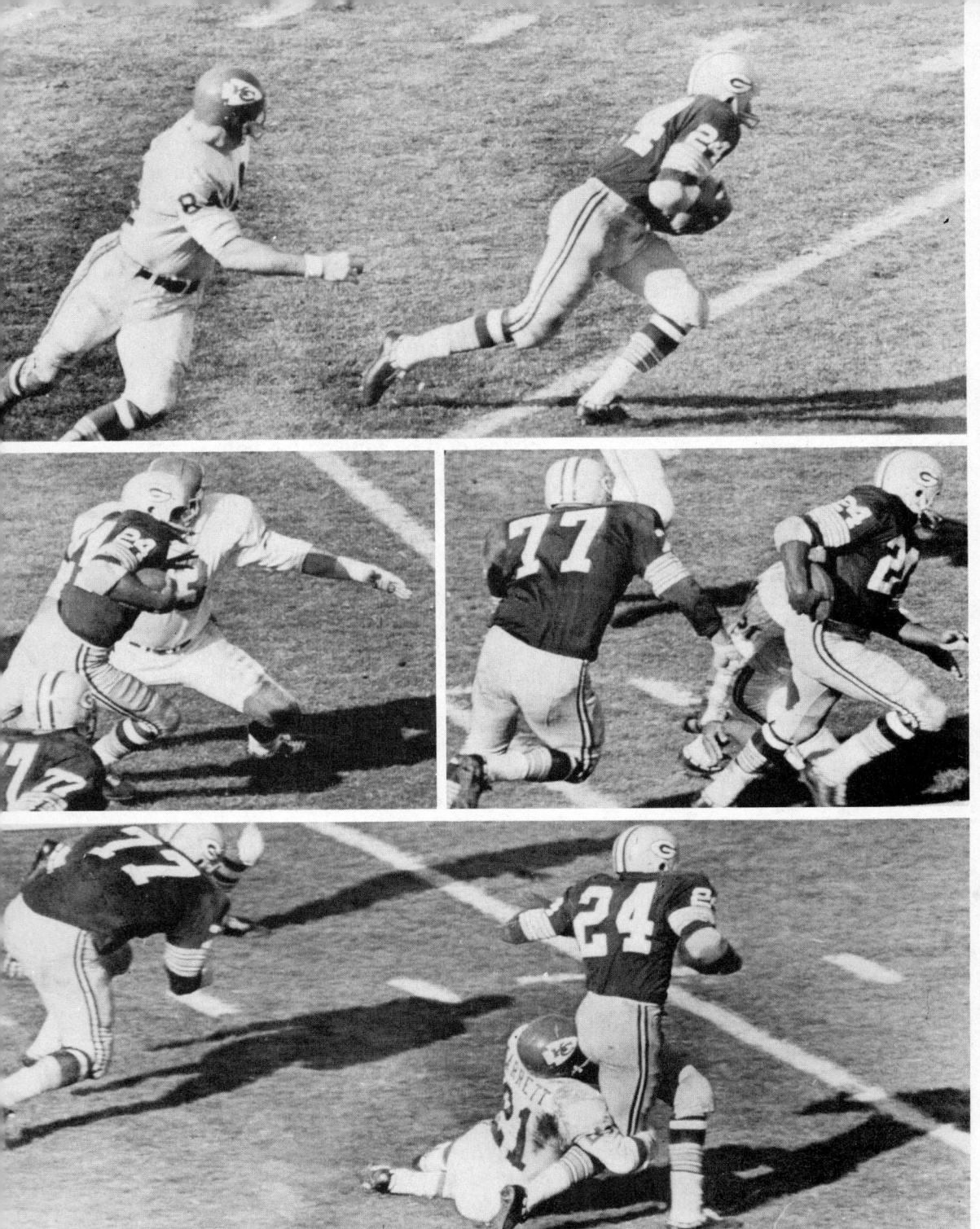

Above: *The turning point: early in the third quarter Willie Wood intercepted a pass intended for Fred Arbanas (84) and returned it 50 yards to the Chiefs' 5. On the next play the Packers ran it in, and the Chiefs could never recover.*

Left: *Icing on the cake: Max McGee scored his second touchdown and the Packers' fourth on a 13-yard pass from Starr. The 34-year-old substitute had caught only four passes during the regular season. In the Super Bowl he more than doubled his output.*

boasted that he was "the greatest," that his forearm smashes had crushed 30 helmets, and that he would inflict similar punishment on the Packers.

"All of his talk—and he says some interesting things—might inspire our downfield blocking," receiver Carroll Dale hinted before the game. Perhaps it did. Late in the fourth quarter, with Green Bay leading 35–10, Donny Anderson headed straight for Williamson on a power sweep. When everyone unpiled, the Hammer had been nailed. The Chiefs lugged him off the field. "That can't be the Hammer," some of the Packers yelled.

Lombardi scored the final jibe. Someone asked him if the Packers had felt intimidated by Williamson's reputation. "Was he out there?" the coach asked innocently. "The only time I noticed him was when they carried him off the field."

But for the most part the winners' locker room was restrained after the game. Most Packers had inoffensive things to say about the Chiefs, dwelling diplomatically on the different styles of play in the different leagues. There was little gloating. The Packers had done what they had been expected to do, and seemed more relieved than proud to have done it. "We didn't play any bush leaguers, and we were happy to accomplish what we did," Wood says. "You could practically hear the giant sigh of relief in the dressing room when the game was over." □

Kansas City	0	10	0	0—10
Green Bay	7	7	14	7—35

GB—McGee 37 pass from Starr (Chandler kick)
KC—McClinton 7 pass from Dawson (Mercer kick)
GB—Taylor 14 run (Chandler kick)
KC—FG Mercer 31
GB—Pitts 5 run (Chandler kick)
GB—McGee 13 pass from Starr (Chandler kick)
GB—Pitts 1 run (Chandler kick)

THE FIRE AND ICE OF GREEN BAY

Green Bay Packers vs. Dallas Cowboys

DECEMBER 31, 1967

In Green Bay on New Year's Eve, 1967, a day better suited for polar bears and penguins than football players, the Green Bay Packers beat the Dallas Cowboys 21–17, capturing their third straight National Football League title. Even by Wisconsin's harsh winter standards, the afternoon's weather was excessive. At game time the temperature was 13 degrees below zero. Bitter Canadian winds whipped across Green Bay's Lambeau Field, plunging the wind-chill factor even lower.

To prevent the field from freezing the Packers had installed what they

Bart Starr (15) burrowed over the goal line from one yard away, right, deciding the 1967 NFL championship game in its waning seconds on a brutally frigid day in Green Bay.

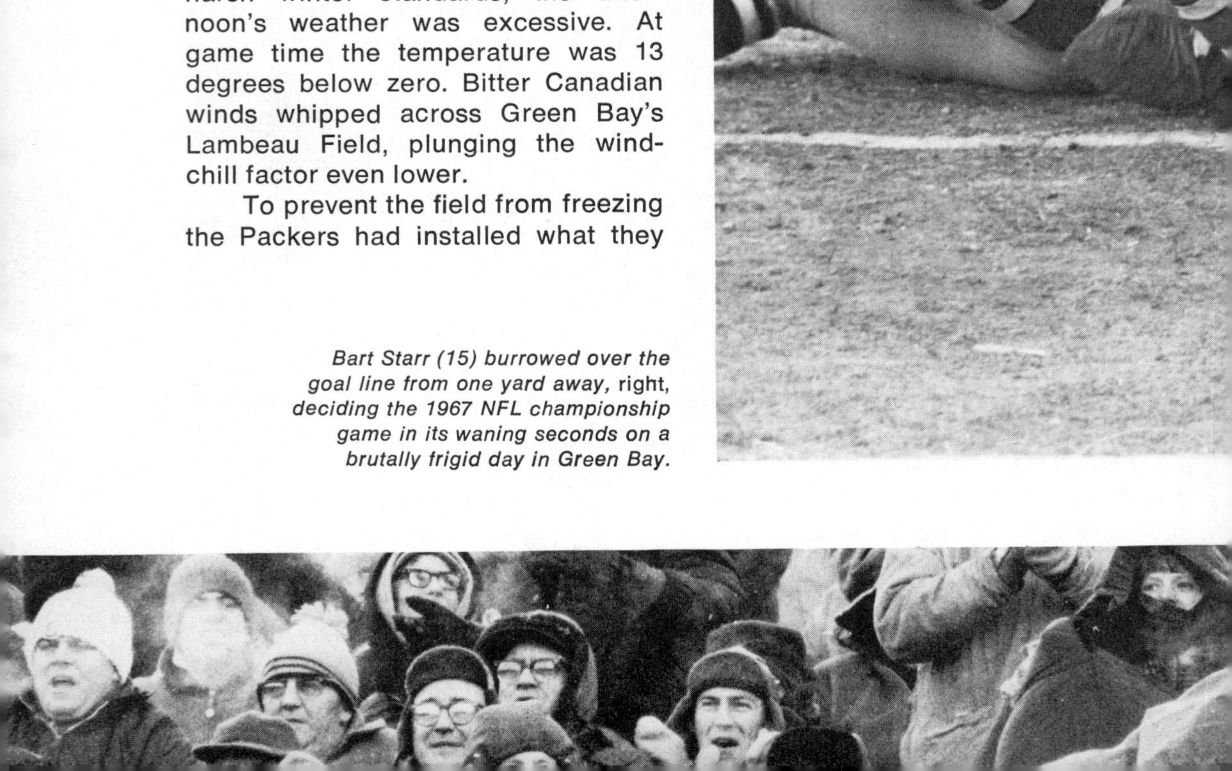

called an "electric blanket," a grid of heating wires six inches beneath the sod. The intense cold put the mechanism out of commission. Thus, on the morning of the game the ground moisture began to harden, leaving part of the field as slick as a skating rink.

The Packers, who lived and practiced in cold weather, were better prepared than the Cowboys for the frigid conditions. If nothing else, they knew enough not to change their game plan or their style of play just because of the weather. Many of the Dallas players remember sitting in their locker room before the game and worrying more about the weather than about the Packers. Quarterback Don Meredith saw his receivers dropping balls during pregame drills, turned to see Bart Starr throwing softer, and tried to do the same. It only ruined his timing.

Green Bay, on the other hand, began their game almost as if it were a warm spring day. On their first possession the Packers drove 82 yards for a touchdown. Dallas helped with two critical blunders—an interference call against Mike Gaechter and a holding penalty on Willie Townes. Starr finished the drive with a 3-yard touchdown pass to Boyd Dowler. Early in the second quarter, Dowler caught another, this for 43 yards, sending Green Bay ahead 14–0.

At this point, the game could have very easily become a rout. But the Packers, uncharacteristically, failed to press their advantage. "We lost our concentration," Starr says. "Maybe we started to think more about the cold and the conditions than we thought about our own execution."

Starr himself was guilty of a rare

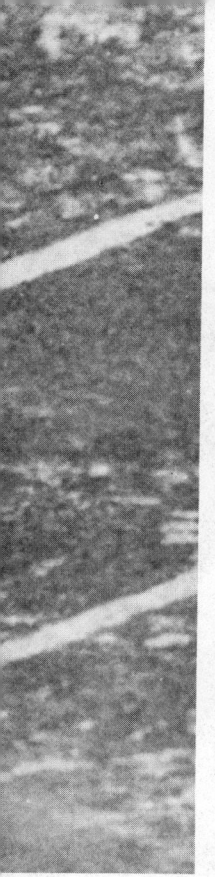

Like the year before, the Packers took an early 14–0 lead and the Cowboys struggled back.
Left: *Boyd Dowler scored the second touchdown, beating Mel Renfro on a 43-yard pass play.*
Above: *Dan Reeves in a Packer's clutches.*

tactical error. With the ball on the Green Bay 26-yard line late in the first half, Starr decided to risk a pass. The Cowboys' coverage was tight, and as Starr scanned downfield, Willie Townes sacked him, dislodging the ball. It slid and skittered into the hands of defensive end George Andrie, who pounded across the goal line for the score. "The receivers couldn't make their cuts on the icy field and I couldn't find anyone to throw to," Starr explains. "I should have pulled the ball to my chest when it was obvious I was going to be tackled, instead of letting it hang out there."

Moments before halftime, Willie Wood muffed a punt at his 17-yard line and Dallas recovered. The Cowboys stalled and settled for a 21-yard field goal by Danny Villanueva. They trailed Green Bay 14–10 at the half.

Early in the second half, Meredith was hit hard by linebacker Leroy Caffey and fumbled on the Packers' 13. The ball was recovered by cornerback Herb Adderley. But the Green Bay offense was suddenly as cold as the day. Time and time again the Packers failed to move the ball. The fifty thousand nervous Green Bay fans huddled numbly in the stands became very quiet.

Halfback Dan Reeves, whose successful outside runs had the Packers on their guard, suggested that Meredith call a "fire pitch." This was a halfback option pass to wide receiver Lance Rentzel. Reeves would fake an outside sweep, drawing the defenders away from Rentzel. Just as planned, Rentzel snared the ball far behind Green Bay cornerback Bob Jeter. De-

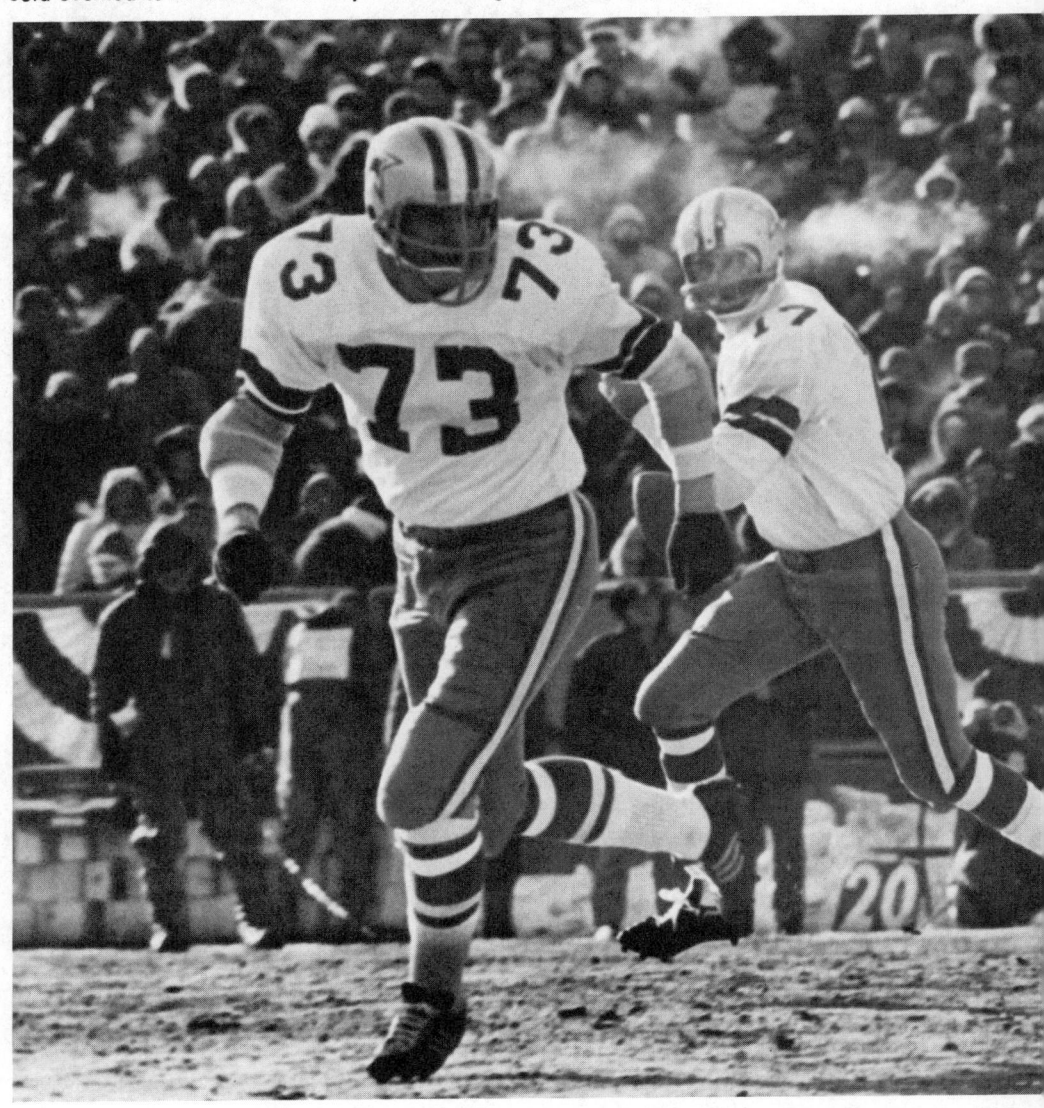

fensive back Willie Wood had noticed Rentzel split wider than usual, but had left him for Jeter to cover. "I didn't react," Jeter says. "It was my job to drop back and protect against any pass."

Rentzel's touchdown made it 17-14 Dallas, and the underdog Cowboys seemed to have their first NFL championship in hand. For ten minutes, Dallas ran out the clock. Meredith was sharp. He completed 6 of 12 pas-

strong Dallas defense had already sacked Starr eight times. Kramer recalled the Packers' other championships. "Maybe this is the end of it all," he remembers thinking. "Maybe this is the year we won't make it."

To loosen the Dallas defense, Starr tossed a screen pass to Donny Anderson. He gained 6 yards. Then Chuck Mercein rushed for 7 yards and a first down. Working methodically, Starr hit Dowler on a 13-yard pass down the middle. "At that point, there was no real hurry," Starr says. "We were quite willing to take anything the Dallas defense was willing to give us as long as we could move the ball."

On the next play, though, Anderson lost his footing and was dropped for a nine-yard loss. Starr didn't panic. He shoveled the ball to Anderson who skated past a tangle of sliding Cowboys to the Dallas 39-yard line. Then Starr lofted a short pass to Anderson. Again, he won the battle of the footing, this time to the Dallas 30 for a first down.

All these plays had gone toward the right sideline. Mercein noticed that the left sideline was unprotected because the Dallas linebackers were dropping too far back. He passed along his observation to Starr, who promptly utilized it. After faking to Dowler over the middle, he threw to Mercein along the left. Linebacker Chuck Howley read the play quickly but slipped and fell. Mercein charged past him and reached the Dallas 11-yard line before he was forced out of bounds. This was the same Chuck Mercein who earlier in the season played for a minor league outfit known as the Westchester Bulls.

ses in the half, a remarkable percentage considering the poor conditions. With four and a half minutes to go, Green Bay took possession on its 32.

Green Bay guard Jerry Kramer glanced nervously at the clock. The

Weeks later, coach Vince Lombardi had somehow plucked him off the roster of the Washington Redskins. Now, in the most important minute of the season, Chuck Mercein had become the man of the moment.

With 71 seconds to play now, Starr called a special "sucker play" he had been saving. Guard Gale Gillingham faked a pulling block in order to draw the defensive tackle out of position. As if on cue, defensive tackle Bob Lilly followed Gillingham down the line. But Dallas coach Tom Landry had prepared the Cowboys' line for the maneuver. Defensive end George Andrie looped around to cover the vacated area. Plunging into Lilly's vacated position, Mercein should have encountered the defensive end, but Andrie slipped and sprawled helplessly. The center and tackle disposed of the Dallas middle linebacker, and Mercein tore through the hole to the Dallas 3.

Anderson ran to the right side for two yards and a first down. Then Starr called the first of three timeouts. In such situations the Packers' best play was "31 Wedge," a halfback plunge between center Ken Bowman and guard Jerry Kramer. Lombardi and Starr decided to use it now.

The temperature had fallen to 18 degrees below zero. Resting in the shadow of the stadium, the playing field was as hard and smooth as a china plate. On the first play Anderson slipped as he took Starr's handoff and fell for no gain. The second play produced the same result. On third down, 16 seconds to go, Starr trotted over to talk with Lombardi.

A field goal would tie the score at 17–17 and force sudden death. Neither quarterback nor coach wanted to try it. Lombardi joked later that he couldn't stand to see the fans shiver through an overtime period. In reality he couldn't stand to see his Packers

settle for second best. Some of the Packers heard Lombardi remark, "If they can't get the ball into the end zone in three plays from the one-yard line, then they don't deserve to be NFL champions."

Starr suggested a quarterback sneak off the "31 Wedge." Lombardi hesitated, then told him to try. It was all or nothing. Both knew the Packers wouldn't have time to kick a field goal if the play failed.

"We had run out of ideas," Starr says of the call.

The quarterback rejoined the huddle and explained what he wanted. Kramer squatted at the line, grinding his spikes into the ice for better traction. The Cowboys tried to do likewise.

"We should have gone to the bench, gotten a screwdriver and gouged out some cleat holes in that ice," Lilly said later.

Starr took the snap and Kramer rammed into tackle Jethro Pugh, driving him back with his left shoulder. Tackle Forrest Gregg flattened Willie Townes, and Starr, hugging the ball, fell through the narrow hole.

Moments later, Lombardi stood in the middle of the steaming dressing room, his frozen face radiant under the television lights. "This is what the Green Bay Packers are all about," he said. "They don't do it for individual glory. They do it because they love one another." □

Dallas	0	10	0	7—17
Green Bay	7	7	0	7—21

GB—Dowler 3 pass from Starr (Chandler kick)
GB—Dowler 43 pass from Starr (Chandler kick)
Dal—Andrie 7 run with fumble recovery (Villanueva kick)
Dal—FG Villanueva 21
Dal—Rentzel 50 pass from Reeves (Villanueva kick)
GB—Starr 1 run (Chandler kick)

THE "HEIDI" AFFAIR

Oakland Raiders vs. New York Jets

NOVEMBER 17, 1968

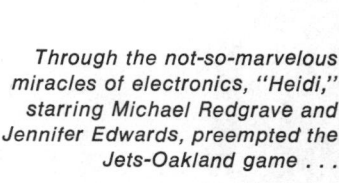

Through the not-so-marvelous miracles of electronics, "Heidi," starring Michael Redgrave and Jennifer Edwards, preempted the Jets-Oakland game . . .

. . . while Oakland was scoring two late touchdowns, including Preston Ridlehuber's kickoff fumble recovery, for a comeback win. Football fans seethed.

It was not the first time a national television network decided arbitrarily to lop off the final minutes of a pro football game. But the notorious "Heidi game" certainly created the loudest stir.

The setting was the Oakland-Alameda County Coliseum, where, in mid-autumn of 1968, the American Football League's defending champs, the Oakland Raiders, faced their bitter rivals, the New York Jets, in a game televised coast to coast. The star attraction was New York's superb

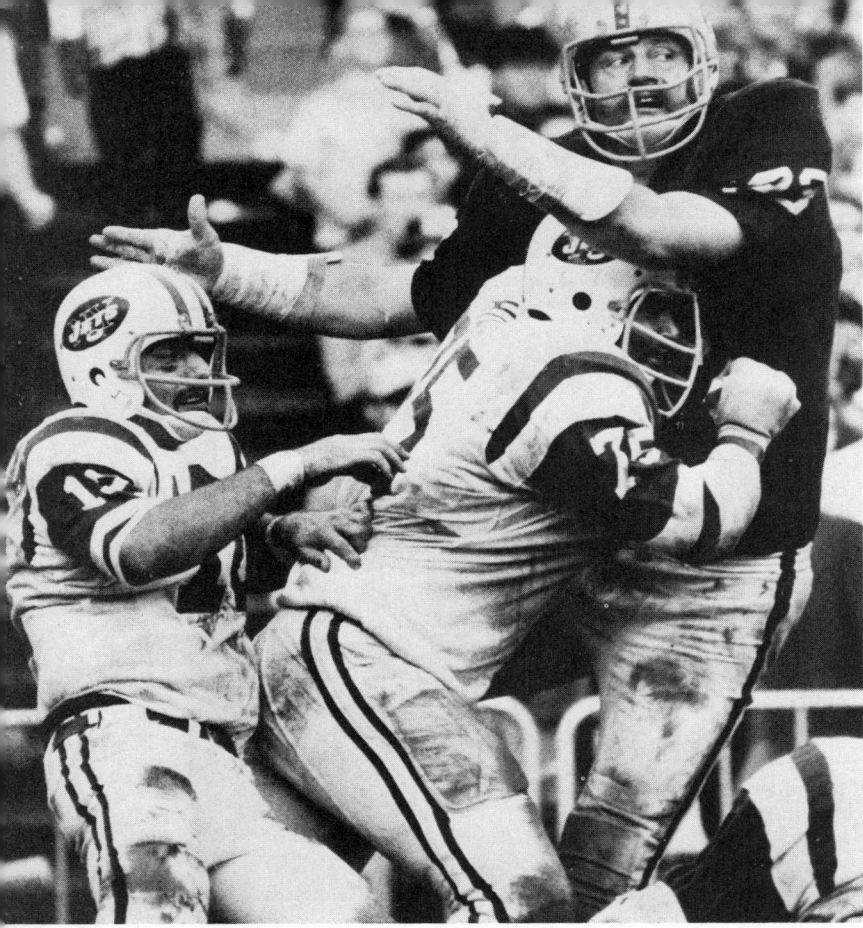

Star billing in the football game went to Joe Namath, whom the big bad Raiders promised to punish. Here, Namath, Winston Hill, and Ben Davidson fought more or less to a draw.

young quarterback, Joe Namath, who was leading the Jets to their first title, and who, under the masterful promotion of Jets' owner Sonny Werblin, had become the glamorous "Broadway Joe," a New York City folk hero. The Oakland Raiders were a rough, swashbuckling crew not known for beneficence toward $400,000 bonus-baby quarterbacks. The Raiders promised to punish Namath. It all made for some pretty good theater.

The game turned out to be even better than advertised. Oakland quarterback Daryle Lamonica threw a pair of touchdown passes, Namath scored once, and the Raiders led 14–12 at halftime. The teams traded touchdowns in the third quarter, but Oakland's two-point conversion increased its lead to 22–19. Then Namath did his thing. He hit Don Maynard with a 50-yard touchdown bomb. Jim Turner's pair of field goals, the last coming with just over a minute to play, gave the Jets a 32–29 advantage. And that's the last anyone east of Denver saw of the game.

They never saw Lamonica toss a 43-yard touchdown pass to Charley Smith with 42 seconds to play. Nor did they see Oakland's Preston Ridlehuber corral Earl Christy's kickoff fumble for yet another Oakland score. Instead of watching Oakland's miraculous 43–32 victory, which ran seven minutes into prime time, millions of bewildered fans saw the tender opening scenes of Johanna Spyri's children's classic, "Heidi."

Sunday games did not usually run more than three hours. When they did, the endings were usually not exciting or important enough to warrant coverage. Earlier that very afternoon, NBC had cut away from a game in progress, Buffalo versus San Diego, to join the start of the Jets-Oakland game. However, for the finish of this game, network executives at NBC sports in New York originally decided to delay "Heidi." But their orders to NBC Broadcast Operations Control could not be communicated because the switchboard was already jammed with calls, these from viewers who anticipated the problem and wanted to express their opinions. So the New York executives called the mobile unit in Oakland and advised it to call Broadcast Operations on its direct line. The contact was made and the message delivered, but Broadcast Operations contended that it needed direct orders to deviate from the schedule and keep the football game on the air. So somewhere in Burbank, California, at a studio controlling the TV feed, the switch was thrown and television viewers were abruptly transported from a howling arena to pretty alpine glades.

Most of them did not want to go. Recording an unprecedented reaction, the NBC New York switchboard lit up completely as tens of thousands of callers tried to voice their protests. Angry fans unable to get through phoned the New York City Police Department, newspapers, other TV stations—anyone who might listen.

Many callers had no idea how the game had ended and were phoning not only to complain but to learn the outcome. They should have stayed tuned. As Klara, the paralyzed cousin, took her first, tentative steps, the final score went rolling across the bottom of the screen. The football fans were indignant when they saw what they had missed. The "Heidi" audience was peeved at having an ambulatory football score intrude on one of the story's more touching moments. Short of pre-empting "Heidi" for a skin flick, NBC could not have managed to alienate more viewers that evening.

NBC's president, Julian Goodman, was forced to issue a public apology before the evening had passed. He claimed that he had been disappointed "as much as anyone" in not seeing the end of the game. He insisted that the network had tried to reconnect the game but that it had ended before the faulty orders could be countermanded. He termed the network's decision to pull the switch "a forgivable error committed by humans who were concerned about children expecting to see 'Heidi'. . . ."

Since the "Heidi" affair, the network's policy has been not to take any game off the air until it has ended. In 1975, NBC spent a fortune promoting "Willie Wonka and the Chocolate Factory," a children's movie, only to run into an overtime game between Washington and Oakland. The game ran forty-five minutes past its allotted time. Angry parents and children who wanted to see the show flooded the network with complaints. The game stayed on. Tough, kid. □

| New York | 6 | 6 | 7 | 13—32 |
| Oakland | 7 | 7 | 8 | 21—43 |

NY—FG Turner 44
Oak—Wells 9 pass from Lamonica (Blanda kick)
NY—FG Turner 18
Oak—Cannon 49 pass from Lamonica (Blanda kick)
NY—Namath 1 run (kick failed)
NY—Mathis 4 run (Turner kick)
Oak—Smith 3 run (Dixon pass)
NY—Maynard 50 pass from Namath (Turner kick)
Oak—Biletnikoff 22 pass from Lamonica (Blanda kick)
NY—FG Turner 12
NY—FG Turner 26
Oak—Smith 43 pass from Lamonica (Blanda kick)
Oak—Ridlehuber 2 run with fumble recovery (Blanda kick)

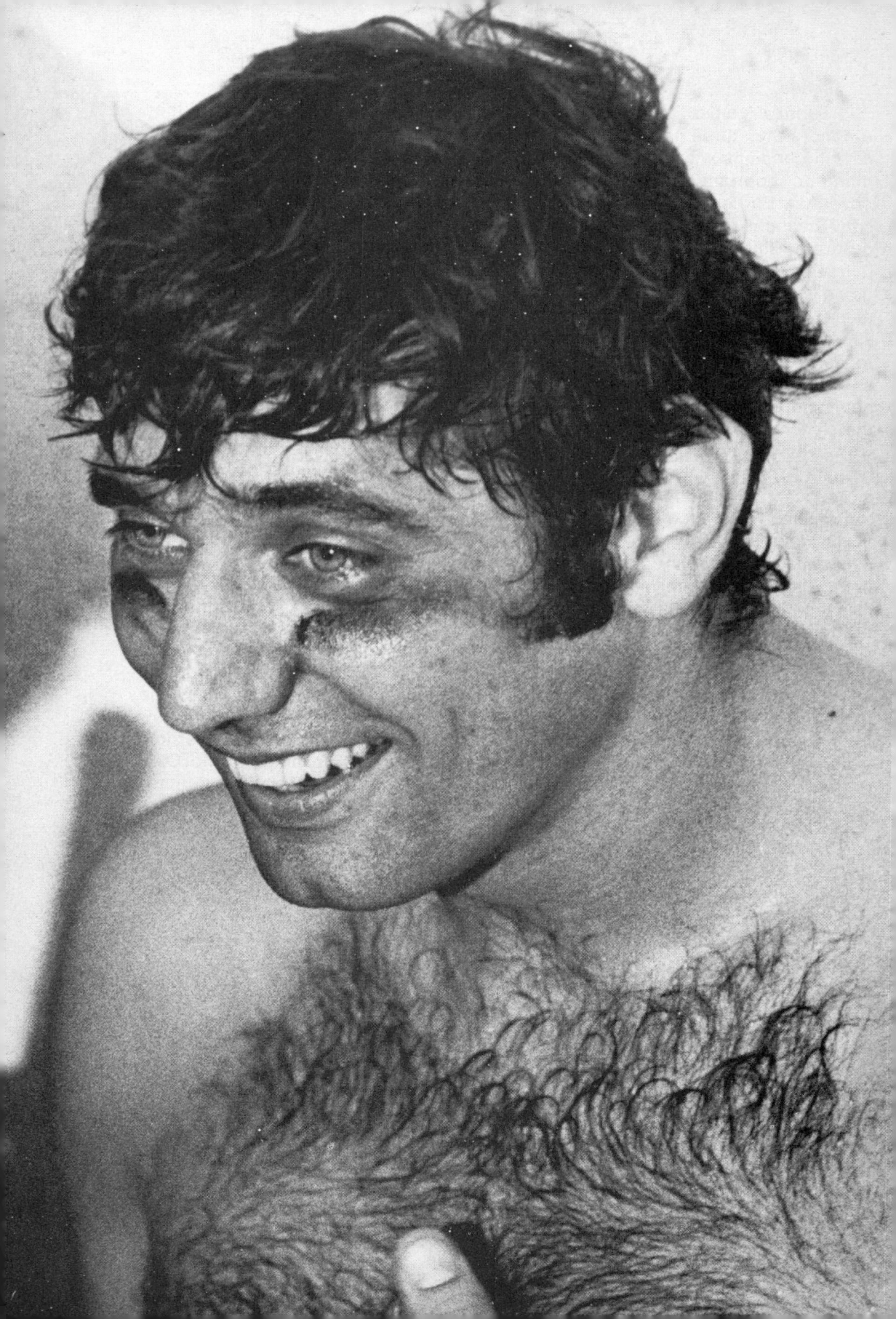

GIVE MY REGARDS
TO BROADWAY JOE

New York Jets vs. Baltimore Colts

JANUARY 12, 1969

Above: *The blueprint for the upset of the decade called for the Jets' Matt Snell (41) to run left at the Colts. Joe Namath (12) hands off, and Winston Hill (75) clears the way. Opposite: Namath aglow: "I told you so."*

Super Bowl III marked a great turnabout in professional football history. From then on, for better or worse, the two rival leagues had to be treated as equals. And the man responsible for the New York Jets' handsome 16–7 embarrassment of the Baltimore Colts, 17-point pregame favorites, was a cool young quarterback named Joe Willie Namath.

Pick an adjective to describe Joe Willie and you pretty much expose your prejudices. There's little middle ground. If you admire him, he's styl-

Snell capped an 80-yard march in the second quarter with this scoring burst from the 4-yard line—the only New York touchdown of the day. Jerry Logan (20) prepares to meet the resolute Jets' running back.

ish, sexy, colorful, brash, hep, and delightful. If you don't, he's conceited, half-witted, boring, arrogant, immoral, and a lout. Never has a football player stirred so many deep emotions. But few have been gifted with Namath's sublime and tested skills. Few have thrown a ball harder than he. Few have had the perfect, quick crossbow release past the ear, or the knack for ferreting out an opponent's weaknesses in the space of an eye blink, or the sheer guts it takes to stand straight up in the pocket on wobbly,

failing knees, waiting out the rush. Namath hasn't always been the most effective quarterback; injuries and bad teams have dogged his career, as they did Sonny Jurgensen's before him. But no one can reasonably deny his skill.

Namath became an instant folk-hero when as a rookie fresh out of Alabama he signed a $400,000 contract with the Jets. Soon he found himself embroiled in the silly controversies that plague most celebrities. Some were attracted by his so-called rebelliousness, though in his many commercial promotions and deals he was about as anti-establishment as J. Paul Getty. Others resented his wealth. The worst people could say of him was that he was a playboy and a rule breaker—"Broadway Joe" of the sports pages, a devout Dionysian carousing down the primrose path. Many players despised him for it.

About a week before Super Bowl III, Namath was unwinding at a favorite Miami watering hole when he fell into a noisy disagreement with Lou Michaels, the Colts' free wheeling defensive end and place-kicker. One word led to another and soon Michaels invited Namath to step outside and settle it. Joe replied by forking a $100 bill on the bar and buying a truce. As if that confrontation wasn't enough, a few days later he told reporters that Baltimore's Earl Morrall, the NFL's most valuable player, wasn't as good as several AFL quarterbacks, including himself. Although this was far from an insupportable opinion, some pretended dismay at his words. Finally, a couple of days after that he told an awards dinner audience, "I guarantee you that we will win on Sunday."

This *was* an outlandish opinion, and it outraged the Colts. No one in the NFL would have risked that insult. The Colts demanded respect. A veteran squad, they were proud of their accomplishments over the years. Hav-

ing fought their way through a long, rugged season with only one loss, they conceded themselves the championship even before it was played. The Baltimore defense was considered peerless. "Wait till Namath tries to figure that out," the critics sneered. "He'll be buried."

But it never happened. Joe was sacked only twice all day, and read the famed Baltimore pass rush as if he were calling it himself. His 235-pound fullback, Matt Snell, veered left on most of his 32 carries, after the New York offensive line repeatedly flattened defensive end Ordelle Braase, linebacker Don Shinnick, and cornerback Lenny Lyles. The Colts never found a way to stop him.

Namath completed 17 of 28 passes for 226 yards, his longest for 39 yards, with no interceptions. The Colts shut off his prime target, Don Maynard, with double-coverage, so he went to George Sauer, working man-on-man against Lyles, eight times for 133 yards. He was flawless and so was his team. While the Baltimore defense fell apart, the underrated Jets' defense played splendidly. New York successfully plugged the middle against the Colts, forcing Morrall to throw into an aroused secondary playing its finest game.

The choreographer of this grand upset was a pudgy elf named Weeb Ewbank. Weeb had coached the Colts in their glory days, leading them to perhaps their greatest victory, the famous 1958 overtime title win against the New York Giants. But a few years later the Colts went into a tailspin and Ewbank was canned. Bitterly disappointed, he switched to the AFL's

One of the biggest surprises of the day was the Jets' pass defense, which intercepted four Colts' passes. Opposite: *Jim Hudson surprises Jerry Hill.* Left: *Johnny Sample (24) out-duels Willie Richardson.*

Jets, where he stressed the same fundamentals he taught the Colts. One of his tenets was let the other team make the mistakes. On this count Baltimore proved most obliging.

On their first possession the Colts rolled to the New York 19-yard line. It was too easy. Willie Richardson, wide open, dropped a pass and Lou Michaels botched a 27-yard field goal. Later, after Ron Porter's recovery of a George Sauer fumble at the New York 12, Morrall passed to tight end Tom Mitchell. The ball struck Mitchell's shoulder pad and caromed back to a waiting Randy Beverly.

There was more grief in store for the luckless Colts. Tight end John Mackey, who never dropped a pass, dropped a sure touchdown at the New York 10. After Michaels' second field-goal miss, a pass to Richardson was nabbed instead by former Colt Johnny Sample. Finally, on a flea-flicker play from Morrall to Matte and back to Morrall, Earl lofted his deadliest spiral right into the paws of Jim Hudson ignoring the Colts' Jimmy Orr, alone in the end zone, gesturing in vain for the ball.

Namath played it cagily indeed. Instead of rushing to the air after Beverly's interception, he paraded his unit 80 yards downfield, mostly on Snell's power running. The key Snell play was called "19 Straight," which Snell ran some 17 times this afternoon for 77 of his 121-yard rushing total. Matt scored on a variation of the above, staggering across the goal line like a man doubled over in a stiff wind.

Early in the second half, Jim Turner garnered the first of three field

Weeb Ewbank chattered (opposite top) and Don Shula grimaced (opposite bottom) as Namath bedeviled the Colts. Right: Pursued by Bubba Smith, Namath cocks to throw.

goals and the Jets led 10–0. Then Namath hit four of seven passes, driving the Jets to the Baltimore 24. Two plays later, he walked off the field grasping his hand, and it was the Jets' turn to fret. However, Namath's injury proved not to be serious—a cramp in his right thumb—and he returned to lead the Jets 63 yards for a final field goal and a 16–0 lead.

At this point, Shula decided it was about time to make a change at quarterback. As Unitas stretched his arm on the sidelines, NFL die-hards took heart. It wasn't 1958 anymore and Unitas was old and rusty, his timing dull, his arm sore, but he was still Unitas and still dangerous. Beverly snatched one of his first passes, but Turner missed a field goal. Then Johnny U. promptly rallied the Colts on an 80-yard touchdown drive. Jerry Hill dashed across for the score and nostalgia throbbed warmly through the Orange Bowl. Then Baltimore recovered an onside kick at the New York 44. Three crisp passes drove Baltimore to the New York 19.

Unitas looked marvelous, but he had spent himself. His next pass was batted aside; another hit the turf. Baltimore needed a field goal and a touchdown to win. Shula wanted the touchdown now, so Unitas passed on fourth-and-five. The ball was badly overthrown and the Colts were finished.

Namath and company had done it, and *easily*. In less than a decade, a team that had once called itself the New York Titans and performed with the grace of a road company burlesque, had come to conquer the haughty NFL. As Joe Willie Namath jogged off the field grinning, he flashed his fans an upraised index finger: Number One! □

New York	0	7	6	3—**16**
Baltimore	0	0	0	7— **7**

NY—Snell 4 run (Turner kick)
NY—FG Turner 32
NY—FG Turner 30
NY—FG Turner 9
Balt—Hill 1 run (Michaels kick)

DEMPSEY BY A KNOCKOUT

New Orleans Saints vs. Detroit Lions

NOVEMBER 8, 1970

It's well known that Tom Dempsey kicked the longest field goal in National Football League history, a sensational 63-yarder with two seconds to play, giving the New Orleans Saints a come-from-behind victory over the Detroit Lions. But Dempsey is special in a way no record can measure. Born without a right hand and with only half a kicking foot, under any definition he could be called handicapped. But he isn't. Rather, he is one of the most intensely competitive, rugged, some would say arrogant players ever to tee up a football. In a game that requires of a player the finest physical equipment, Dempsey has had to make do with less. He is not resentful.

"I'm lucky," he says. "I was born this way so I never had to worry about losing anything. I accepted my life as I became aware of it, thanks in great part to my father. He played with me and made sure I competed in every sport. It's because of him that I'm not sensitive about my foot and my arm. I take pride in my accomplishments."

Dempsey trotting on and off the field is a familiar sight to fans around the league. A special shoe, which looks something like a boxing glove, encases his stump foot. On the street he wears normal shoes, stuffing tissues into the part where the toes should be. When he kicks, his short right arm flaps outward for balance,

When New Orleans' Tom Dempsey kicked a 63-yard field goal that beat Detroit, above, Saints and Lions alike agreed that as a field-goal kicker Dempsey, opposite, was anything but handicapped.

like any kicker's. But it has only two fingers. "Seven out of ten isn't bad," Dempsey says with a smile, surveying the fingers on both hands.

For Dempsey, the talents he has, not what he lacks, are important. He has made countless tackles on kick-offs during his NFL career. Once, when he was in the minors at Lowell, Massachusetts, he played two positions, tackle and linebacker, for an entire game. "I'd like to play full-time now," he says. "But those days are past."

Dempsey was not always a kicker. He played defensive end in high school. At Palomar Junior College, he was a shot-putter and a wrestler. When the coach doubted that he could make the football squad, Dempsey took up kicking. "I wanted to show him I could do something for the team," Dempsey says. "So one day I tried it in practice and found out I could do it. The coach let me play then, and pretty soon I was playing offense and defense."

Soon he won a tryout with Lowell's team in the Atlantic Coast Football League. He easily made the team. At that time, in 1967, he kicked barefooted with a strip of tape across his stump. NFL rules required that he wear a shoe, so when he reported to the San Diego Chargers the following season, he had one specially made.

Dempsey's defect works to his

143

Missing three fingers on [his] right hand and the toes o[f his] right foot, Dempsey seem[s] awkward as he kicks. But the handicaps have not h[urt] his kicking and may even[?] have helped it.

advantage as a kicker. The front of his toeless foot is flat and hard, and he does not have to lock his ankle when he kicks. A normal foot must be held firm throughout the sweep of the leg on a place-kick. Dempsey's foot is already locked, in a sense, because there is no instep. The contact is flush and the ball sails, though not always straight. "I chart my kicks and study the angles I miss from," he says. "I've modeled my kicking after Lou Groza, but I try to follow my own style. I don't go out to *try* field goals; I go out to kick them."

Dempsey has his detractors. In 1968, the Chargers demoted him to the taxi squad, then waived him outright after a dispute over a special kicking shoe Dempsey disliked and claims he was forced to wear. Another reason San Diego may have dropped him was his growing reputation as a goof-off. "I admit I broke curfew a few times," Dempsey says. "But I was no troublemaker. I was very serious about football. I always knew I could kick. But when [coach] Sid Gillman put me on waivers, I was afraid people would decide I just couldn't do it."

The Saints, who trained next door to the Chargers and who knew a good thing when they saw it, signed Dempsey as a free agent. Coach Tom Fears was suitably impressed when Dempsey booted a 54-yard field goal against Denver late that summer. Fears even considered using Tom to place-kick rather than punting from the midfield area. His range was phenomenal. He regularly boomed kick-offs across the end zone or, if he wanted, chipped the ball so high that a player could barely return it. Dempsey was so good that the Dallas Cowboys' general manager, Tex Schramm, asked the NFL for a ruling on Dempsey's odd shoe. The league rule said only shoes "of stock manufacture available for retail sale" were permissible. But the league bent the rule a little in Dempsey's case.

Dempsey has had his slumps, as every high-grade kicker has. In the month before his 63-yarder against Detroit, his record had faded to a mediocre 5 for 15. Perhaps only the presence of a new head coach, J. D. Roberts, who had signed the week before and wasn't yet up to date on all his players, gave Dempsey a chance for the record. With 18 seconds to play, Detroit kicker Errol Mann struck an 18-yard field goal, giving Detroit a 17–16 lead. The game seemed lost. But Al Dodd ran back the kickoff to the Saints' 28-yard line, and quarterback Billy Kilmer found Dodd with an aerial. The receiver skipped out of bounds at the Saints' 45 with two seconds to play. Roberts collared assistant coach Don Heinrich and asked, "What's next, Don?"

"We've got to go for the field goal," Heinrich said.

Roberts told Dempsey to give it his best shot. Dempsey nodded. Holder Joe Scarpati squatted a yard farther back than usual to give Dempsey a bit more time. "I knew I could kick it sixty-three yards," Dempsey says. "But I wasn't sure I could kick it straight. There was pressure and I felt it, but I tried to shut it out of my mind. I kicked a line drive from twenty-four yards out earlier in the game and it was blocked. I wanted to get it up."

Some of the Detroit players laughed about the field-goal attempt; one didn't even bother to rush. Defensive tackle Alex Karras did rush, hard and fast, barely missing it with his hand. As the ball soared up and away, Detroit assistant Bill McPeak muttered, "Oh my God!" He knew.

A minute later, while general delirium raged around the Sugar Bowl, linebacker Wayne Walker told New Orleans' Danny Abramowicz as the two walked off the field together, "Dempsey didn't kick that football. God did." So much for God-given handicaps. ☐

Detroit	0 7	7	3—17
New Orleans	3 3	3	10—19

NO—FG Dempsey 29
Det—Farr 10 run (Mann kick)
NO—FG Dempsey 27
Det—Sanders 2 pass from Munson (Mann kick)
NO—FG Dempsey 8
NO—Barrington 4 run (Dempsey kick)
Det—FG Mann 18
NO—FG Dempsey 63

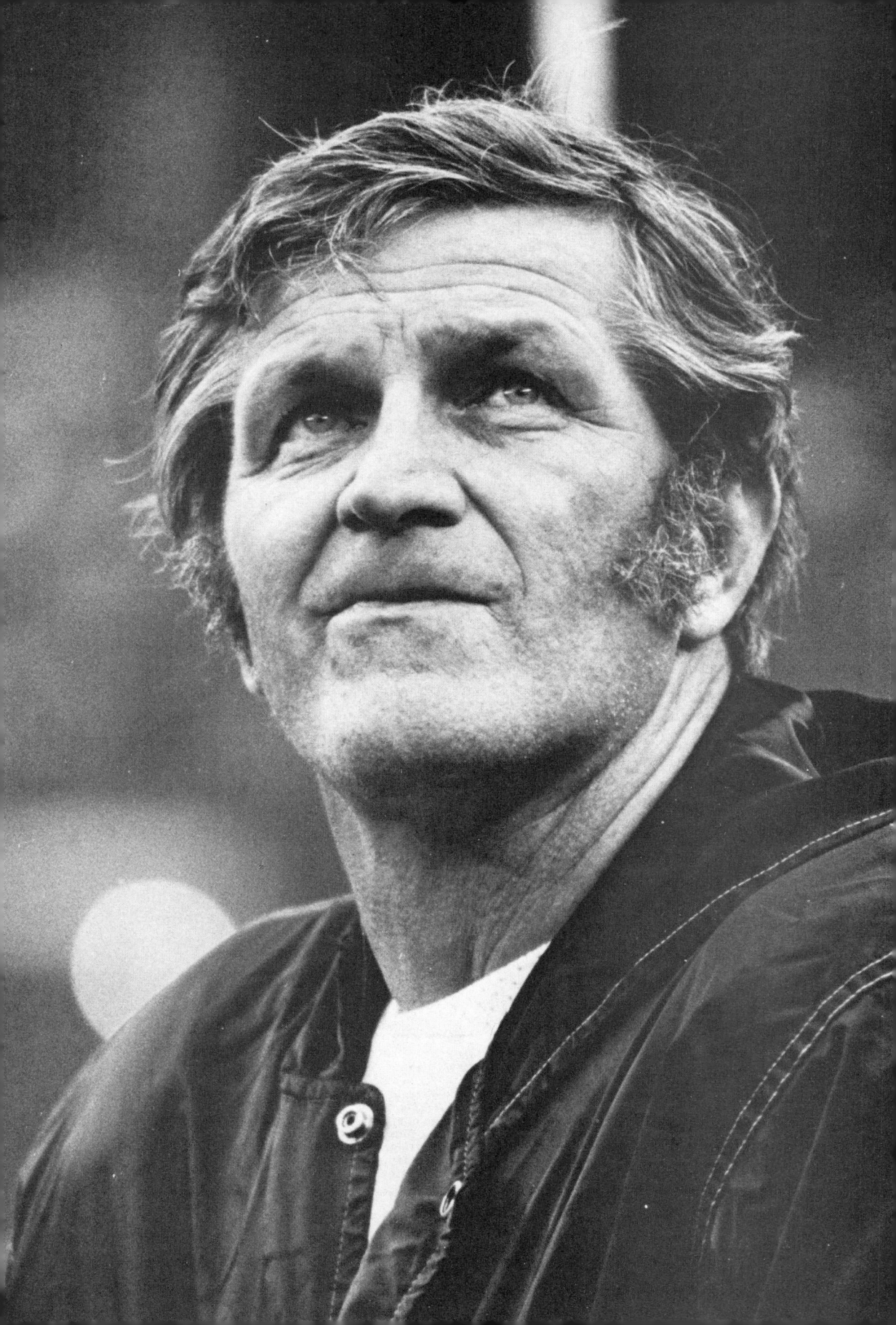

BLANDA:
STILL KICKING

**Oakland Raiders vs. Pittsburgh Steelers,
Kansas City Chiefs, Cleveland Browns,
Denver Broncos, San Diego Chargers**

1970

From the moment ageless George Blanda joined the Oakland Raiders at the onset of the 1967 season, last-minute heroics became his stock in trade. Today he is known mainly for his uncanny clutch field goals. But, lest we forget, there was also a five-game stretch during the 1970 season when old George did it both ways, as a quarterback and a kicker, spurring the Raiders to four critical wins and a tie.

He was younger then, 43, an age at which most pro football players are well into retirement and second careers. Through 1976, George Blanda had labored for 27 seasons in professional football. It is almost inconceivable that anyone will ever match this service record.

Much has been made of Blanda's celebrated longevity on the field. His secret, if it can be called a secret, has been resolute moderation. Since he broke in as a rookie with the Chicago Bears in 1948, Blanda exercised frequently, watched his weight, and, for these reasons, perhaps, managed to avoid the crippling injuries that shorten many careers. He is not an excitable type, nor is he given to moody introspection. He enjoys the game as a game, not as some overblown life-death struggle, and perhaps it is just this happy perspective that has given him an advantage over his younger, more impressionable colleagues. News feature writers and television flacks have called him "superman," a label that plainly puzzles old George. If Blanda has an edge over anybody else in the sport, it is that he knows his limits so well.

Blanda drew much media attention in his distinguished career as a kicker and quarterback, but nothing like the adulation he got in 1970. Old George found himself celebrated in song and verse, television specials, and magazine spreads. "Blanda for

*In this 1972 picture the signs of age were beginning to
mark George Blanda's face. His kicking leg remained young,
however, and the Oakland Raiders were more than satisfied.*

147

Mayor" buttons appeared on normally apolitical lapels. He agreed to peddle Dodge trucks on television for a fat fee. (Some other endorsements he rejected.) He was praised and feted and showered with awards. Some attributed to Blanda a mini-boom in church attendance in the environs of Oakland, where Raiders' fans were heard to swear, "If he makes this one, I'll go back to church!"

Surprisingly, Blanda was placed on waivers before the 1970 season. No one claimed him. No one wanted a 43-year-old substitute, except the Raiders. However, they needed the roster space to test younger talent. Once the youngsters flopped, Blanda quietly returned. He sat on the bench and watched the second quarter of a 7–7 deadlock with the Pittsburgh Steelers when a chronic bad back forced quarterback Daryle Lamonica to the sidelines. Until then, Lamonica had guided the team with indifferent success—two wins, two losses, and a tie. Coach John Madden told Blanda, "George, you're going in. Throw to Ray Chester over the middle."

This he did, expertly, for a touchdown, but a penalty nullified it. Nevertheless, hardly all was lost. From the bench Blanda had noticed that the Steelers' defenders left the middle wide open and failed to cover the deep left side, where receiver Warren Wells ran most of his patterns. On the next series Blanda called a play-action pass, sending Wells far downfield to the left. The ball, Wells, and cor-

nerback Mel Blount converged simultaneously, but Wells prevailed, grabbing the ball and scoring. Later Blanda booted a field goal, then fired a touchdown to Chester at the end of the half. He hit Chester again in the second half. Oakland won 31–14.

Twice Blanda caught the Steelers blitzing. Both times he threw touchdown passes. In all his years of football, there was nothing old George hadn't seen. Fans sometimes forget that such old-timers as Johnny Lujack, Y. A. Tittle, Bobby Lane, and Charley Conerly were rookies in 1948, the year Blanda broke in with the Bears.

A week after the Pittsburgh game, the Raiders journeyed to Kansas City for the first of their annual brawls with the Chiefs. This one was a hell raiser. The Chiefs led 17–14 with eight seconds to play and Oakland squatting on the Kansas City 41. In jogged Blanda from the sidelines, patiently unlimbering his old, cold leg. Ignoring the chilly wind blowing steadily in his face, he fixed his eyes upon the spot on the 48-yard line where Lamonica readied the ball, then banged it directly between the goal posts, mere inches above the elongated fingers of 6-foot 9-inch Morris Stroud, who had leaped up from underneath the crossbar in a vain attempt to block the kick.

The resultant tie did wonders for the Raiders' morale, propelling Oakland into first place in the American Football Conference Western Divi-

Last-minute gems: On November 22, 1970, Blanda beat the San Diego Chargers with a 16-yard field goal seven seconds before the game ended, opposite top. Four weeks earlier he had victimized the Kansas City Chiefs similarly, from the 48-yard line with three seconds left, opposite bottom.

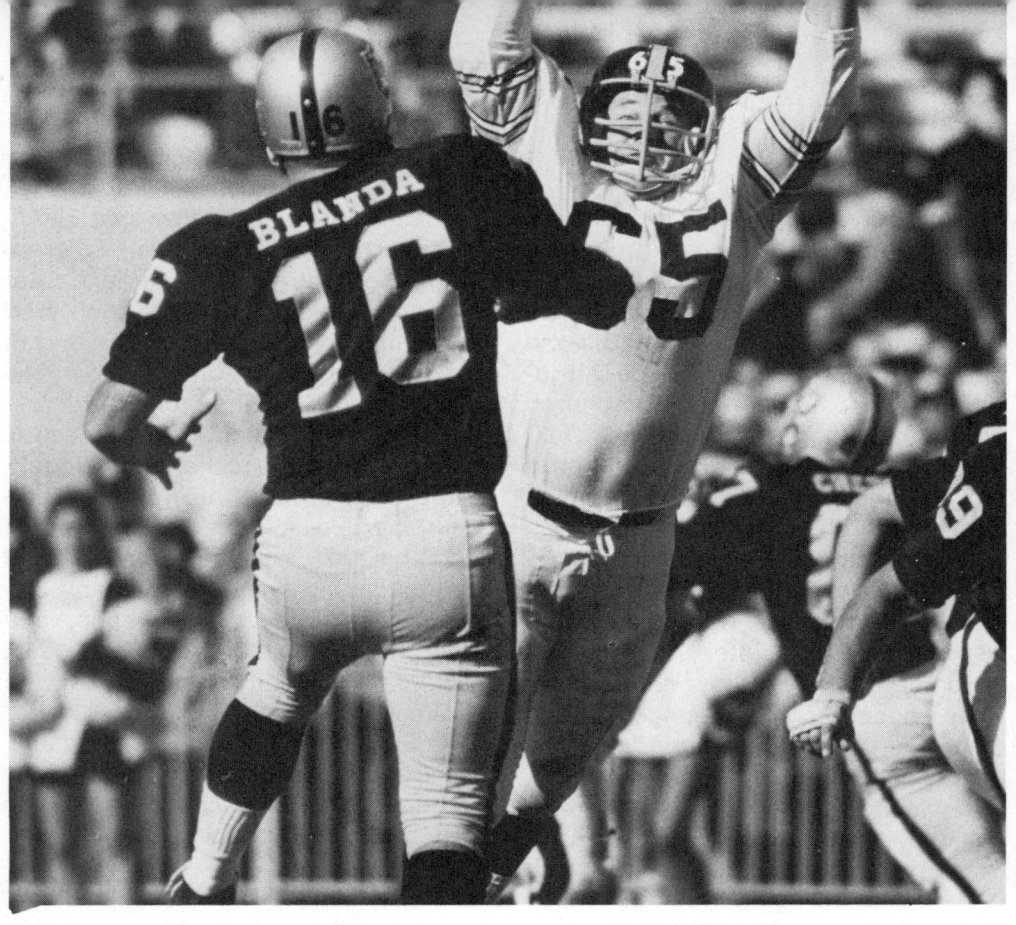

sion. Blanda's locker overflowed with telegrams and letters from the envious over-40 set. "ON BEHALF OF ALL THE OTHER SENILE OLD WRECKS, WE SALUTE YOU!" read one. But a Kansas City spoilsport carped, "BACK TO THE OLD FOLKS HOME, YOU PHONY!"

Next week, the Raiders finessed Cleveland 13–0 until the second quarter, when the Browns began a 17-point comeback. Then Lamonica damaged his shoulder and Blanda replaced him, tossing an interception on his first play. Cleveland kicked a field goal with four minutes to go. Unperturbed, Blanda returned, deftly eluding a spirited Cleveland pass rush, flinging a tie-making touchdown to receiver Warren Wells with 1:34 to play.

After defensive back Kent Mc-

Cloughan picked off a Cleveland pass, the Browns shoved Blanda and the Raiders out of field-goal range. But with nine seconds to go and no timeouts left, George spun a nine-yard pass to Hewritt Dixon who dodged out of bounds. Then old George won the game with a 52-yard field goal.

Against Denver and later San Diego, it was more of the same. Trailing the Broncos 19–17 with a minute to go, Blanda drove the Raiders across the field, winning on a 20-yard touchdown pass to Fred Biletnikoff. He finished off the Chargers on a last-second chip shot from the 19-yard line.

"It was easy," Blanda says. "Anyone could have kicked that field goal. It kind of embarrassed me that everybody made so much fuss about it. I've

Opposite: *Against Pittsburgh on October 25, 1970, Blanda seemed not to appreciate the dangers that Lloyd Voss (65) posed to a 43-year-old man.* Right: *Playing kid to coach John Madden, who is nine years younger.*

kicked field goals; I've missed field goals. I've thrown touchdown passes that won games. I've had passes intercepted that lost games. What is there left that I can get excited over?" Ah, the serenity of age. □

October 25, 1970
Pittsburgh   0   7   7   0—14
Oakland   7   17   7   0—31
Oak—Chester 37 pass from Lamonica (Blanda kick)
Pitt—Pearson 2 run (Mingo kick)
Oak—Wells 44 pass from Blanda (Blanda kick)
Oak—Blanda FG 27
Oak—Chester 19 pass from Blanda (Blanda kick)
Pitt—Hughes 12 pass from Bradshaw (Mingo kick)
Oak—Chester 43 pass from Blanda (Blanda kick)

November 1, 1970
Oakland   0   7   7   3—17
Kansas City   0   7   3   7—17
KC—Hayes 4 run (Stenerud kick)
Oak—Chester 3 pass from Lamonica (Blanda kick)
Oak—Chester 8 pass from Lamonica (Blanda kick)
KC—FG Stenerud 33
KC—Taylor 13 pass from Dawson (Stenerud kick)
Oak—FG Blanda 48

November 8, 1970
Cleveland   0   10   7   3—20
Oakland   3   10   0   10—23
Oak—FG Blanda 9
Oak—Smith 27 pass from Lamonica (Blanda kick)
Oak—FG Blanda 42
Cle—Kelly 10 pass from Nelson (Cockroft kick)
Cle—FG Cockroft 42
Cle—Scott 63 run (Cockroft kick)
Cle—FG Cockroft 32
Oak—Wells 14 pass from Blanda (Blanda kick)
Oak—FG Blanda 52

November 15, 1970
Oakland   7   3   7   7—24
Denver   0   3   3   13—19
Oak—Wells 36 pass from Lamonica (Blanda kick)
Den—FG Howfield 47
Oak—FG Blanda 32
Den—FG Howfield 44
Oak—Dixon 46 pass from Lamonica (Blanda kick)
Den—Whalen 10 pass from Liske (kick failed)
Den—Liske 1 run (Howfield kick)
Oak—Biletnikoff 20 pass from Blanda (Blanda kick)

November 22, 1970
San Diego   7   0   7   3—17
Oakland   0   7   7   6—20
SD—Garrison 5 pass from Hadl (Mercer kick)
Oak—Smith 3 run (Blanda kick)
SD—Garrison 15 pass from Hadl (Mercer kick)
Oak—Smith 1 run (Blanda kick)
Oak—FG Blanda 16
SD—FG Mercer 11
Oak—FG Blanda 19

THE BLOOPER BOWL

Baltimore Colts vs. Dallas Cowboys

JANUARY 17, 1971

Super Bowl V was an untidy light comedy showcasing some of the wildest play ever seen in a National Football League championship game. The eighty thousand fans packing Miami's Orange Bowl and millions more watching on national television loved every awkward minute of it. There were a record 11 turnovers, including five fumbles, six interceptions, countless gaffes and mental lapses, dropped passes, tipped passes, passes flung unhesitantly into the ground, and to cap the madcap day, probably

152

Tumultuous Super Bowl V came to a tumultuous end when, with nine seconds left in the game, Baltimore's Jim O'Brien kicked a game-winning 32-yard field goal.

the hardest, most vicious hitting, and the tightest and most arresting finish in Super Bowl history.

The zany performance was a surprise considering the depth and polish of the Baltimore Colts and the Dallas Cowboys, veteran squads supposedly inured to playoff pressures. With Vince Lombardi gone and the Green Bay Packers in decline, these Colts and Cowboys represented the best of the old NFL. An aging team, the Colts were running out of time to avenge their embarrassing 1969 Super Bowl defeat by the New York Jets. Baltimore, along with the Cleveland Browns and the Pittsburgh Steelers, had shifted to the AFC under a league realignment plan introduced the year before. The Colts settled in quite nicely, slugging their way into first place in the AFC East with an 11–2–1 mark and beating out the Cincinnati Bengals and the Oakland Raiders for the conference crown.

The Colts' quarterback and inspi-

The Colts went with Earl Morrall,
below pressured by Larry Cole
(63), after Johnny Unitas,
opposite with Morrall, repaired
to the sidelines with bruised
ribs from a George Andrie tackle.

ration was a tight-lipped veteran named John Unitas, now nearing the end of his fabulous career and beset with nagging injuries and a fallow arm. Early in the game, Unitas received a painful shot from defensive end George Andrie and retired for the afternoon with damaged ribs. His replacement was nearly as old, Earl Morrall, a shambling, shy, crew-cut individual with clear dark eyes. The NFL's all-time best journeyman quarterback, Morrall was unjustly pegged a "loser" for the Baltimore failure in Super Bowl III.

The Cowboys, too, had quarter-back troubles. Craig Morton nursed a chipped elbow and couldn't throw accurately short or long. But their inside running attack was sturdy and swift, and their celebrated "Dooms-day Defense" was the league's stingi-est. Dallas' biggest problem was lingering defeatism from the heartbreaking losses to Green Bay and Cleveland in the sixties. Although they were perennial contenders, this was the Cowboys' first trip to the Super Bowl, and they were still beset by the conventional wisdom that they "couldn't win the big ones."

On the night before the Super Bowl, a raiding party of noisy, drunken Cowboys' rooters attempted to plaster the hallway outside the Colts' hotel rooms with Dallas pennants. Aroused by the commotion, coach Don McCafferty angrily scattered the revelers. But he was too upset to sleep the rest of the night. It was only the start of a frazzling day.

In the first quarter, cashing in on a Baltimore fumble, Dallas scored two fast field goals. Unitas answered with

In a game of goofs, Dallas' Duane Thomas, opposite, committed perhaps the biggest when he fumbled on the Colts' 1-yard line. Baltimore's Eddie Hinton, left, battling Mel Renfro, bounced one pass off Renfro to teammate John Mackey for a score.

a delicate spiral that winged off receiver Eddie Hinton's wrist, kissed the fingertips of defensive back Mel Renfro, and settled comfortably into the arms of Baltimore's John Mackey, who took it the rest of the way for a touchdown. The extra point was botched, leaving the game tied 6–6. Morton's heave to Duane Thomas put Dallas back ahead, 13–6.

After Unitas was hurt, Morrall drove the Colts to the Dallas 2-yard line. Three straight runs netted one yard, but McCafferty shunned the easy field goal, ordering a pass to tight end Tom Mitchell. Morrall's fourth-down toss nose-dived into the turf. "If we had lost, that would have been the worst call I made all season," McCafferty said later.

The second half opened ingloriously with the Colts fumbling the kickoff at their 21-yard line. Dallas recovered and on the play moved the ball down to the 1. "My God!" linebacker Mike Curtis thought, "if they score here, we're going to lose just like we did to the Jets!"

On the first play from scrimmage, as Duane Thomas swam through a pile of bodies, the Colts' Jim Duncan screamed "Fumble!" The officials obediently presented the Colts with the ball, though there was some dispute as to who had recovered. Dallas claimed it had been their center, Dave Manders. "If we'd made that touchdown, the game was all over," coach Tom Landry says. "There was no way Baltimore could have caught us with a 26–6 lead."

Morrall presently revived an old Baltimore Colts' flea-flicker play. Morrall pitched the ball to Sam Havri-

157

Opposite: *Herb Adderley collars Baltimore's Tom Nowatzke.* Right: *In a friendlier gesture Nowatzke grasps Baltimore coach Don McCafferty, whose day of ups and downs began early that morning when some Cowboys' fans invaded his hotel corridor.*

lak, who was supposed to return it to the quarterback, but pressured by Bob Lilly, Havrilak couldn't pitch it back to Morrall. So he reared and lofted the ball to Eddie Hinton downfield. Defensive back Cornell Green pounced on the receiver at the Dallas 8. The ball slid free, merrily flopping across the end zone while Colts and Cowboys fell over one another in vain and comical pursuit.

Baltimore finally did score the tying touchdown after Rick Volk's interception of a deflected Morton pass. With the ball at the Dallas 2, Morrall handed off to fullback Tom Nowatzke, who smashed across for the touchdown. "I lowered my head and told myself, 'It's either you or me, brother,'" Nowatzke recalls.

That made it 13–13 with time running out, but Dallas still had a chance to win. With 1:58 left, Bob Hayes fielded a punt at the Baltimore 48. A field goal was likely, but then a holding penalty shoved the Cowboys back to their 27. Morton boldly sailed the ball downfield to Dan Reeves. The perfect throw hit Reeves' fingers the very instant that Jerry Logan smashed into Reeves. The ball floated to linebacker Mike Curtis, who dashed to the Dallas 28.

With 59 seconds to go, Morrall cagily ground down the clock to nine seconds, then called for time. Field-goal kicker Jim O'Brien fretted at the sidelines about blowing the game. "I hoped it wouldn't come down to me to win it," O'Brien says. "Who needed that kind of pressure? The money is just as good if somebody else wins it for you."

"For God's sake, Earl, talk to the

kid," McCafferty whispered to Morrall.

Morrall, less than chatty himself, trotted back to the huddle. "Just hit it straight for the center of the posts and don't worry about it," Morrall barked.

O'Brien nodded. Earlier in the week, he had dreamt vividly about a field goal winning the game. "But the dream wasn't in technicolor so I had no idea which team kicked it," he says. "Then a couple of days later, my mother, who dabbled in fortune-telling, called and said we'd win by a small margin. I had begun to doubt her."

Guard Dan Sullivan stared at O'Brien. "You scared?" Sullivan asked.

"Let's get this thing over with," O'Brien replied.

Across the line, the Cowboys chirped loud insults. O'Brien ignored them. The Colts said the same things in a practice drill. It was nothing. The eighty thousand fans drowned out everything. He silently studied his spot at the 32-yard line. Center Tom Goode snapped the ball to Morrall and O'Brien clubbed it through the posts.

"The whole thing made me cry," O'Brien says.

At the same time, Lilly tore off his helmet in anguish and frustration and hurled it fifty yards toward the Dallas bench. It was one of the better throws of the day. □

Baltimore	0	6	0	10—16
Dallas	3	10	0	0—13

Dal—FG Clark 14
Dal—FG Clark 30
Bal—Mackey 75 pass from Unitas (kick failed)
Dal—Thomas 7 pass from Morton (Clark kick)
Bal—Nowatzke 2 run (O'Brien kick)
Bal—O'Brien FG 32

THE LONGEST DAY

*Miami Dolphins vs.
Kansas City Chiefs*

DECEMBER 25, 1971

On Christmas Day, 1971, the Miami Dolphins and Kansas City Chiefs played the longest game in National Football League history. At stake was the chance to play for the American Conference championship, the ticket to the Super Bowl. It took two sudden-death overtime periods to decide the winner. For sheer drama this game has never been topped.

In the first quarter the Western Division champion Chiefs overwhelmed the inexperienced young Dolphins, winners in the AFC East. Kansas City shut off fullback Larry Csonka, then picked apart the Miami zone defense with short passes, running plays, and occasional traps and draws. Jan Stenerud kicked a 24-yard field goal. Then linebacker Willie Lanier intercepted a pass, and quarterback Len Dawson converted the turnover into a score with a soft 7-yard touchdown pass to Ed Podolak. The Chiefs led 10–0 at the end of the first quarter, and the fifty thousand fans

*The end at last—after Garo Yepremian's
field goal decided the longest NFL
game. Holder Karl Noonan (89) called
the play; Larry Csonka (39) thanked God.*

packing Kansas City's rickety Municipal Stadium were delighted.

But on the series after the Chiefs' touchdown, the Dolphins began to rebound. A 5-yard third-down penalty against Kansas City gave the Dolphins a first down at their 44-yard line. With the Chiefs intent on stopping Csonka and halfback Jim Kiick, quarterback Bob Griese threw a quick sideline pass to receiver Paul Warfield, who sidestepped a tackler and sped to the Chiefs' 21-yard line. "That might have been the key to the whole game," Lanier says. "The Dolphins got a new life when it looked like we could have taken over and maybe scored again. Then they broke a big play. It gave them a lot of confidence."

Griese's 16-yard pass to tight end Marv Fleming set up Csonka's 1-yard touchdown plunge. Then Podolak fumbled at the Kansas City 12, and Garo Yepremian booted a field goal, tying the score at halftime.

Yepremian had been informed the night before that Stenerud had been selected over him to be the American Football Conference's kicker in the Pro Bowl. The choice angered the Miami kicker, and he resolved to demonstrate on the field the next day what he considered his superior credentials. "It was the coaches' fault," Yepremian fumed. "I decided I'd show them and Stenerud

that there was a mistake . . . that I would kick better than he did all that day."

Yepremian would indeed kick better than Stenerud in the Miami-Kansas City playoff, and to devastating effect.

The Chiefs opened the second half as they had the first, controlling the ball for nearly ten minutes and dominating the game. Dawson mixed his offense cleverly, grinding out 75 yards in 15 plays. Fullback Jim Otis carried the last three times, bulling one yard for the touchdown.

Dawson was forced to rely on his running backs throughout the game. With Miami's tough zone defense keeping receivers Otis Taylor and Elmo Wright effectively double-covered, running back Podolak became the Chiefs' main man. He not only ran off tackle and around end but caught passes and returned punts and kickoffs. Podolak alone accounted for 350 of his team's 606 total yards.

The Miami offense was more diverse. After the Kansas City touchdown, Griese started a drive with a 23-yard pass to Howard Twilley. Csonka and Kiick rushed the ball to the Chiefs' 39-yard line. Then Griese threw to Warfield at the 7. Jim Kiick scored and Yepremian's extra point tied the score 17–17. There was a minute to play in the third quarter.

Right: *Jim Kiick's one-yard run tied the score 17–17.*
Above: *Jan Stenerud blew his chance to win the game in regulation time.*

Nick Buoniconti's fumble recovery stopped a Kansas City drive but the ensuing Miami march died when Jim Lynch intercepted a pass at the Chiefs' 9-yard line. Now it was Dawson's turn for the big play. He hit Wright with a 63-yard bomb down the middle that perched Kansas City virtually on top of the Miami goal line. Podolak took a pitchout and swept 3

yards for the score. With 6:30 to go, Stenerud's extra point made it 24–17 Chiefs.

Mercury Morris returned the kickoff to the Miami 29-yard line. Griese passed to Fleming for 13 yards, called a reverse, then a pass, then another pass, 17 yards to Warfield at the Chiefs' 41. Csonka ran a draw. Tight end Jim Mandich caught a short pass. On third-and-four, Warfield streaked down the sidelines, gathering in the ball for a 26-yard gain. Twilley caught a pass at the 5-yard line. Then Griese called a hook pattern to Fleming in the end zone. Scrambling away from a strong pass

rush, Griese managed to hit Fleming for the touchdown. With 1:36 to play, it was tied again, 24–24.

Though exhausted from all his heavy-duty running, Podolak somehow hauled Yepremian's kickoff 78 yards to the Miami 22. Curtis Johnson caught him from behind, saving a touchdown and, as it turned out, the game. Yet Kansas City was well within Stenerud's field-goal range. The Kansas City fans were confident that Dawson needed only to keep the ball and run down the clock to ensure the win. On third down Podolak lost three yards on a right side sweep. So to spot the ball for the field-goal at-

Ed Podolak, above, starred for the Chiefs, accounting *for more than half his team's total offense. Otis Taylor lateraled to him on a spur-of-the-moment, flea-flicker play in the third quarter,* opposite.

tempt, Dawson knelt on the 31-yard line, near the right hashmark, Stenerud's favorite position.

Stenerud was nervous. In this game all his kicks had hooked left. He decided to adjust the kicking angle. "The snap was perfect," he recalls. "But I had been getting under the ball too much, shooting the ball to the left. I hit it there again. It went high and nice. I thought it might be good. Then it wouldn't come around."

Later in the week, after the meaning of that miss had sunk in, he watched the replay on television. "It made me sick all over again," he says. "I couldn't sleep that night

thinking about it, though I went to sleep easily on the night of the game. I felt like hiding. I never again wanted to play football. It was unbearable, totally unbearable."

The overtime began with another sparkling kickoff return by Podolak, this one to the Chiefs' 46. Five plays later, Stenerud tried another field goal. Linebacker Nick Buoniconti batted it aside. Then Yepremian failed on a 52-yard attempt. As the first overtime period ended, the weary teams shifted sides. A second overtime, a sixth quarter, would be needed.

By this time the Chiefs had entirely smothered the Miami running at-

tack. Griese had only one play left in his repertoire. "It was a roll trap that went against the flow," Griese says. "Kiick and I would start to the right with Jim going behind Csonka. I'd hand Larry the ball and he'd get lead blocks from [tackle] Norm Evans and [guard] Larry Little. Csonka always liked that play."

The fake was perfect. Linebackers Willie Lanier and Jim Lynch raced toward Griese and Kiick while Csonka

and his two-man escort tore through the other side of the line. Csonka rumbled downfield to the Kansas City 36. Cautiously, Griese ran the ball into the line. On fourth down Yepremian and holder Karl Noonan jogged onto the field. Garo nicked a spot for the ball on the 37-yard line. As soon as Noonan set it, Yepremian kicked. He watched it soar high and straight. "As soon as I kicked it, I knew it was good," he remembers. "I jumped up

Left: *Garo Yepremian gets it past Emmitt Thomas (18) and over Jim Lynch (51) and,* below, *seems to know before anyone else that it's good.*

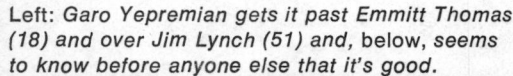

and didn't even look at the goal posts. Then I realized this was the most important field goal of my life, so I thought, 'Turn around and see what happens.' "

Eighty-two minutes and 40 seconds after the opening kickoff, referee John McDonough raised both hands to signal "Good." For a few seconds, Yepremian thought to search for the kicking tee so that he would be ready for the next kickoff. Then he realized there would be no kickoff. This seemingly interminable game was finally over. □

Miami	0	10	7	7	0	3—27
Kansas City	10	0	7	7	0	0—24

KC—FG Stenerud 24
KC—Podolak 7 pass from Dawson (Stenerud kick)
Mia—Csonka 1 run (Yepremian kick)
Mia—FG Yepremian 14
KC—Otis 1 run (Stenerud kick)
Mia—Kiick 1 run (Yepremian kick)
KC—Podolak 3 run (Stenerud kick)
Mia—Fleming 5 pass from Griese (Yepremian kick)
Mia—FG Yepremian 37

IN GOD WE TRUST

Pittsburgh Steelers vs. Oakland Raiders

DECEMBER 23, 1972

If in this universe of ours there lurks a heavenly spirit who wagers on professional football games, then he must have gone for broke one December Saturday in Pittsburgh, Pennsylvania. The occasion was the final play of a 1972 American Football Conference playoff pitting the surprising Pittsburgh Steelers against the powerful Oakland Raiders. Father John Duggan, an Irish priest who served for several years as unofficial chaplain and confessor to the Pittsburgh squad, recalls entering the locker room before the game, as was his habit, to mumble a brief benediction. As he casually turned the leaves of his Bible, his eyes fell upon a random line: "Stand firm and wait for the victory of the Lord."

Hours later, savoring anew fresh memories of the Steelers' instant upset, a victory brought about with but five seconds remaining in the game by fullback Franco Harris' so-called "Immaculate Reception," Father Duggan openly marveled at the ways of the Lord. "I didn't think we'd have to wait *that* long," he mused.

From the outset it was apparent that this game was something special. The Steelers, unrelieved losers for more than a quarter century, had at long last reached a National Football League playoff, principally because of a sturdy defense and an adequately rebuilt offense headed by a fine young quarterback, Terry Bradshaw. The Raiders, however, remained heavily favored until starting quarterback Daryle Lamonica came down with the flu. His timing stuttered and his passes lacked their normal zing. Midway through the last quarter, he was replaced by his backup, Ken Stabler. Without a passing attack to share the burden of taming the ferocious Pittsburgh defense, the Raiders' running backs spent much of the afternoon locked in the arms of Pittsburgh linemen Dwight White and "Mean" Joe Green.

However, the Steelers didn't take advantage of the Oakland failures. Their offense stalled repeatedly. The Oakland line smothered rookie sensation Franco Harris, who had gained more than 1,000 yards rushing that season. Coach Chuck Noll's passing attack never got off the ground. The game stayed scoreless.

Despite the evidence that points would be hard to come by in this contest, late in the second quarter Noll

Art Thoms (80), Gerald Irons (86), and Jack Tatum (31) weren't the only ones who couldn't believe Franco Harris' "Immaculate Reception." The entire football world reeled in incredulity.

*The most bizarre play of this and perhaps
any championship game: Terry Bradshaw, to Frenchy
Fuqua and Jack Tatum (double touch), to Franco Harris.*

disdained an easy field-goal try. The Steelers were repulsed on fourth down for no gain. Noll was furious. "If I had a third leg, I would have kicked myself," he said.

In the second half Pittsburgh broke through, moving on three crisp Bradshaw passes to Oakland's 11-yard line. Roy Gerela booted an 18-yard field goal for a 3–0 lead. Then Stabler, upended by Pittsburgh's L. C. Greenwood, fumbled, and Gerela's quick 29-yarder put the Steelers ahead 6–0 with 3:50 to play.

On his last shot at a score, Stabler knew he couldn't scramble against the Steelers' tight defense. So on fourth-and-one, he slipped the ball to running back Charley Smith, who

wove forward for four yards. Then he tossed a series of hit-and-miss passes, culminating in a long, sweet spiral to receiver Mike Siani at the Pittsburgh 30. Wary of another pass, the Steelers called a safety blitz. Seeing Stabler hesitate in the backfield, rookie tackle Craig Hanneman lurched after him, forgetting that his assignment was to guard against the outside run. Stabler neatly reversed himself and dashed into the end zone, leaving poor Hanneman looking like a stranded commuter waiting for a bus. George Blanda's extra point put Oakland ahead 7–6 with 73 seconds to play.

"My God!" defensive end Dwight White thought to himself. "Was all this

It was a very merry Christmas for Bradshaw, top, the Steelers, and their fans; a heartbreaking one for Oakland, particularly for coach John Madden, bottom.

for nothing? Is this the way the whole damn thing is supposed to end?''

Blanda's kickoff nicked the goal posts, preventing a return. On two passes Bradshaw maneuvered his team to the 40-yard line, but linebacker Jack Tatum swatted down his next two throws. On fourth-and-10 with 22 seconds to play, Noll called for a pass to Barry Pearson. It wasn't a promising call, as unpromising as the Steelers' chances at that moment.

Up in the mezzanine Steelers' owner Art Rooney slowly left his seat and headed for the elevator. Never before had his team come so close to winning a playoff. The forty years of futility left him deeply disappointed. He didn't want to watch anymore. "I figured we had lost," he says. "I wanted to get to the locker room early so I could personally thank the players for the fine job they'd done all season."

Pittsburgh's last play was to be a

174

short pass to Pearson over the middle with Franco Harris remaining in the backfield to block. But the play fell apart when Oakland defensive ends Tony Cline and Horace Jones reached the backfield fast, forcing Bradshaw to duck and scramble. Suddenly, it was painfully clear to the fifty thousand Steelers' fans jamming Three Rivers Stadium that Oakland was about to nail down the victory.

Harris instinctively turned downfield, waving his hand and yelling for the ball. Bradshaw ignored him, scanning for Pearson first, then spotting and firing to his halfback John ("Frenchy") Fuqua near the Oakland 35. Jack Tatum saw Fuqua stretch for the ball and lit into him hard with a frightfully loud clap that sent the ball ricocheting backward, still airborne—directly at Harris.

"I wasn't supposed to be there," Harris says. "But I started running to block for Frenchy. I saw him go up with Tatum for the ball, then I saw it fly out from their collision. I thought to myself, 'Oh no! Wow! This is it!' The ball kept coming straight at me. From there it was all instinct. I reached and caught the ball below my knees and never broke stride. The timing was perfect, too perfect ever to be planned. John McMakin gave a good block and Jimmy Warren tried to tackle me high near the ten-yard line, but slipped away."

Bradshaw never saw Harris catch the ball. All he remembers is his despair at Fuqua's miss. Then he heard the crowd scream and saw Harris sprint across the goal line. As he craned his neck looking for a penalty marker, he was engulfed by happy spectators.

Rooney stood waiting for the elevator when a stadium guard shouted, "You won it! You won it!"

"Are you kidding?" Rooney asked the man.

"No, no," he replied, "listen to that crowd."

Puzzled, Rooney descended to the empty locker room. Up on the field no one was quite sure whether the game had been won by Oakland or Pittsburgh, so bizarre was the last play. Referee Fred Swearingen did not signal a touchdown. He checked with his fellow officials, then phoned Art McNally, chief of all NFL officials, who had been sitting in the press box. The problem was: did Fuqua slap the ball back to Harris; or did Tatum, or Tatum and Fuqua together, touch it before the catch? If only Fuqua touched the ball, the catch was illegal. Otherwise, it was a touchdown.

Swearingen had been watching the quarterback and did not see the catch. Neither did two other officials. But umpire Pat Harder and field judge Adrian Burk, both former NFL players, claimed there had been double-touching (both Tatum and Fuqua) and therefore the pass was legal. Nevertheless, instead of making the call immediately, Swearingen phoned McNally upstairs. "I just wanted to do what was right," he says.

McNally and Swearingen watched together as the play reran on special television screens. "We call it double-touch," Swearingen said. "What do you think of the decision?"

"You're right," he was told.

To this day Raiders' fans grouse about the call. Tatum insists he never touched the ball. But all the protests in the world can't change the outcome now. That is to say, not without a bit more Divine meddling. □

Oakland	0	0	0	7—	7
Pittsburgh	0	0	3	10—	13

Pitt—FG Gerela 18
Pitt—FG Gerela 29
Oak—Stabler 30 run (Blanda kick)
Pitt—Harris 60 pass from Bradshaw (Gerela kick)

Below: On the same day that the Steelers stunned the Raiders, the Dallas Cowboys effected a miracle of their own with a 17-point final quarter that beat the San Francisco 49ers. Right: Roger Staubach (12) and Ron Sellers (88) celebrated their winning touchdown.

WITH A LITTLE HELP FROM THEIR FOES

Dallas Cowboys vs. San Francisco 49ers

DECEMBER 23, 1972

One could go a long way toward answering the perplexing riddles of competitive sports by determining just how much winners do to win games and how much losers do to lose them. Consider for example a 1972 National Football Conference playoff matching the Dallas Cowboys against the San Francisco 49ers at Candlestick Park. With 1:48 to play in the third quarter, the 49ers led 28–13 and appeared to have the game well in hand. The Cowboys looked terrible. Quarterback Craig Morton and the vaunted Dallas offense weren't getting anywhere. Morton already had coughed up the football twice—an interception and a fumble, both leading to easy 49ers' scores. So head coach Tom Landry yanked him, substituting Roger ("the Dodger") Staubach, and the Cowboys rallied for a 30–28 victory. The question is: did Roger really spin a mira-

177

Guided by John Brodie, above, and sparked by Vic Washington's return of the opening kickoff for a score, right, the 49ers assumed a 28–13 lead.

cle, or did the 49ers sit on their lead and blow it?

The game opened happily enough for the hometown crowd with a torrid 97-yard kickoff return for a touchdown by the 49ers' Vic Washington. Shortly thereafter defensive end Tommy Hart and cornerback Windlan Hall proceeded to scissor Morton in two, and he obligingly fumbled the ball over to the 49ers at the Dallas 15. Larry Schreiber trotted in for the touchdown, first of his three, and the home team led 14–3. After Schreiber scored again and the Cowboys'

Toni Fritsch kicked his second field goal, the veteran Lance Alworth voodooed San Francisco cornerback Jim Johnson, sprinting downfield on a 28-yard scoring pass from Morton.

Strangely, the Cowboys felt confident. They had moved the ball well against the solid 49ers' defense and didn't seem discouraged by their turnovers. The miscues continued early in the third quarter when halfback Cal-vin Hill fumbled at the Dallas 1-yard line, San Francisco recovered, and Schreiber collected another touchdown. With only 15 minutes to play, San Francisco led 28–13.

Landry mulled it over and decided he wasn't yet ready to pull his starting quarterback. Staubach, the Cowboys' regular starting quarterback, had been sidelined with an injured shoulder and Morton had

Larry Schreiber, scoring opposite, accounted for three 49ers' touchdowns.
Dallas encouraged the early San Francisco dominance,
relinquishing the ball on such miscues as Craig Morton's fumble, below.

guided the Cowboys to the playoffs, so Landry decided to give Craig one more chance. On third down he lofted a high spiral straight to Bob Hayes, running free at the goal line. The ball smacked off his hands, costing a touchdown. It wasn't Morton's fault, but that miscue compelled Landry to act. "When that play missed, I felt we had to have a change," Landry says. "It had been the same pattern for nearly three full quarters. Morton wasn't that bad. The turnovers were killing us. I felt the only chance we had was to get Roger in there. He has a way out there. He knows how to turn things around."

As Staubach loosened his arm on the sidelines, Morton walked over and gave him a hug of encouragement. "The fact that he was rooting for me deep down gave me just the shot of

*With 1:31 left Roger Staubach passed to Billy Parks for a score,
bringing the Cowboys to within a touchdown of the lead.
One onside kick later, Dallas was knocking on the door again.*

confidence I needed," Staubach says. "It really meant more to me than anything else."

At first, the 49ers' fans were delighted with Landry's substitute. Staubach appeared to be even worse than Morton. He was sacked four times and finally fumbled. The 49ers might have scored again, but Bruce Gossett muffed a 32-yard field goal, only the second time he had missed from that range the entire year. It was a miss that acrimonious 49ers' fans would long remember.

Slowly, the Cowboys struggled back into contention. Hill galloped 48 yards on a draw play, and after a pass to Billy Parks, San Francisco was charged with a 15-yard penalty. On fourth-and-long, Fritsch booted a 27-yard field goal. 28–17.

Landry was amazed by his team's high spirits, as the Cowboys trailed by 11 points with four minutes to play. "It was unbelievable the way they refused to give up," he says. "They kept saying, 'If we can get one touchdown, we can win.' "

Perhaps they were merely putting up a good front. Guard Blaine Nye, for one, wasn't very optimistic. "I don't think many of us believed we had a chance once the clock passed five minutes to play," Nye says. "Roger hadn't played much that year, so I guess we all lost sight of what he can do."

The turning point was a poor punt by the 49ers' Jim McCann. It wobbled only 17 yards. Cliff Harris corralled it at the San Francisco 45 and Roger made the most of the advantageous field position. He flipped two passes to Walt Garrison for 16 yards. Park nabbed a pass at the 20. Then he zipped into the end zone on a post pattern, beat cornerback

Bruce Taylor, and gathered in Staubach's pass for a touchdown. With 90 seconds to go, the Cowboys trailed 28–23, much to the dismay of the 49ers' rooters.

But San Francisco played it cool. "The 49ers showed hardly any concern at all after we scored that touchdown," Staubach recalls. "A team that confident can shake you up. Their players knew that all they had to do was get the ball and hang onto it. We had one timeout left and realistically, there wasn't much we could do once that was gone. We needed a break."

Probably everyone at Candlestick expected Fritsch to try an onside kick. The ball dribbled the required 10 yards, deflected off the chest of San Francisco's Preston Riley, and nestled snugly in the arms of the Cowboys' Mel Renfro. "The odds against pulling that off must be a thousand to one," Nye says. "But once we did, I knew there was no way we wouldn't score."

"It was like we deserved it," Staubach says. "It was all positive thinking down there. Everyone knew we were going right back out again."

Three thousand miles away in Pittsburgh, Pennsylvania, Franco Harris, whose "Immaculate Reception" had destroyed the Oakland Raiders an hour earlier, watched the Dallas comeback on television. "I was as tense and as excited as anyone else watching the game," Harris says. "I couldn't believe what I was seeing."

With a minute left, Staubach fell back to pass, couldn't find an open receiver, and danced upfield to the San Francisco 29. Billy Parks seized a high pass, skipping out of bounds at the 10-yard line. The clock was halted with 56 seconds to go.

While Parks had sprung across

the sidelines in making the last reception, tight end Ron Sellers had found himself wide open in the middle of the field. "I've got a curl-in across the middle," Sellers told Staubach.

The primary receiver on the next play was Parks, but Staubach told Sellers to be ready as an alternate. "I heard what Sellers said and I kept it in mind," Staubach says. "He was right where he said he'd be."

So was the ball. Sellers caught it

square in the stomach, whereupon he reeled off a little jig of joy. Even the habitually sober-faced Landry broke into a relieved smile at that.

The Candlestick crowd was silent and angry. San Francisco's John Brodie had about thirty seconds to pull off a field goal. On fourth-and-two, he hurled the ball to Vic Washington at the 49ers' 45. Then he fired another to Preston Riley at the Dallas 30. It looked for a moment as if San Fran-

The winner: Ron Sellers eluded Windlan Hall in the end zone, and Staubach drilled it to him. The Cowboys had scored two touchdowns in about a minute, overcoming a 28–16 deficit.

cisco might yet salvage the game, but then a yellow penalty flag fell near the line of scrimmage. Tackle Cas Banaszek was charged with holding. The 49ers were finished.

While the mournful crowd shuffled home, Landry dashed down the Candlestick runway, brandishing the game ball and screaming "Whoopee!" Blaine Nye strolled behind him, smiling sweatily but not once glancing at the shell-shocked 49ers. "I felt so sorry for those guys when the game was over, I couldn't even look at them," he says. □

Dallas	3	10	0	17—30
San Francisco	7	14	7	0—28

SF—V. Washington 97 kickoff return (Gossett kick)
Dal—Fritsch FG 37
SF—Schreiber 1 run (Gossett kick)
SF—Schreiber 1 run (Gossett kick)
Dal—FG Fritsch 45
Dal—Alworth 28 pass from Morton (Fritsch kick)
SF—Schreiber 1 run (Gossett kick)
Dal—FG Fritsch 27
Dal—Parks 20 pass from Staubach (Fritsch kick)
Dal—Sellers 10 pass from Staubach (Fritsch kick)

THE DAY OF THE DOLPHIN

Miami Dolphins vs. Washington Redskins

JANUARY 14, 1973

On the brink of a perfect season, the Dolphins lapsed into buffoonery when Garo Yepremian (1) recovered his blocked field goal and tossed it to the Redskins' Mike Bass (41), who scampered for a touchdown. Except for that aberration, Super Bowl VII went as the whole season had for the Dolphins—just swimmingly.

I'm no miracle worker," Don Shula told a 1970 press conference on the day of his selection as head coach of the Miami Dolphins, a four-year-old expansion team with a miserable 15–39–2 record. "I don't have a magic formula. I'm not a person with a great deal of finesse. I'm about as subtle as a punch in the mouth."

Three seasons later, at the conclusion of a neat, surgically clean 14-7 execution of the Washington Redskins in Super Bowl VII, Shula's

Howard Twilley (81) scored the first touchdown
of the final game, beating Pat Fischer (37)
on a 28-yard pass play. Washington never caught up.

Dolphins had rewritten the record books, becoming the first championship team in NFL history to win every game of the season, something such storied teams as Vince Lombardi's Green Bay Packers, Paul Brown's Cleveland Browns, and George Halas' Chicago Bears never achieved. Only the 1934 and 1942 Bears had finished the regular season unbeaten, but both of those teams were defeated in the championship game.

An undefeated season wasn't the Dolphins' primary goal. Winning the Super Bowl was. Shula already had lost two Super Bowls and dreaded becoming the first coach to lose three of them. The coach's estimable ego forbade anything short of total excellence and success. This conviction infected his players, who had dropped the Super Bowl to the Dallas Cowboys a year earlier and who now feared losing nearly as much as Shula did.

The Dolphins' summer training camp resembled a kind of religious revival meeting. Players loudly vowed to win every game as if they were proclaiming their faith in God. An injury to quarterback Bob Griese in the season's fifth game showed their goal to be achievable. His replacement until the Super Bowl was 38-year-old Earl Morrall. Earl was hardly as flashy as Griese, but he was smart and seldom made mistakes.

Still, the undefeated mark did not come easy. There were several close calls, including a 16–14 last-second victory over the Minnesota Vikings, a 24–23 triumph over the Buffalo Bills, a title-clinching 28-24 win over the New York Jets, and a riveting 13–0 finale against the Baltimore Colts. In the playoffs, the Dolphins quietly disposed of the Cleveland Browns and the Pittsburgh Steelers, and moved into the Super Bowl.

"As we progressed through the season unbeaten, it became more and more evident that no matter how many games we won, we wouldn't be successful until we won that seventeenth game," Shula says. "I really had mixed emotions when we were fourteen and nothing. I was proud, but I honestly felt that neither I nor the team had accomplished anything. I knew that if the Super Bowl ended and we were sixteen and one, I would be a loser. A sixteen-and-one record was not good enough. It had to be seventeen and nothing."

Those close to Shula report that his preparations for this game were no different than for any other. But privately, he worried keenly about mistakes, about the unwelcomed bounce of a ball or an official's poor call. He had great confidence in his team, particularly since Griese was able to play, with Morrall ready to spell him. But Shula was rankled by constant reminders in the Los Angeles newspapers of his Super Bowl losses. The owner of the Los Angeles Rams, Carroll Rosenbloom, his former boss in Baltimore and current critic, glibly predicted that Shula would "choke" in the big one. Rosenbloom had never forgiven Shula for the Jets' upset in Super Bowl III and for Don's later defection from the Colts to the Dolphins..

Yet in the end, it was Redskins' coach George Allen, and not Shula, who wilted under the pressure. Allen, a brazenly effective leader, especially distrusted the press. He fretted daily over the mounting distractions his team faced: media interviews, phone calls from well-wishers, the commotion at the hotel, where friends, ene-

Opposite: *Bob Matheson (53) and Jake Scott (13) sandwiched Charley Taylor (42), and Scott intercepted.* Above: *Larry Csonka (39) gave Bob Griese plenty of time to throw.*

mies, fans, and reporters milled about asking questions. He also barred the players' wives from joining their mates until after the game. "I wish they'd stop at Chicago and stay there," Allen fumed. "They have the rest of their lives to be together, but there's only one Super Bowl."

Despite the eccentricities of their coach, the Redskins were a formidable opponent. The oldest team in the league, they proudly dubbed themselves "the Over-the-Hill Gang." They had methodically crushed Green Bay

and Dallas in the playoffs and rolled into the Super Bowl as three-point favorites. Their single most reliable weapon was the slashing inside running of halfback Larry Brown. Once a team anticipated the run, the Redskins threw bombs to receivers Charley Taylor, Roy Jefferson, and Jerry Smith.

On their own behalf, the Miami offense, led by Larry Csonka and Jim Kiick and fronted by the finest offensive line in the league, established an all-time league rushing record of

2,960 yards. The so-called Miami "No-Name Defense," featured such stars as Nick Buoniconti, Manny Fernandez, Jake Scott, and the "53 man," Bob Matheson. In long yardage situations, Matheson either rushed as a lineman or dropped back with the linebackers.

Washington had beaten Miami in the preseason with Sonny Jurgensen at quarterback. But against the Giants, Jurgensen destroyed his heel and was finished for the season. His replacement was Billy Kilmer.

Allen insists that the game's deciding play was the Redskins' failure to recover a fumbled punt at the Miami 37-yard line late in the first quarter. "We felt we had to get on the board early against them," Allen says. "If we had gotten the ball, we would have scored and it would have been a different ball game."

But it was the Dolphins who scored first, briskly marching 63 yards and scoring when Griese hurled a 28-yard pass to Howard Twilley, who flew through cornerback Pat Fischer. Kilmer's attempted reply was a short, play-action dump pass to Brown. He expected Buoniconti to crowd the line, but he didn't; Matheson did. Buoniconti drifted back, casually picked off the loose spiral, and chugged to the Redskins' 27-yard line. Kiick and Csonka plowed ahead for 6 yards, and Griese hit tight end Jim Mandich at the 2. Kiick squirted between the blocks of Larry Little and Jim Langer, and at halftime the score stood 14–0.

Washington's offense remained somnambulant in the second half. Curt Knight scuffed a 32-yard field goal, and Kilmer's looping 10-yard toss to Jerry Smith in the end zone fell into the hands of safey Jake Scott, who darted to the Redskins' 45.

Miami now came up with their most entertaining miscue of the sea-

Opposite: *If the Dolphins had an underrated unit, it was not their "No-Name Defense" but, like most teams, their offensive line, anchored by guards Larry Little (66) and Bob Kuechenberg (67). Here they escort Mercury Morris around end.* Right *and* far right: *the coaches— Don Shula and George Allen.*

son. As the little Cypriot field-goal kicker, Garo Yepremian, readied himself for a 42-yarder, big Bill Brundige sliced through the line, punching the ball straight back to Garo, who held it quizzically for a moment, as if intending to take a bite out of it. He waddled uncertainly to his right and, sensing imminent pain and catastrophe, tried to do with the queer object what the Americans did—throw it. But the ball refused to cooperate, fluttering churlishly off on its own directly into the path of Washington's Mike Bass, who fled downfield with it and scored.

Suddenly, the Dolphins' perfect season seemed in jeopardy. Shula swallowed his bile and hollered the requisite encouragements. Griese didn't fail him, coolly wasting the clock until Miami was forced to punt with 83 seconds to play. The Redskins went nowhere. Facing a 70-yard campaign with no timeouts, Kilmer didn't even come close. Fittingly, he was

sacked on the game's final play by defensive ends Bill Stanfill and Vern DenHerder. "I knew that was the ball game," DenHerder says. "Stanfill just went crazy after the play, grabbing me, hugging me. Then I realized we were still on top of Kilmer. We were kind of thrashing around on top of the poor guy and the referee said, 'If you hit Kilmer again, this game might not be over.'"

Miami won the Super Bowl and well-deserved accolades for their undefeated season. For Shula the old emptiness, the fears and doubts about losing the big one, had vanished. He rode happily off the field on the shoulders of his champions. □

Miami	7	7	0	0—14
Washington	0	0	0	7— 7

Mia—Twilley 28 pass from Griese (Yepremian kick)
Mia—Kiick 1 run (Yepremian kick)
Wash—Bass 49 fumble return (Knight kick)

VINTAGE JUICE

Buffalo Bills vs. New York Jets

DECEMBER 16, 1973

Before Jim Brown became a movie star, he earned his keep pounding out yards on a football field for the Cleveland Browns. A matchless performer, he rushed for 1,863 yards in 1963, a record that observers believed would stand for decades.

At the peak of his career, Brown once spent a Sunday afternoon deftly demolishing the San Francisco 49ers at chilly Kezar Stadium. Up in the bleachers, a flock of wide-eyed kids gazed enraptured at their idol. To watch Brown in his prime, his body a continuous curving black muscle thrashing repeatedly into the line, was a cherished privilege. No other fullback could produce such awesome moves, or the ability to power inside so boldly, shrugging off tacklers left and right like a restless panther bounding through dry underbrush.

After the game, so the story goes, a couple of the kids dropped into a malt shop across the street to trade stories about their hero when Brown himself walked in the door. The kids stared shyly, a little embarrassed, as the man ordered an ice cream. One of them started strutting like Brown and

mimicking a few of his moves, and the others cheerfully followed suit. Then the show-off sauntered up to the man and said, "Mr. Jim Brown, some day I'm going to break all your records. You wait and see."

That confident kid, O. J. Simpson, was better than his word. Today, in the age of O. J., big Jim Brown seems a distant memory. O. J. Simpson is the ultimate open field runner, combining and improving upon the talents of such past greats as Brown, Gale Sayers, and Elroy ("Crazylegs") Hirsch. Like Hirsch, Simpson is a dangerous, sure-handed receiver whose ability to grab a ball while he is running full tilt, weaving side-to-side without breaking stride or losing speed has blown open many a close game. Like Brown, Simpson is strong and durable. But most of all like Sayers, whose brilliant career was aborted by injuries, O. J. is master of the standing, exploding start at the snap, rocketing out of the backfield, spinning, whirling, and cutting past defenders with sublime, charismatic grace and rhythm.

Dancers are the artists most

Gazing at the action or creating it, O. J. Simpson
projects a superstar's sense of serenity.
After a few dry years, the Juice began to flow in 1972.

195

often compared to a Simpson or Sayers. Gale was the sleeker of the pair, a spidery, long-legged classicist. Simpson retains these traditional lines, but there is something jazzier and meaner about the Juice. Sayers belongs to the ballroom, Simpson to Broadway and the disco scene.

Simpson started out at City College of San Francisco, winning immediate raves and the chance to transfer to the University of Southern California, where he shattered just about every record for a college halfback en route to the coveted Heisman trophy. Selected first by the Buffalo Bills in the 1969 college draft, he languished for three miserable seasons with a second-rate squad, his talents wasted by an indifferent coach.

In 1972, while O. J. contemplated an early retirement, Buffalo selected Lou Saban as its new head coach. Saban's preposterously simple plan was to rebuild the laggard Bills' offense around its stellar running back. O. J. responded with an excellent season, his finest ever as a professional, leading the league with 1,251 yards rushing. Better things were promised for the following year. In summer training camp, O. J. confided to his roommate and on-field protector, guard Reggie McKenzie, that he expected to gain 1,700 yards in 1973.

"Why not make it an even two thousand?" McKenzie jested.

"You're on," O. J. replied with a laugh.

He wasn't kidding. In the season's opener, he exploded for 250 yards, a single-game record, and suddenly everyone knew this was the special season always predicted for Simpson. A countdown commenced, and after many weeks of dogging Brown's record pace, Simpson needed only 61 yards in the season's finale against the New York Jets to eclipse Brown's 1,863. Everyone

O. J. Simpson broke two historic barriers against the Jets. The first was Jim Brown's single-season rushing record of 1,863 yards. Referee Bob Frederic marked the occasion.

counted on O. J. to smash the record. Simpson was so excited he couldn't sleep. "He was uptight and that just wasn't his style before a game," McKenzie recalls. "He kept tossing and turning all night, muttering, 'I wish we could get this thing over with.' "

So did coach Saban. He wanted O. J. to have his record, but not if it meant risking serious injury. The coach, along with everybody in the press box, from the Bills' assistant

Right: *Dashing past roommate Reggie McKenzie and, hopefully, through New York's Delles Howell.* Opposite: *Galloping away from the pack.*

coaches to statisticians and sports-writers, kept a running tally of Simpson's total yardage throughout the game.

"We came out on the field for our first series thinking about the record," Buffalo quarterback Joe Ferguson remembers. "I think all of us wanted to get it over with, then settle down to the business of winning the game." A victory for the Bills would have meant a playoff spot for them if the Cincinnati Bengals had lost their game that day, to the Houston Oilers. The Bengals won that day, but not before the Jets-Bills game concluded, so Buffalo felt the added pressure.

Regardless of the circumstances, Simpson was the Bills' number-one offensive weapon. On his second play

he whisked around right end for 30 yards. He might have shattered the record then and there had he not slipped on the snowy Shea Stadium turf at the New York 34-yard line. This moved his total past the 5,000-yard mark. Then, five plays later, a 6-yard jaunt left him just 4 yards short of the record. Jim Braxton, the Bills' big blocking fullback, carried the last four times for the touchdown.

"O. J. was pretty pooped," quarterback Ferguson says. "We had worked him hard and they were beginning to look for him on every play. I knew that he would make it okay. O. J. wasn't pushing us in the huddle. We knew we had the Jets set up pretty well."

After the Buffalo score, the Jets

overshifted to the strong side of the Buffalo line, moving strong safety Burgess Owens so close that he functioned as a kind of fourth linebacker. But the Jets, though they dearly wanted to win the game for their retiring coach, Weeb Ewbank, simply could not prevent the inevitable. "We kept trying to mix them up," Jets' linebacker Paul Crane recalls. "We tried everything and it didn't work. They came to get a record and they got it."

Ferguson heard on the sidelines that Simpson needed only four more yards. He decided to call "27," Simpson's favorite play. Braxton faked a dive up the middle. The guards pulled out, escorting Simpson around the end. Linebacker Ralph Baker saw the play unfold. "We were in a five-under,

an undershift, and he ran right into the strength of the defense," Baker says. "He didn't get a lot of yards, but he had what he wanted."

The play netted 6, and Simpson had finally surpassed Brown's old standard—1,866 yards! Referee Bob Frederic halted the game and presented Simpson with the ball. O. J. embraced Saban and congratulated his teammates.

Near halftime, O. J. galloped 13 yards for a touchdown. Moments later, Bill Cahill hustled a punt back 51 yards for a score and Buffalo led 21–7. With the Bills safely ahead, everyone settled back to see if O. J., now with 1, 910 yards, could top 2,000 before the game, and season, ended. Early in the second half, he dashed 9

Opposite: *Seven yards on his thirty-fourth carry of the day brought him over 2,000 yards for the season.* Left: *In the locker room afterward he gathered his offensive mates around him to share the glory.*

yards for 1,919. Then, on the next series, he gained 3, lost 3, and gained 8 more. Next, he tore around right end for 25 yards. In the press box, pencils danced down columns of numbers and word was sent to coach Saban: O. J. needed less than 50 yards to break the magic 2,000 mark.

"I got something to fire you guys up," Ferguson told his mates in the huddle. "The Juice needs only fifty yards!"

Nobody said a word. Nobody even looked at Simpson. Nobody had to.

He added 8 yards on that series, and on the next swept around right end for 22. He added 9 more, then 5, swelling the total to 1,996. Now everyone turned statistician. Ferguson sensed he was close. He saw a player hold up four fingers. He knew how close.

The Shea Stadium lights flick-ered on, brightening the raw winter day. O. J.'s thirty-fourth carry was to be led by his pal McKenzie. Catquick, Simpson bolted through the ragged wound in the New York line, churning for 7 yards—2,003 for the season! The remaining spectators gave Simpson a rousing ovation.

Later, on television and at a press conference, O. J. graciously introduced every member of his offensive line. It was a considerate gesture by a class guy, who, incidentally, plans to follow Jim Brown into an acting career, and outshine him there, too. □

Buffalo	7	14	7	6—34
New York	7	0	0	7—14

Buf—Braxton 1 run (Leypoldt kick)
NY—Barkum 48 pass from Namath (Howfield kick)
Buf—Simpson 13 run (Leypoldt kick)
Buf—Cahill 51 punt return (Leypoldt kick)
Buf—Braxton 1 run (Leypoldt kick)
Buf—FG Leypoldt 12
Buf—FG Leypoldt 11
NY—Caster 16 pass from Namath (Howfield kick)

BOB WINDSOR: THE PRICE OF HEROISM

New England Patriots vs. Minnesota Vikings

OCTOBER 27, 1974

The scoreboard clock at Metropolitan Stadium in Bloomington, Minnesota, showed 11 seconds to play. Beneath it, the Minnesota Vikings' veteran defense squad gathered along the 10-yard line. It was the final play of the afternoon and the Vikings knew it would be a pass, probably between the 5-yard line and the end zone. They needed only to knock it down, sack the passer, or intercept the ball and their lead would be secure.

Until the fourth quarter, the game had been a tight, low-scoring affair. The surprising New England Patriots sprinted to a 10–0 lead early in the game. But then the Vikings shut down the New England offense and surged ahead 14–10 on touchdowns by halfback Chuck Foreman and quarterback Fran Tarkenton, the latter coming with only 90 seconds to play.

Across the way, the Patriots broke their final huddle and moved to the line of scrimmage. Quarterback Jim Plunkett had selected his best play, a "94 Pass," sending five receivers against the Minnesota defense. It

After New England's Bob Windsor scored the winning touchdown against Minnesota, above, *his teammates piled on in exultation,* opposite, *unaware that he had just sacrificed his knee.*

Two yards away the right knee buckled, and Windsor knew he was hurt. Nevertheless, he lunged for the goal line and made it. Paul Krause (obscured) and Jackie Wallace (25) defended.

was the same call that had succeeded moments before when receiver Randy Vataha caught a 50-yard bomb at the Minnesota 10. The Vikings were wary of Vataha now and double-teamed him. They failed to notice tight end Bob Windsor. He hesitated at the snap of the ball, as if to block, then raced through the middle.

Plunkett glanced at Vataha, saw the double-coverage, then spotted Windsor running free at the 2-yard line. He fired the ball and Windsor caught it, spinning off balance, unable to see free safety Paul Krause lunge at his legs. He felt his right knee buckle and instantly knew the cartilage was torn. He also knew that he hadn't quite reached the end zone. With a frantic, animal thrust, he wrenched his leg from Krause's grasp and fell into the end zone. As his teammates piled on in joy, Windsor nearly fainted from the pain.

Thus the Patriots upset the mighty Vikings. But what happened to Windsor? He had ripped the medial ligament in three places in his right knee. His season was over in game number seven. What on earth would drive a man to do such a thing? "It's not the money, that's for sure," Windsor says. "We want to win. It's our nature because we are competitors, every one of us, or we wouldn't be playing.

"I look back at that play now and sometimes I think it is funny the way I reacted. The moment I left the line I wanted nothing more than to get into the end zone. That's all I thought about. Nothing else mattered. My subconscious must have told me when I got hit, 'You caught the ball, you tore up your knee, so you might as well get the touchdown. It'll hurt a lot worse if you get this far and don't score.' "

He lunged. He gave no thought to the days of anguished rehabilitation, of the physical pain and mental anxiety that would come once he returned to the game, wondering if his knee would hold or buckle again. Returning after serious surgery, a player spends countless hours alone in rehabilitation and therapy, soaking in daily whirlpool baths, raising weights attached to the leg, jogging up and down stadium steps, rebuilding confidence along with the limb.

Tucker Frederickson, a gifted runner who was the top draft pick of the National Football League back in 1965, had his promising career wiped out by knee injuries. So did Gale Sayers, the Chicago Bears' brilliant running back, who might have set untold records had he stayed healthy.

"You worried about getting hurt again after the first operation because you didn't know whether or not you could stand the rehabilitation process," Frederickson says. "Then after it happened a couple more times, you stopped worrying because it didn't matter. You knew that if you ever got hurt again, there just wouldn't be a next time."

Bob Windsor's wife had suffered a serious knee injury in a softball game six months before the Minnesota game. At the time he couldn't understand why she took such a long time to recover. She was still on crutches when she went to the airport to meet him returning from the game. She didn't know about his injury and was shocked when he hobbled up on his own crutches and gave her a very understanding kiss.

"When it happened to me, I realized how tough it was," he says. "The tough part was the inactivity. It tore me up inside not to be a part of the team on the field. It's one reason why a guy will go through a knee operation and all that goes with it. He just has to get back out there."

Windsor remembers John Thomas, an outstanding offensive guard and a teammate on the San Francisco 49ers, whom he played for before the Patriots. Thomas destroyed both knees on an extra-point play—ligaments and cartilage. He was confined to a wheelchair for more than six months and never played again.

"I always remembered John whenever I thought of myself getting injured," Windsor says. "It's not something a player thinks too much about, though all of us realize that it could happen in an instant. You see the other guy get it and say, 'He's hurt. That's too bad. A damn shame.' Then you put it out of your mind. It's not supposed to happen to you."

When Windsor reported to training camp a year later, his knee wasn't quite ready. He could run straight ahead but found it difficult to shift rapidly from side to side, as any receiver must do. The knee was sore and stiff and the daily drills caused great pain. Coach Chuck Fairbanks was very patient, allowing him to progress at his own pace. All the while he put off the most excruciating test—breaking the adhesions that had formed since surgery.

"There is no easy way," he says. "I'd heard of a guy who planted two poles in the ground, tied himself to them, and then had someone bend him backward as far as he could go. That didn't do him any good. He just made the knee worse. I didn't play until the fourth preseason game. On the third play I got crunched by three tacklers. My adhesions broke at that instant. Maybe that was the easy way because it was out of my control. I was positive that I had ripped the knee apart again. But it didn't happen. Gradually the pain and swelling decreased. The knee became stronger. I played in every game during the 1975 season."

There is no happy ending to this story. No one, not even Windsor knows what will happen. He can tell you when it will rain because his knee gets a twinge. Whenever he caught the ball in a crowd during the 1975 season, he felt damn scared. His once precise cuts aren't as sharp as before. His consolation is that in a game most people have long forgotten his big play brought a victory. Was it worth it? Don't ask. □

New England	3	7	0	7—17
Minnesota	0	0	0	14—14

NE—FG Smith 37
NE—Schubert 10 pass from Plunkett (Smith kick)
Minn—Foreman 3 run (Cox kick)
Minn—Tarkenton 3 run (Cox kick)
NE—Windsor 10 pass from Plunkett (Smith kick)

IT SHOULD HAVE BEEN THE SUPER BOWL

Oakland Raiders vs. Miami Dolphins

DECEMBER 21, 1974

The television network publicity office hailed the 1974 playoff game between the Oakland Raiders and Miami Dolphins as "the real Super Bowl," though the big game was still three weeks away, and as it turned out, neither team would make it there. Nevertheless, the publicists had justification for their hyperbole.

The Dolphins had played in the Super Bowl for three consecutive years and won the last two after losing their first one, to Dallas in 1972, two seasons after Don Shula became their coach and rescued them from the junk pile of the NFL's expansion lot. Only Vince Lombardi's great Green Bay Packers had won two Super Bowls in a row, and they had not come close to extending the streak to three. Now the consensus held that the Dolphins would win that third Super Bowl if they could overcome the Raiders. If not, Oakland would be

Champs at last, or so it seemed
after Oakland dethroned Miami.
John Madden holds the ball aloft.

the oddsmakers' pick to go all the way.

The Raiders had lost just two of their fourteen games. They had seemingly yawned their way through a season, as if nothing else mattered but the chance to scotch their rapidly growing reputation as a team that "couldn't win the big one." Six seasons before, they had played and lost to the Packers in Super Bowl II and were acclaimed the power of the future in the old American Football League. In six of the next eight seasons, they would come within one game of returning to the Super Bowl, an unmatched record in pro football for futility at the brink of success.

The man responsible for putting this team together, managing general partner Al Davis, once a successful coach of the Raiders as well, had made getting to the Super Bowl an obsession in the Oakland organization. A winning season, even a championship one, was considered all but meaningless unless the team played the seventeenth game of the year, the one for the NFL title.

Obviously, the Raiders would be more than primed for this confrontation with Miami, but they had no monopoly on extra motivation. Sportswriters balleyhooed Miami's quest for the unprecedented third straight, particularly since many felt that the Dolphins' dynasty was not likely to extend beyond this year. Miami was about to lose its rampaging fullback, Larry Csonka, the main cog in the offensive engine that had propelled the team to a perfect season in 1972 and

the next year had shredded the Minnesota Vikings' famed defense in the Super Bowl. Csonka had joined a splendid but aging wide receiver, Paul Warfield, and running back Jim Kiick in signing a multi-million dollar package with the new World Football League. All three were playing out their contracts with the Dolphins.

The Dolphins had a well-coordinated and experienced defense, which after two seasons as the backbone of the world champions belied its nickname, "the No-Name Defense." Each member was well known now, and rightfully so. Under Shula the Dolphins had brought back to the pros a college-style defense called "the 53 Defense," named after the jersey number of Bob Matheson, the man who transformed it from the standard 4-3 by becoming an extra lineman or linebacker when he entered the game. The Miami defensive unit wove a pass defense so cohesive that it gave opposing quarterbacks nightmares in long-yardage situations. And even when not confronted with the 53 Defense, a quarterback faced a tricky, talented resistance.

The Raiders had a more wide-open offense than the Dolphins. But like the Dolphins they could chew up a defense, with such runners as Marv Hubbard, a 228-pound fullback who played every game in a state of perpetual fury, and swift, tricky Clarence Davis. Oakland felt it could match Miami's passing game with its wide receivers—Cliff Branch, who was fast enough to run through the Dolphins'

zone, and tenacious Fred Biletnikoff, a pass receiver whose style recalled that of Baltimore's no-speed, great-hands wonder, Raymond Berry.

Quarterback Ken ("the Snake") Stabler directed this show—an able, deft, and daring young left-hander who could stimulate an offense to strike as quickly as his nickname implied. He worked behind a line that considered itself every bit as good as Miami's and had more than a few supporters for its claim.

Though the Raiders' defense was suspect, having finished the season ranked seventh in the American Conference with more than 300 yards allowed per game, the team's offense more than compensated. The Raiders had averaged almost 340 yards total offense during the season.

Clearly, this would be a lively of-fensive show, to the delight of foot-ball fans, whose grumbling had begun to mount in recent years over what they deemed to be the defenses' undue domination of playoff games. Offense was in great demand and it would be in great supply this day. By the time the game ended a nation of television viewers and fifty-five thousand spectators in Oakland's Coliseum were limp from three hours of fireworks. It wasn't the Super Bowl, but it should have been.

Miami's Nat Moore made the bombastic claims of the network pub-licists seem conservative when he ran back the opening kickoff 89 yards for a touchdown. Then the teams battled evenly until Stabler's 31-yard pass to halfback Charley Smith helped forge a 7–7 tie in the second quarter. Garo Yepremian's 33-yard field goal made

In their 1974 playoff game, the Dolphins and Raiders produced a better played and more exciting contest than many Super Bowls. Opposite: Larry Csonka plows ahead. Left: Ken Stabler scrambles.

the score 10–7 Miami at intermission.

Midway through the third quarter, the offenses broke through again. First the Raiders regained the lead on Stabler's 13-yard pass to Biletnikoff, but Griese answered with a 16-yard touchdown pass to Warfield. Yepremian missed the extra point and Miami had only a two-point lead, 16–14, which it widened to 19–14 on Yepremian's 46-yard field goal.

Two plays later the fun began. With the Raiders at their 28-yard line, Stabler sent Branch down the left sideline. Branch made a diving catch, barely eluding cornerback Henry Stuckey, who skidded past him trying to play the ball. When Stuckey failed to touch him, Branch jumped up and ran in for the score. "I knew in professional football you can get up and run again if you haven't been touched,"

Branch explained. "I practice it whenever I go down on my own. I try to get back up and run a few yards. That was one time when it paid off."

When George Blanda kicked the extra point, Oakland led 21–19 with 4:37 to play. It was only the start of one of the most hair-raising finishes in NFL history.

Griese ran the ball at the Raiders' weak defense, and did so well— perhaps too well—that in two and a half minutes he had Miami in front again. The score came on a twisting, dodging, tackle-breaking 23-yard run by rookie back Benny Malone. Somehow he stayed on his feet and avoided the sideline as he threaded his way for the score. Yepremian hit the extra point this time, and with 2:08 to go, Miami led 26–21.

At times like these Miami's de-

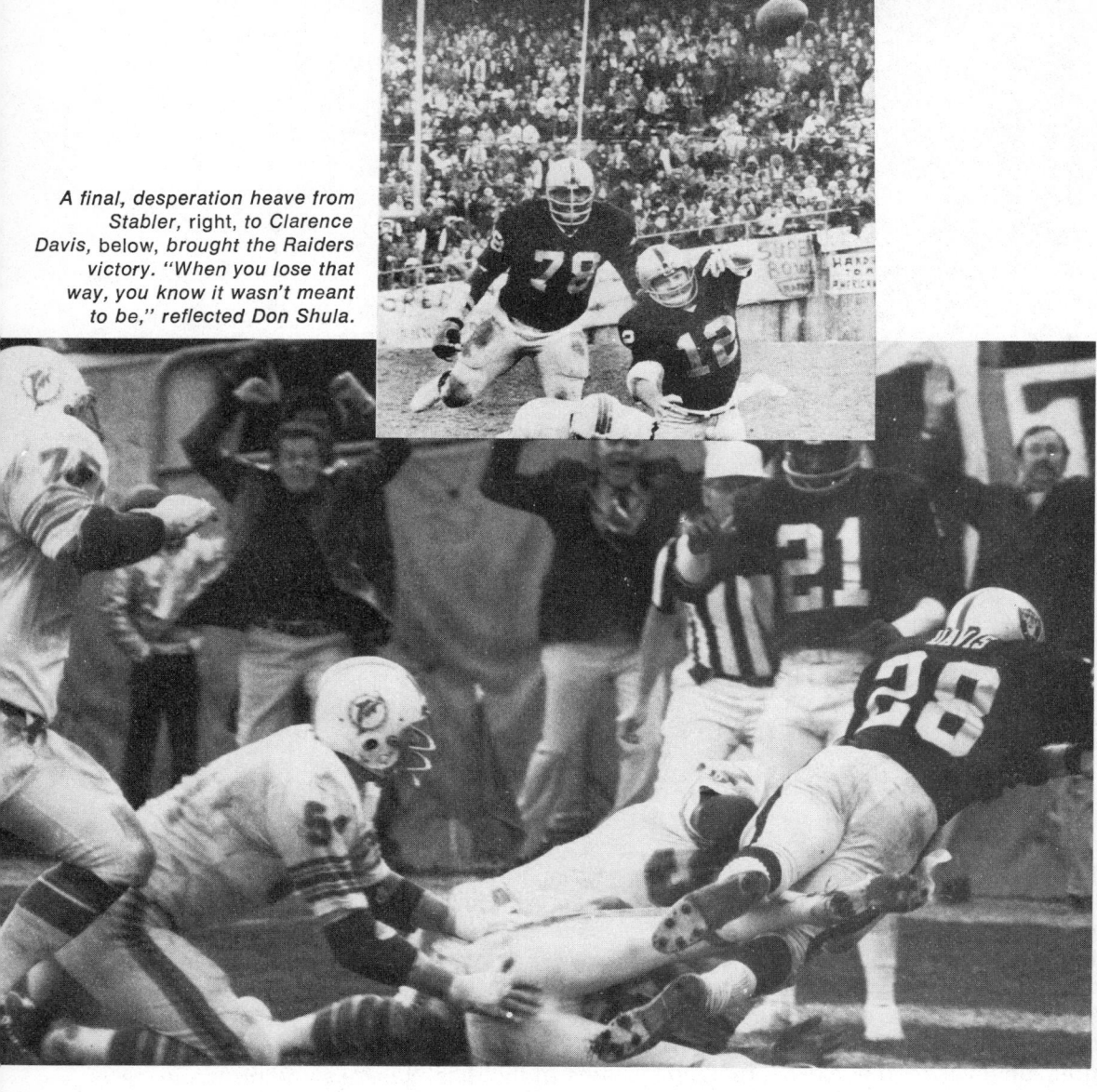

A final, desperation heave from Stabler, right, to Clarence Davis, below, brought the Raiders victory. "When you lose that way, you know it wasn't meant to be," reflected Don Shula.

fense seemed impregnable. A quarter-back faced the seemingly impossible dual challenge of fighting off an unrelenting clock and a Miami defense that surrendered only the stingiest yardage. Eventually, the quarterback would become so impatient that he would lead his team into Miami's pass-snaring defensive web. The 53 Defense preyed on imperfectly thrown balls or poorly run pass patterns.

Stabler didn't panic. His passes were perfect, his receivers precise in their patterns. He worked the middle of the field and used two timeouts; he worked the sidelines and stopped the clock automatically. With less than a minute to play, he stood third-and-one at the Dolphins' 14. He had one time-out left.

He trotted to the sidelines to confer with coach John Madden. "If we threw a pass to save the timeout, but missed, it would have been fourth down and the whole season riding on one play," Madden said. "So I called a running play and then decided to use the timeout to stop the clock."

Clarence Davis slipped off tackle for six yards and a first down at the Dolphins' 8. Thirty-five seconds to play. "We had four chances to complete a pass, and each time the clock would stop if we didn't make it," Madden explained. "We had the only shots we could have wanted in this situation."

They needed only one.

Stabler stepped into his huddle and called his play. It sent Biletnikoff into one corner of the end zone. Tight end Bob Moore would delay for two counts, blocking the linebacker to deceive the Dolphins into thinking a run was coming. That would allow the running backs, following the hashmarks into the end zone, to get a step on their defenders.

Stabler coolly took the ball from center Jim Otto and hurried into the passing pocket. He peered downfield and, in the blur that is the quarterback's three-second view of the developing pattern could not see any receiver open. The pressure of the Miami rushers began to collapse his protective pocket. Suddenly, defensive end Vern Den Herder grabbed him. The lineman's hands slipped down Stabler's legs and began to jerk at his ankles, pulling his feet from beneath him.

"I saw Kenny was in trouble," said Clarence Davis, who had run down the right hashmark. "I came back to help. I didn't know if he'd see me or not."

As Stabler went down, he saw Davis with just enough room between him and the Miami defenders around him. At that moment he didn't recognize Davis, much less stop to consider that he was the least proficient of the Raiders' pass receivers. He just sent the ball fluttering vaguely toward him.

"We got it!" Shula thought to himself as he watched Stabler throw off-balance, the ball looping toward the end zone and three Dolphins tensing to jump for it as if it were a basketball rebound.

"I had my hands on it but he had it too," Miami linebacker Mike Kolen remembers.

Somehow, Clarence thrust his 5-foot 10-inch frame above the Miami players and grabbed the ball. His arm was underneath it, and Kolen's was on top of it. Desperately, Davis wrenched the ball free and clutched it to his chest in the end zone for the winning score.

"I didn't know I was that strong," he says. "It was pure concentration because suddenly I knew we wouldn't get another chance."

When he tumbled to the grass, the clock showed 26 seconds left. "When you lose like that, you know it wasn't meant to be," Shula said later. "Your dreams go down the drain. It was the toughest loss I've suffered since I've been coaching."

And so the dream of winning three straight Super Bowls vanished. Once, after he lost his first two Super Bowl games, the critics had said that Shula "couldn't win the big one." He had experienced the fulfillment of destroying that myth. Now the Raiders had done the same. And the "real Super Bowl," though its victor would never reach the real Super Bowl, had more than satisfied its buildup. □

Miami	7	3	6	10—26
Oakland	0	7	7	14—28

Mia—Moore 89 kickoff return (Yepremian kick)
Oak—Smith 31 pass from Stabler (Blanda kick)
Mia—FG Yepremian 33
Oak—Bilentnikoff 13 pass from Stabler (Blanda kick)
Mia—Warfield 16 pass from Griese (kick failed)
Mia—FG Yepremian 46
Oak—Branch 72 pass from Stabler (Blanda kick)
Mia—Malone 23 run (Yepremian kick)
Oak—Davis 8 pass from Stabler (Blanda kick)

WHEN IRISH EYES ARE SMILING

Pittsburgh Steelers vs.
Minnesota Vikings,
Dallas Cowboys

JANUARY 12, 1975, JANUARY 18, 1976

Sometimes there is justice in this world. In January 1976, the Pittsburgh Steelers defeated the Dallas Cowboys 21–17, becoming the third team in National Football League history to capture two successive Super Bowls. After forty long, dreadful, losing seasons, the once-lowly Steelers had put together a pair of championships like a matched set of pearls, much to the delight of their 75-year-old owner and patriarch, Anthony J. Rooney.

In the interim Rooney and the Steelers suffered the trials of Job. There weren't even many close calls —only two. In 1947, Pittsburgh and the Philadelphia Eagles tied in the standings, and a playoff was required to settle the Eastern Division race. The teams met in Philadelphia and

The Pittsburgh Steelers won two straight Super Bowls. The first showcased their defense, the second the acrobatic Lynn Swann.

Opposite: *Clutching the Super Bowl trophy in one hand and the game ball in the other, Steelers' owner Art Rooney seemed a bit misty-eyed, to the delight of Pete Rozelle, after Super Bowl IX. Below: Terry Bradshaw throws before "Too-Tall" Jones can reach him.*

the Eagles romped 21–0. Late in 1963, the Steelers needed a single victory over the New York Giants to reach their first NFL championship game. It was no contest. The Giants breezed 33–16 and Pittsburgh finished fourth. Everyone complimented old man Rooney on his perseverance and good sportsmanship, but he didn't try to hide his disappointment. "Losing is like a death in the family," Rooney said. "When you come home from a losing trip, it's like there's a body on the plane."

But in the early seventies, the Steelers underwent a steady, dramatic reversal of form. Through a series of excellent high draft picks, coach Chuck Noll rebuilt the team entirely, adding such talented players as "Mean" Joe Green, Terry Bradshaw, Franco Harris, and Lynn Swann. In 1974, Pittsburgh snatched the American Conference crown from the powerful Oakland Raiders and trooped into Super Bowl IX at New Orleans the sentimental choice to beat the Minnesota Vikings. Fans across the country wanted Art Rooney to go out a winner in his twilight years.

He's a fussy old softy, this Arthur J. Rooney—his face a wad of freckled dough chomping on a wet cigar. Stories are legend about his kindness and generosity. Mostly they tell of his lifelong habit of listening patiently to the hard-luck tales of total strangers, then quietly peeling off a roll of G-notes for their troubles. Once a Pittsburgh church needed money for an orphanage. Rooney, just returned from a rich payoff at Saratoga, heard about it and told the pastor he wanted to help. He proceeded to count out ten $1,000 bills.

"I hope you came by this honestly," said the startled priest.

"Sure, father," Rooney replied. "I won it on the horses."

Rooney is reputed to have amassed the beginnings of his great wealth one lucky weekend at Saratoga Race Track in upstate New York. Though he insists the figure is exag-

Left: *Dallas' Preston Pearson finds a seam in the Pittsburgh defense.* Below: *The ball seems suspended as Franco Harris (32) fumbles. After a decade of mostly anticlimactic Super Bowls, the Cowboys and Steelers made Super Bowl X the thrilling finish it was supposed to be.*

gerated, he supposedly won more than $370,000. He used $2,500 of that money to purchase a semipro football team called the Pittsburgh Pirates and bought his way into the fledgling NFL. To this day Rooney has invested heavily in horseracing. His family owns a 125-horse stable in Maryland and controls half a dozen racetracks on the East Coast. But his heart has always belonged to his beloved team.

A marvelous, witty yarn spinner, Rooney spends hours reminiscing about his old football cronies. Among his less than successful coaches were the authoritarian Dr. Jock Sutherland —"the players used to consider Sunday their day off, because that's when we'd play a game"—and the somewhat obstreperous Johnny McNally, alias "Johnny Blood," a particular favorite of Rooney's, who coached the Steelers in the late thirties.

"He may have been the only

Opposite: *Steve Furness captures Roger Staubach.*
Right: *Lynn Swann outleaps Mark Washington and hypnotizes the football.*

coach in history who had the players looking out for him," Rooney recalls. "John couldn't have been in any other organization but ours. He didn't believe in fundamentals or curfews. He always wore tennis shoes, summer and winter, and often would ride to practice on a motorcycle. The players really worried about him and looked after him. . . ."

Rooney's players, hardly world beaters, were always among the most colorful in the league. Walt Kiesling, Joe Bach, Bill Dudley, Bobby Lane, Buddy Parker, Gene ("Big Daddy")

Lipscomb, and a kid quarterback named Johnny Unitas, who was let go —"too dumb" said his coach—all toiled for Pittsburgh at one time or another. So did Byron ("Whizzer") White, who later graduated to the United States Supreme Court.

When Rooney departed for Super Bowl IX, he left behind the same, snug 12-room town house where he had lived with his family for 37 years. The Irish neighborhood has decayed badly, but Rooney would never think of moving. He grew up across the street. A diverse entourage of pals and

hangers-on accompanied the old man to New Orleans. Included among them was the entire Three Rivers Stadium ground crew *plus* their families. Rooney handled all the arrangements. It wasn't his first football sally down to Bayou land. He remembered a time back in the thirties when the Steelers transferred a home game with the Cleveland Rams to New Orleans because of a heavy snowstorm. A promoter promised to fill the stadium. Cleveland agreed to the switch as long as Rooney paid the travel expenses, which he did.

"I was told that the mayor of New Orleans, a fellow named Maestri, would get behind the game," Rooney says. "Now I had been active in politics and knew what some of those mayors could do. But when I got to New Orleans and met the major, he didn't know anything about the game. He'd never heard of Whizzer White or the Steelers. He thought we had come down to play Tulane. When the game started, there was no one in the stands. The promoter told us New Orleans was a late-arriving crowd. Well, we're still waiting for it to show up."

The turning point of Super Bowl X came in the fourth quarter when Pittsburgh scored a safety on Reggie Harrison's block of Mitch Hoopes's punt, narrowing the Dallas lead to 10–9.

As the day for Super Bowl IX drew near, Rooney's sons, Art and Dan, who now ran the club, watched their father bask nobly in the limelight. "This is my father's week," Dan said. "He's been waiting forty-two years. None of us are jealous."

"You know," the old man told a reporter the day before the game, "I'd rather have a team in the Super Bowl than a horse in the Kentucky Derby."

The question of the day was whether Pittsburgh's "steel curtain" defense could successfully entangle Fran Tarkenton's scrambling offense. After many bruising seasons with the Giants, Tarkenton, at age 34, wasn't the fleet runner he once had been. But his arm was still sound, and he was always a threat to dash downfield. Noll devised a special defense to contain him. It was so effective that Tarkenton was never a factor, completing only 11 passes for 102 yards. Once, nailed by defensive end L. C. Greenwood, Fran fumbled in his own end zone and the Steelers gained a safety.

Up in the press box, Rooney quietly nodded. He never doubted that his team would win. When fullback Franco Harris, whose 158 yards rushing set a Super Bowl record, sprinted 9 yards for a touchdown, the old man didn't bat an eye. It was his day, but nothing to get excited about.

As in past Super Bowls, a succession of blunders cost the Vikings two touchdowns. Within easy scoring range, Tarkenton threaded a pass over the middle to receiver John Gilliam. Gilliam was popped by Glen Edwards and the ball flew straight up, dropping like a parachute into the hands of Pittsburgh's Mel Blount. Later, Mean Joe Green wrestled the ball away from Chuck Foreman at the Steelers' 5-yard line.

The Vikings kept the game interesting when Matt Blair blocked Bobby Walden's punt in the end zone and safety Terry Brown flopped on top of it for a touchdown. Up in the press box a cloud of angry cigar smoke registered the old man's displeasure. He shouldn't have worried. Bradshaw quickly drove the Steelers to a clinching touchdown. En route, a key play set off the day's only controversy. Tight end Larry Brown nabbed a 30-yard pass, fumbled, and Minnesota recovered. But the officials ruled the play completed before the fumble. Minnesota coach Bud Grant and a television replay said otherwise, but again, it was a Rooney day. On third-and-two, Bradshaw lofted a touchdown to Brown. That would do it.

Upstairs, the old man slowly left his seat. "Better go get the big silver thing," he said.

One year later only the opponent changed. The Vikings were aced out of their fourth Super Bowl by Roger Staubach's expert "Hail Mary" touchdown pass in the waning seconds of the 1975 NFC finale. The Dallas Cowboys, after a year of rebuilding, were a sharp young team, featuring a curious old formation, "the Shotgun." Staubach, the quarterback, would stand six or seven yards behind the center, ready at the snap to scramble or throw without bothering to backpedal.

Pittsburgh steamed into Miami's Orange Bowl heavy favorites, having lost but two games all season. They were the league bullies now, a brawling, muscular, hard-hitting crew that depended on Franco Harris' legs and a wonderfully balanced defense. "Win the battle of the hitting," Noll preached. "Do whatever it takes to win."

The game turned out closer than expected, more exciting by far than most other Super Bowls, which had tended to resolve themselves in dreary, drawn-out routs. Staubach opened the scoring with a nifty, over-the-middle touchdown heave to speedy Drew Pearson. "The Cowboys showed us three different sets on that play," moaned linebacker Andy Russell. "Half of us were going one way, half another."

Fortunately for the Steelers, their offense wasn't nearly as confused. Wide receiver Lynn Swann, the recipient of a mild concussion courtesy of the Oakland Raiders in the AFC title game, nabbed a 32-yard pass deep in Dallas territory. Bradshaw's flip to

tight end Randy Grossman evened the score. Dallas replied with a 36-yard field goal and led at halftime 10–7.

The game remained stalemated until early in the fourth quarter. As Dallas rookie Mitch Hoopes prepared to punt from his own end zone, Pittsburgh's Reggie Harrison plowed through the line, catching the ball flush on his face. It caromed past the end line for a safety.

"We like to think those are nine-point plays," Noll says. But the Steelers couldn't quite pick up a touch-

The end: the irrepressibe Lynn Swann iced the game by gliding past Mark Washington for a perfectly thrown touchdown pass from a cool-under-fire Terry Bradshaw.

down after taking the Cowboys' kickoff, and had to settle for Roy Gerela's field goal and their first lead of the afternoon with scarcely six minutes to play.

Gerela booted another after Mike Wagner's interception, but with Staubach's reputation for instant miracles, the 15–10 advantage seemed less than secure. So on third-and-four, Bradshaw decided to throw a bomb to old reliable Lynn Swann. Landry guessed a pass too, ordering a fully-rigged rush of the quarterback. For a few violent seconds all hell flew at Bradshaw, gallantly feinting and weaving, the ball leaping from his hand the very instant he was powdered from the blind side by defensive tackle Larry Cole. Swann never broke stride, gliding gracefully into the end zone, two steps ahead of a stumbling, cursing Mark Washington. Bradshaw never saw it. Led groggily off the field, he had no idea until much later, when someone told him in the dressing room, that his pass had produced a touchdown.

Staubach answered with a desperate 34-yard touchdown pass to rookie Percy Howard, who slipped past the fallen Mel Blount. But time was running out.

"We didn't want to give them a big play again," Noll says. "They needed a touchdown to beat us and I felt our defense could prevent that." It did. Staubach's futile prayer to Pearson was batted down by all of six Pittsburgh defenders in the end zone. His last try was intercepted by Glen Edwards, and Mr. Rooney's shelf gained another nice trophy.

"You know, this is even better than the day I got married," Rooney told a friend. "Getting married I took for granted." □

Pittsburgh	0	2	7	7—16
Minnesota	0	0	0	6— 6

Pitt—Safety (White dropped Tarkenton in end zone)
Pitt—Harris 9 run (Gerela kick)
Minn—T. Brown recovered blocked punt (kick failed)
Pitt—L. Brown 4 pass from Bradshaw (Gerela kick)

Dallas	7	3	0	7—17
Pittsburgh	7	0	0	14—21

Dall—D. Pearson 29 pass from Staubach (Fritsch kick)
Pitt—Grossman 7 pass from Bradshaw (Gerela kick)
Dall—FG Fritsch 36
Pitt—Harrison safety, blocked punt out of end zone
Pitt—FG Gerela 36
Pitt—FG Gerela 18
Pitt—Swann 64 pass from Bradshaw (kick failed)
Dall—P. Howard 34 pass from Staubach (Fritsch kick)

ANY STIFF COULD HAVE DONE IT

Raiders vs. Colts

December 23, 1977

"**A**ny stiff could have done it...."

That was easy for Dave Casper to say at the time. Moments before—43 seconds into a second overtime quarter—he had caught a very difficult 10-yard touchdown pass from quarterback Ken Stabler, and that catch had given the Oakland Radiers a 37–31 victory over the Baltimore Colts in the semifinals of the 1977 American Football Conference playoffs. The game marked only the fourth time in pro football history—one day short of the sixth anniversary of its last occurrence—that two teams had played as long.

Playing into overtime always increases the suspensefulness of any game, but this had been such a symphony of big plays and come-from-behind drama, culminating in 16 minutes of icy anticipation, that it became something very special: "A game," Oakland coach John Madden was moved to admit afterward, "where you really hate to see a loser."

"That was the most exciting game I ever played in," Stabler says today, and he carries a half dozen or so around in his memory that could qualify just as easily for that honor. "I like the challenge of overtime, but only if you win. Then it's fine."

He obviously loved the challenge of this game because it got better as it got older, and then it got downright scary. It had big plays right from the start—a 30-yard touchdown run by the Raiders' Clarence Davis with only a half minute to play in the first quarter for a 7–0 Oakland lead, followed two minutes later by Bruce Laird's 61-yard interception return

for a tie-making score—and it had the spectacular performance of Casper. He caught only four passes, but three of those were touchdowns. The other was a 42-yard over-the-shoulder beauty that was a combination of Joe DiMaggio playing centerfield and Dave Casper playing the superb pass catcher.

His first catch was an eight-yard touchdown toss from Stabler during the Raiders' first possession in the third quarter. It gave Oakland a 14–10 lead that lasted precisely 16 seconds, or for as long as it took the Colts' Marshall Johnson to return Earl Mann's kickoff 87 yards for a touchdown and a 17–14 Baltimore advantage.

Back came Oakland less than four minutes later. Following Ted Hendricks' block of David Lee's punt, Stabler in three plays found Casper with a ten-yard TD pass, Casper's second catch.

This was Oakland's third lead, but it lasted only four-and-a-half minutes into the fourth quarter when, after cornerback Lester Hayes interfered with Glenn Doughty in the end zone, the Colts got the ball at Oakland's 1-yard line. It took three tries, but Ronnie Lee finally barged over for the score, and for the third time the Colts had the lead, 24–21.

Then the game got out of control. In four plays, including a pass interference call against Colts' cornerback Nelson Munsey that put the ball at Baltimore's 1-yard line, Oakland's Pete Banaszak scored, and the Raiders led 28–24.

Forget that lead. Bert Jones brought his team 73 yards in four plays, the last being Lee's 13-yard touchdown run, and Baltimore led for the fourth time, 31–28, with half the last quarter still to play.

Here the Colts made a decision that probably cost them the game: Coach Ted Marchibroda abandoned their wide-open style and tried to sit on the lead. Baltimore never made another first down the rest of the day.

Stabler did just the opposite. There was 2:55 to play when he began driving the Raiders from their 30-yard line. Casper provided his 43-yard dandy that put the ball at Baltimore's 14-yard line with just over a minute to play. That was catch number three.

"That was the game's key play," Stabler says. "It put us in position to get a tie and go into overtime. Had he not caught the ball, we were still a long way off with not much time to get home."

A bigger play than his winning touchdown?

"Absolutely," Stabler insists. "In the overtime, we were on the ten-yard line, and if we'd missed on the touchdown, there was another chance, and if that missed, then we could have kicked the field goal and still won the game. Without Dave's catch in that last minute, we might never have played the other scene."

Three plays later Oakland was at the Colt's 5-yard line, facing a fourth-and-one with a half minute to play. Madden had two choices: Go for the first down, and then try to score a touchdown and win in regulation time; or kick the field goal for the tie and take his chances in overtime. "I couldn't let the whole season hinge on going for a first down," he says. "I had to go for the tie, although emotionally I wanted the first down and the victory. Sometimes, though, it's more difficult to do what's right."

Then it was Mann's turn to sweat. "I was nervous, apprehensive, everything else," he said. "I'd missed field goals before in my career, but I knew this was one I absolutely had to make. All I could think

Raider wide receiver Cliff Branch drops behind Colts' Nelson Mansey to make an acrobatic catch of a long Ken Stabler pass.

of was that the kick was worth a half-million dollars, because that was what we'd make if we got into the conference championships the following week. And what made it worse, I knew it would all happen in just one point four seconds — the time it took the ball to get from the center to my holder, Dave Humm, and then for me to kick it."

The 22-yard kick sailed cleanly through the uprights, and everyone awaited the drama of overtime. The Colts won the toss and received the kickoff, but their offensive fire had fizzled. During the overtime, they made only 12 yards in three possessions, never going beyond their 40-yard line. But Jones did miss tight end Raymond Chester in the open, and that play, he still feels, might have ended the game.

Oakland was fortunate in another situation as well. Late in the first extra quarter Cliff Branch fumbled after catching a pass, and a wild scramble ensued at the Raiders 37-yard line. Both teams signalled the ball was theirs, but when the officials finally dug into the pile of players, they said that Oakland tackle Henry Lawrence had the ball.

The Colts players on the field screamed bloody murder that Lawrence stole the ball from one of their players as the pile was being opened and after the whistle had blown. Instead of having a golden opportunity to win the game, Baltimore then was set back to its 15-yard line by Ray Guy's punt, couldn't move, and punted back to the Raiders 42-yard line.

Stabler was master now. Cleanly and cleverly, he drove his team, twice coming to third down plays and each time making the precise yardage—a third-and-one run by Banaszak and a third-and-nineteen pass to Branch, who made a sliding catch at Baltimore's 26-yard line. He then passed for eight yards to Fred Biletnikoff, and Banaszak added five more on a run. The quarter ended with Oakland at the 13-yard line.

During the fifth quarter, the Raiders had had the wind advantage, but Mann had missed a 48-yard field goal. Madden decided, after Branch's catch, to forget about the wind "and just stay solid and take our chances in the next quarter. Banaszak ran on the first play of the sixth quarter to the ten-yard line, and we saw the Colts were playing exclusively for the run, particularly when we had three tight ends in the game. So we decided to fake the run and throw to Casper."

"The play was called a K–17, and it was designed for me all the way," Casper says. "Their cornerback [Munsey] was playing for the run, and I faked inside, then went outside."

But it was not really that easy. Casper had to fight off a linebacker before he was clear in the left corner of the end zone. Stabler, with the option of throwing the ball away if the play could not succeed, had nearly abandoned the play, throwing the ball high and forcing Casper to reach up and out to snare it.

"That was my centerfielder's instincts again, and I played it like a ball hit over my head," he said afterward. "Heck, any stiff could have done it, and I'm glad I was the stiff who did."

Oakland	7	0	14	10	0	6	**37**
Baltimore	0	10	7	14	0	0	**31**

Oak—Davis 30 run (Mann kick)
Balt—Laird 61 interception return (Linhart kick)
Balt—FG Linhart 36
Oak—Casper 8 pass from Stabler (Mann kick)
Balt—Johnson 87 kickoff return (Linhart kick)
Oak—Casper 10 pass from Stabler (Mann kick)
Balt—R. Lee 1 run (Linhart kick)
Oak—Banaszak 1 run (Mann kick)
Balt—R. Lee 13 run (Linhart kick)
Oak—FG Mann 22
Oak—Casper 10 pass from Stabler (No kick)

Top: *Otis Sistruck pressures Bert Jones as he tries to run with the pigskin.*

Bottom: *Oakland coach John Madden shouting instructions to Pete Banaszak while sending him into the action.*

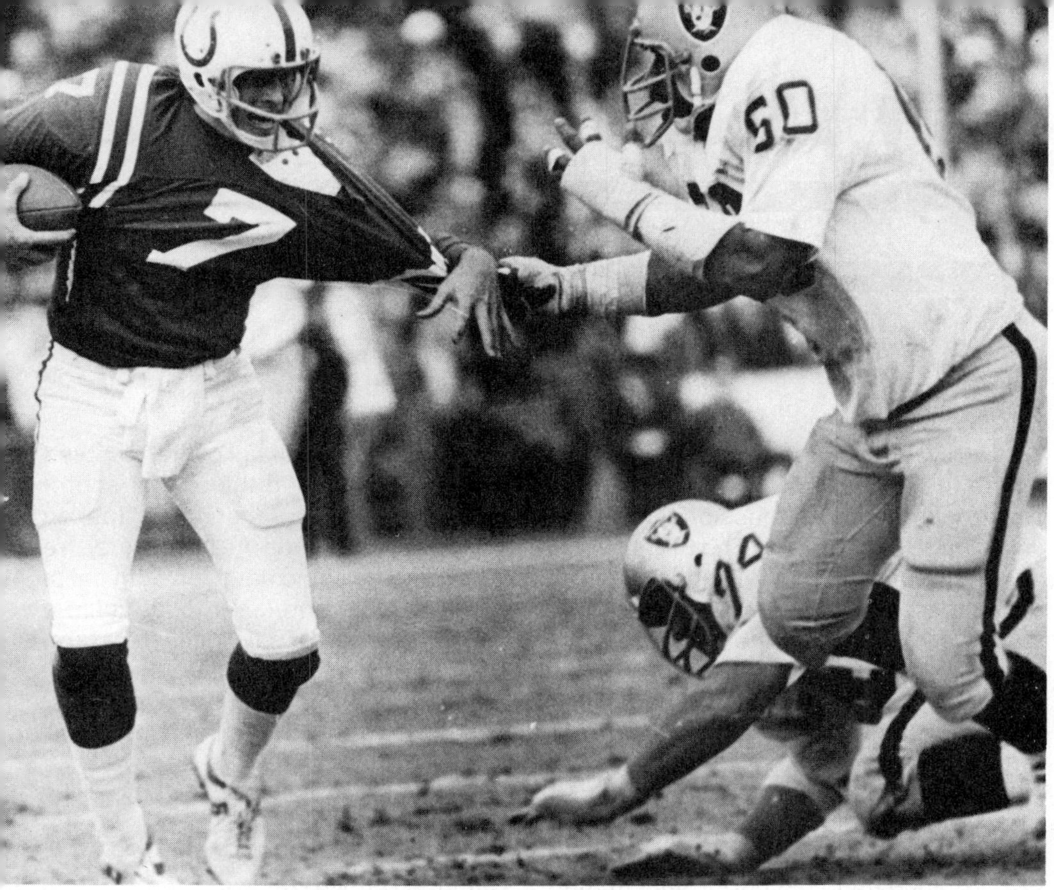

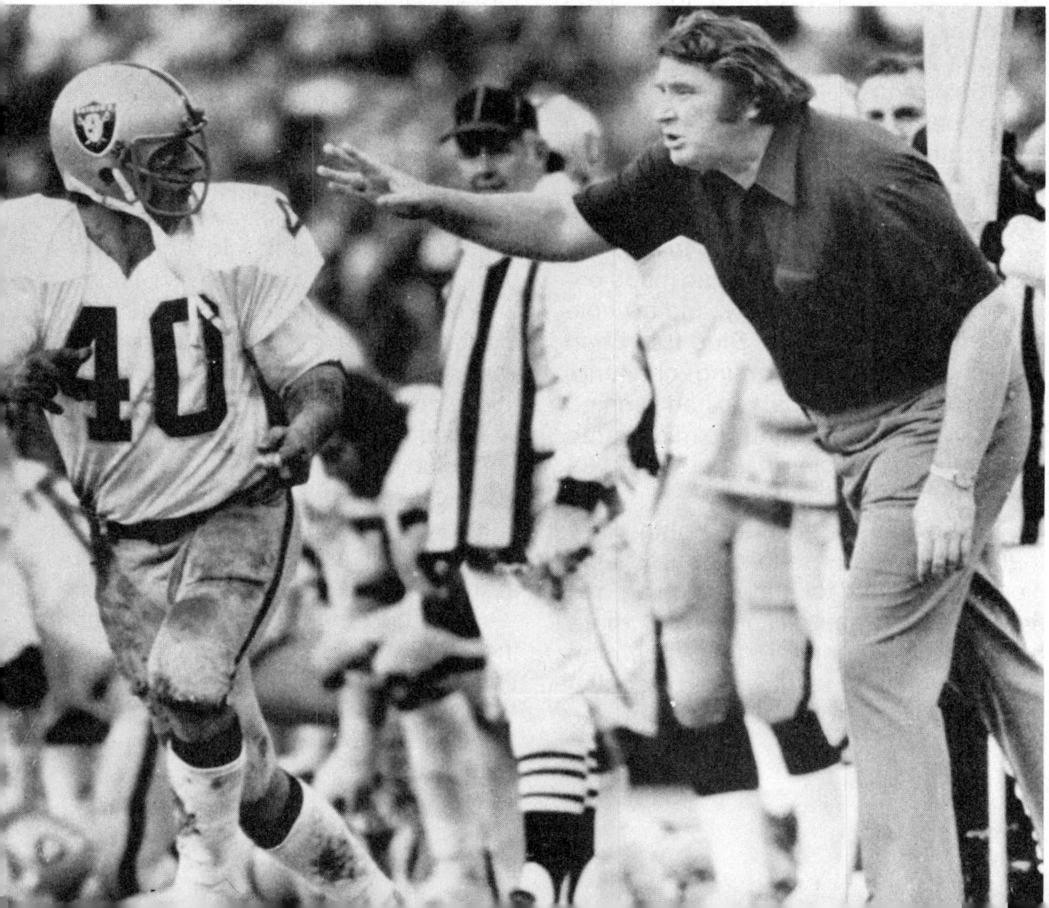

LUV YA, BLUE; LUV YA, EARL

Oilers vs. Dolphins

November 20, 1978

Earl Campbell flashed onto the NFL scene in 1978 with the burden any star rookie carries into professional football when he's referred to as The Franchise.

Call someone The Franchise and the skeptics immediately come out of the woodwork to scoff — the I-told-you-so guys who are never satisfied. With luck, he can survive, be successful, and raise a good team to the status of a great team.

The last was pretty much the common judgment Campbell's rookie year unfolded in Houston. As he piled up big performance upon big performance, the ranks of the believers grew, forcing the skeptics and agnostics to draw their wagons into a circle for one last stand: Monday night, November 20, 1978, when the rugged Miami Dolphins came to Houston for a nationally televised game. This would be the final, the acid test.

When the game ended with a 35–30 Houston victory, Campbell had made believers of an entire country, and a whole new era called Luv Ya, Blue had been born the singing, screaming, chanting, and cheering partisans who had jammed the Astrodome that night. He had scored four touchdowns and amassed 199 yards rushing in 28 carries.

But it was that twenty-eighth carry that blew away any doubts about his abilities—an 81-yard touchdown run around the right end when millions everywhere had to be wondering just how the man could even stand up. It was an electrifying play not only for its distance but also for the fact that no Miami player troubled him once he passed the line of scrimmage. Despite the battering he'd taken in 27 previous running attempts, he looked as if he could have run right out of the Astrodome and kept going until he reached his mother's tidy little rose farm 200 miles away in Tyler.

Even Don Shula, the Dolphins' coach who had done it all and seen it all in nearly two decades as a player and coach in the NFL, was a bit awestruck by that performance, the first time he'd ever had to play against this man-machine. "Campbell is everything they've said and more," Shula said afterward. "I don't know how much Houston is paying him but he's worth every cent."

In that Boom Town, U.S.A., the Oilers had shelled out a hefty $1.2 million for their rookie, and the Texas-sized shootout that night fit in with the awesomeness of the city, the contract, and the expectations of those screaming Texans with their blue pom-poms. Their team was fighting for a division title with Pittsburgh and looking for its first playoff berth in nine seasons. Going into the game, Campbell was the second-leading rusher in the NFL. Who was number one? Delvin Williams of the Dolphins.

Before the game, the supercharged atmosphere had gripped even the players. Carl Mauck, Houston's veteran center, said to Campbell, "We need four touchdowns to win tonight. You do that and the defense promises to hold Williams under one hundred yards."

"It was a joke, yes and no," Mauck

Earl Campbell's successful struggle for a three-yard gain against the Miami defense.

says. "I knew if Earl was running the way he could, Miami wouldn't be on the field long enough for Williams to roll it up. And that's exactly how it worked out."

Well, almost. The Oilers did shut down Miami's running game, holding Williams to 73 yards. But Dolphins quarterback Bob Griese almost undid the entire plot. He completed 23 of 33 passes for 349 yards, and had Miami ahead 7–0 the first time he had the ball, on a 10-yard pass to Nat Moore.

Campbell came back on the next drive with one yard and his first touchdown. Houston quarterback Dan Pastorini gave his team a 14–7 lead in the second quarter with a 15-yard pass to Mike Barber. But back came Griese and the Dolphins, and Williams polished off a long drive with his only touchdown of the game. The score was tied 14–14 at the half.

Miami's defense had done a good job to that point, holding Campbell to just 44 yards. But Earl began his all-out as-

sault by leading the Oilers to a 21–14 third quarter lead with a six-yard TD run. Miami's Leroy Harris matched that score a bit later, and the teams again were tied, 21–21, as the fourth quarter began.

Disaster in the form of Dolphins defensive end A. J. Duhe struck the Oilers early in the final quarter when he tackled Pastorini for a safety in the end zone. Miami led 23–21, and then had the ball at its 45-yard line following the free kick.

"But we didn't get anything," Griese says, "and that was the key series that cost us the game. Houston had a good defense, too good to allow us to score every time we had the ball."

And Houston also had Earl Campbell.

Campbell plunging through for first quarter touchdown.

Starting on their 20-yard line, the Oilers and Campbell pounded away. Twice there were crucial third down plays, and both times Campbell burst off tackle, once for eight, then for six yards. "I had him all lined up on the first third down call, and he just went right past me," said Dolphins linebacker Steve Towle, noting that the play looked like a re-enactment of a chewing tobacco commercial the two had done even before Campbell had played his first NFL game. The punch line of that ad was former Dallas fullback Walt Garrison yelling to Towle, "Try roping him." Even that wouldn't have worked on this occasion.

Campbell finished the drive by dipping inside, then cutting to the outside and running 12 yards for the touchdown, giving Houston the lead for good.

Griese was undaunted and started driving the Dolphins again until, with about three minutes to play, his pass to tight end Andre Tillman was tipped away by defensive back Mike Reinfeldt and intercepted by linebacker Steve Kiner— but at Houston's 7-yard line. A lost fumble or bad punt from the end zone and Miami still could be in good position to win.

There was 3:05 to play, and Oilers coach Bum Phillips wanted not only to get the ball from his end zone but also to eat up as much time as possible doing it. After Tim Wilson pounded four yards to the 11, Campbell took over. Three yards, then four yards on third-and-3, and then another yard on first down to the 19.

That totaled 27 carries for the game, three in a row against a desperate Miami defense that battered at their tormentor each time he touched the ball. No matter. Back he came again in the same play that the Dolphins had failed to stop on Houston's last touchdown drive—a sweep to the right, with the option of cutting upfield whenever he saw an opening. For an instant, it appeared that he'd be thrown for a loss back at the 15-yard line as Miami safety Tim Foley flashed into the backfield. But he groped help-

lessly at Campbell's heel, and Earl made his turn upfield. Looking anything but the back who had worked so brutally, he just reached back, turned on his afterburner, and took off up the sidelines.

"Ten more yards and I'd never have made it," Campbell said afterward, belying the fact that he had looked so fresh zooming down the sidelines.

"Man, how did you do that?" asked Wilson, the first of a horde of Houston players who streamed to joyously embrace Campbell as he stood, bent over at the waist, trying to catch his breath.

When he finally got back to the beach, one of Houston's tackles, Greg Sampson, who had thrown a key block on the play, knelt in front of him and said gently, almost reverently, "Helluva run, man."

And then he added: "You won the game." And the hearts and minds of any disbelievers who still wondered just how good Earl Campbell could be realized he was indeed The Franchise.

| Miami | 7 | 7 | 7 | 9—30 |
| Houston | 7 | 7 | 7 | 14—35 |

Mia—Moore 10 pass from Griese (Yepremian kick)
Hou—Campbell 1 run (Fritsch kick)
Hou—Barber 15 pass from Pastorini (Fritsch kick)
Mia—Williams 1 run (Yepremian kick)
Hou—Campbell 6 run (Fritsch kick)
Mia—L. Harris 1 run (Yepremian kick)
Mia—Safety (Duhe tackled Pastorini in end zone)
Hou—Campbell 12 run (Fritsch kick)
Hou—Campbell 81 run (Fritsch kick)
Mia—Cefalo 11 pass from Griese (Yepremian kick)

SUPE XIII

January 21, 1979

One Super Bowl worthy of the ballyhoo which preceded it was Super Bowl XIII between the defending NFL champion Dallas Cowboys and the Pittsburgh Steelers on January 21, 1979. Though the Steelers won, 35–31, the game had a rollicking rhythm that kept 80,000 fans in Miami's Orange Bowl and more than 100 million television viewers in a frenzied state from the opening kickoff until one final, futile on-sides kick was smothered by Pittsburgh's Rocky Bleier with just 22 seconds to play.

The game was not a pure gem. It was a flawed diamond really, and the flaws cost the Cowboys dearly. But even those flaws—a dropped pass in the end zone by Jackie Smith, one of the best tight ends ever to play in the NFL; a wrong pass-interference call; and a misdirected kickoff that was fumbled and lost by a defensive tackle, Randy White, who was playing on the kick return team—fit perfectly into the vibrant theatre that unfolded on that muggy, gray day.

The final product was worthy of the pre-game hype, which seemed even more intense than that for previous Super Bowls, because for once the teams were the best the NFL had to offer. One of which would even be acclaimed the best team of the seventies, the first to win three Super Bowls.

Pittsburgh's quarterback Terry Bradshaw began his demonstration of football genius early. In seven plays, following John Banaszak's fumble recovery at the Steelers 47-yard line, he put Pittsburgh ahead 7–0 on a 28-yard touchdown pass to John Stallworth, who was left uncovered when three Dallas defenders followed the other wide receiver, Lynn Swann. That kind of play—opportunistic, aggressive, and wide open—characterized the entire game, producing what many believe to be the best first half of football ever played in a Super Bowl.

Dallas tied the score after Ed ("Too-Tall") Jones recovered a fumble by Bradshaw when he was sacked by Harvey Martin at Pittsburgh's 41-yard line. On the third play, Roger Staubach passed to Tony Hill, running unmolested on the left side, for a 39-yard touchdown on the first quarter's final down.

Three plays later, the Cowboys blitzed again. This time Henderson knocked the ball loose from Bradshaw's hands and linebacker Mike Hegman snatched it away and ran 37 yards for the score and a 14–7 lead. "When Thomas hit him, he tried switching the ball from his right to his left hand," Hegman recalls. "Then I hit him and took it out of his arms. After that touchdown, I thought we were on our way."

Bradshaw didn't, because three plays later he passed to Stallworth on a short inside hook pattern, and after one move to get past defensive back Aaron Kyle, the Steelers wide receiver outran two other Cowboys for a 75-yard touchdown.

Pittsburgh's defense—the Steel Curtain—then took command and allowed Dallas just 16 yards for the second quarter. Near the end, Mel Blount intercepted Staubach's pass, and Pittsburgh had a shot for another score at its 44-yard line. Bradshaw made the most of it.

He totalled 50 yards in two passes to Swann (who caught seven for 124 yards in the game) to put the ball at the Cowboys 16-yard line. Franco Harris got nine more on a trap. With just 26 seconds to

Above: *Harvey Martin bearhugs Redskin's John Riggins after he took a quick pass from Joe Theismann.*

Opposite: *Rocky Bleier scores a touchdown for the Steelers as Lewis attempts to break up a Bradshaw pass.*

play in the first half, Terry rolled out to his right and looped a pass to Bleier in the end zone, just over linebacker D. D. Lewis, to give Pittsburgh a 21–14 halftime lead.

So much for conventional football.

On its second possession of the third quarter, the Cowboys were at Pittsburgh's 10-yard line, with third-and-3, when Landry sent in Jackie Smith as an extra tight end, indicating a running play. Staubach sent halfback Tony Dorsett in motion to the right, and fullback Scott Laidlaw stayed put in the backfield, so Pittsburgh keyed its defense to either a run by him or a swing pass to Dorsett. But after a fake to his backs, Staubach threw to Smith in the end zone, and there wasn't a Steeler within ten yards of him. Instead of the game's easiest touchdown, this 16-year NFL veteran dropped the ball! "Jackie was so wide open, I could have punted the ball to him," Staubach said afterward. "I took something off it because I didn't want to drill it through his hands. Maybe if I had thrown it harder, he would have caught it. I think he anticipated the ball coming harder than it did, but I threw it low because he got deeper in the end zone than I anticipated, and I kind of lobbed it."

Smith's only moment of Super Bowl glory, after years of outstanding play with St. Louis, evaporated in that moment, to be replaced by anguish. But he never tried to excuse his blunder.

The Cowboys defense still had control in the fourth quarter when, with less than ten minutes to play, on a second-and-5 play at Pittsburgh's 45-yard line, Bradshaw was forced to hurry a pass to Swann down the right sideline. Cowboys cornerback Benny Barnes was with him step-for-step and jockeyed with him to make the catch. Both went down, and the official closest to the play waved it off as an incomplete pass.

But field judge Fred Swearingen, watching from about 15 yards away in the middle of the field threw his flag: pass interference against Barnes. Pittsburgh had a first down at the Cowboys 23-yard line, and three plays later, Harris pounded 22 yards through the middle on a trap play for a touchdown. The Steelers led 28–17.

The penalty became the game's most crucial call, and as NFL commissioner Pete Rozelle later admitted, an incorrect one. Barnes recalled afterward, "The call should have gone against Swann. He shoved me, knocked me down, and then tripped over me."

The Cowboys' luck stayed bad. On the ensuing kickoff, Noll instructed Gerela to boot the ball deep, but he slipped kicking it, and it bounced along the ground where White tried to grab it. He was playing with a cast on one hand and never got a good grasp before the ball was stripped loose by Tony Dungy. Dirt Winston recovered for the Steelers at the Dallas 18-yard line.

On the next play, Swann made a leaping catch in the end zone for Pittsburgh's final touchdown and a 35–17 lead with 8:09 to play. There was instant celebrating on the Steelers' bench because their third Super Bowl victory was secured. Or so they thought.

In situations like these, Staubach always was most dangerous, and Roger again gave it his best shot. With 6:51 to play, he drove Dallas 89 yards, completing all five of his passes and even scrambling 18 yards on a third-and-11 play, before capping the eight-play drive with a 7-yard TD pass to tight end Billy Joe DuPree. The Steelers then led 35–24. Time left: 2:27.

Rafael Septien's on-sides kick was bobbled by Dungy—who had caused White's fumble—and Dallas recovered at the Steelers' 48-yard line. Pittsburgh now was desperate, but Staubach couldn't be stopped. He completed five of seven passes—the last on the ninth play of this drive to Butch Johnson for a touchdown—to carve the deficit to four points with 22 seconds to play.

Terry Bradshaw dropping back to pass.

There was a sense of panic among the Steelers when Septien again nudged the ball to his left. This time, though, it bounced evenly toward Bleier, who in this special situation was on the front line of Pittsburgh's return team. "Just before the kick, one of the guys said, 'Watch out for the dribble kick.' I decided that if it came hard at me, I'd let it go through so one of the guys behind me could get it," he recalls. "Fortunately, the ball took no bad bounces, and being an old third baseman, I knew how to handle those easy grounders."

Pittsburgh	7	14	0	14—**35**
Dallas	7	7	3	14—**31**

Pitt—Stallworth 28 pass from Bradshaw (Gerela kick)
Dall—Hill 30 pass from Staubach (Septien kick)
Dall—Hegman 37 fumble return (Septien kick)
Pitt—Stallworth 75 pass from Bradshaw (Gerela kick)
Pitt—Bleier 7 pass from Bradshaw (Gerela kick)
Dall—Septien 27
Pitt—Harris 22 run (Gerela kick)
Pitt—Swann 18 pass from Bradshaw (Gerela kick)
Dall—DuPree 7 pass from Staubach (Septien kick)
Dall—Johnson 4 pass from Staubach (Septien kick)

SAY A PRAYER

Cowboys vs. Vikings, 1975
Redskins vs. Cowboys, 1979
Cowboys vs. Cardinals, 1980
Browns vs. Vikings, 1980
Cowboys vs. Falcons, 1981

The phenomenon began on a frosty December Sunday in 1975 when the Dallas Cowboys trailed the Minnesota Vikings 14–10 in a playoff game at Metropolitan Stadium in Bloomington, Minnesota. The scoreboard clock behind the field's open end zone showed there were only 25 seconds to play.

In a word, it was desperation time for the Cowboys.

That's what Dallas wide receiver Drew Pearson was thinking before he broke off the line of scrimmage at the 50-yard line, gave Vikings cornerback Nate Wright a little inside fake, and then raced down the sideline toward that end zone. The fake didn't take and Wright stayed with him.

Cowboys quarterback Roger Staubach, standing in the shotgun formation, had taken the long snap from center Kyle Davis and watched Pearson in his foot race with Wright. Then seeing Vikings defensive end Jim Marshall break into his vision, he threw the ball. It was not his most picturesque pass, more of a dying quail, but that unintentional lack of trajectory and distance became the key to what a second later would for all time be known as the Hail Mary Pass.

Pearson, looking back, saw that the ball would not reach the end zone, so he slowed up, then tried to reach back and catch it at the five-yard line. At that moment, Wright collided with him and fell to the ground, the ball appearing—at least

Cowboys' Drew Pearson nailing Staubach's 50-yard touchdown pass with 24 seconds left in NFC playoff game, 1975.

to the 45,000 in the stadium and the millions more watching on television—to slither past Pearson's right leg and fall incomplete.

But it hadn't!

In the next instant, Pearson was skipping into the end zone with the ball in one hand, caught in some magical moment of instant reaction and, after an anxious glance to get the official's signal for a touchdown, triumphantly waving the ball. Then he hurled it into the mass of disbelieving Vikings fans.

Dallas	0	0	7	10—**17**
Minnesota	0	7	0	7—**14**

Minn—Foreman 1 run (Cox Kick)
Dall—Dennison 4 run (Fritsch kick)
Dall—FG Fritsch 24
Minn—McClanahan 1 run (Cox kick)
Dall—D. Pearson 50 pass from Staubach (Fritsch kick)

The Cowboys, more than any other team (and maybe that's why they've become known as America's Team), seem most blessed in these hair-breadth finishes. First it was Staubach. Then in 1980, his succesor, Danny White, carried on the tradition. And at its shrine, where it all began, Metropolitan Stadium, the Vikings found the same kind of salvation when Tommy Kramer and Ahmad Rashad combined for their own version in another 1980 game against Cleveland.

More than anything, the play gives any team trailing by a touchdown or less the one ingredient that sustains: hope.

Every season there are a few "thousand-to-one shots," but somehow Dallas has a better sense of the dramatic when it comes their turn to act. Another good example was the final game of the 1979 season against the Washington Redskins where a playoff berth awaited the winner.

When the last quarter began, the Cowboys led 21–17. With less than four minutes left, Washington had what appeared to be an insurmountable 34–21 lead. The Cowboys, however, recovered Clarence Harmon's fumble, and three

plays later Staubach passed to Ron Springs for a touchdown to cut the deficit to 34–28. Then the Cowboys' defense—and the defense always is an important partner in setting up these miracle finishes—forced Washington to punt, so with 1:46 to play and in possession of the ball at their 25-yard line, the Cowboys had one final chance with the game and the playoff berth riding on the outcome.

In five plays, Staubach's passes had Dallas at the Redskins' 8-yard line with less than a minute to play. With 50 seconds left, he passed to Tony Hill in the end zone, but Washington defensive back Ray Waddy broke up the play. Staubach tried Hill again, this time with 46 seconds to play. Instead of the inexperienced Waddy on the coverage, the NFC's best cornerback, Lemar Parrish, picked up Hill when he left the line of scrimmage.

Who's covering and how good he may be don't mean much when it's Hail

Washington	10	7	0	17—**34**
Dallas	0	14	7	14—**35**

Wash—FG Moseley 24
Wash—Theismann 1 run (Moseley kick)
Wash—Malone 55 pass from Theismann (Moseley kick)
Dall—Springs 1 run (Septien kick)
Dall—P. Pearson 26 pass from Staubach (Septien kick)
Dall—Newhouse 2 run (Septien kick)
Wash—FG Moseley 24
Wash—Riggins 1 run (Moseley kick)
Wash—Riggins 66 run (Moseley kick)
Dall—Springs 26 pass from Staubach (Septien kick)
Dall—Hill 8 pass from Staubach (Septien kick)

Mary time, and in that instance, Staubach rifled the ball to Hill over Parrish for the winning touchdown. "Roger just knew that he could win in that type of situation," Landry says. "There was something in him that brought out his best when everything seems hopeless."

When Staubach retired after the 1979 season, many felt the day of the Hail Mary pass was gone in Dallas, but Danny White had become a willing convert. When the Cowboys played in St. Louis against the Cardinals on November 2, 1980, they trailed 24–21 with 1:52 to play and the ball at their 31-yard line.

Six plays later, it was fourth-and-5, with 46 seconds to play, and the ball at the Cardinals 28-yard line. On the sideline, wide receiver Tony Hill stood next to Landry and joined with White in planning for that one last deciding play. "I told the coach I could beat [cornerback Roger] Wehrli in the corner," Hill recalls. "So they called a desperation play to me, deep in the left corner of the end zone."

White sent Hill into the left corner and seemed to loop the ball, hoping that with Hill's great leaping ability he could out-jump Wehrli if the play was close. Hill caught it over his shoulder but with Wehrli nearly inside his jersey.

When the Cowboys played the Atlanta Falcons in the second round of the NFC playoffs on January 4, 1981, Drew Pearson was the man again. Once more the clock was inside 50 seconds. Dallas was trailing 27–24, and the ball was at Atlanta's 23-yard line.

This time the play was a quick post pattern to Pearson where, White says, "I thought only he could get it." And, of course, Pearson did just that—leaping to cradle the ball in his midsection with defensive backs Rolland Lawrence and Tom Pridemore just inches away—though White later admitted, "I didn't really think he would get it. He made a great catch."

Dallas	3	7	0	20—**30**
Atlanta	10	7	7	3—**27**

Atl—FG Mazzetti 38
Atl—Jenkins 60 pass from Bartkowski (Mazzetti kick)
Dall—FG Septien 38
Dall—DuPree 5 pass from White (Septien kick)
Atl—Cain 1 run (Mazzetti kick)
Atl—Andrews 12 pass from Bartkowski (Mazzetti kick)
Dall—Newhouse 1 run (Septien kick)
Atl—FG Mazzetti 34
Dall—D. Pearson 14 pass from White (Septien kick)
Dall—Pearson 23 pass from White (Pass failed)

This miracle business is not the sole property of the Cowboys. The Vikings staked their own claim in the most dramatic finish of any game during the 1980 season in a December 14 contest against Cleveland from almost the same spot on the same field where Staubach

struck his first miracle five years before.

The Vikings, like Cleveland, were in the midst of a playoff battle, but trailed 23–9 with only 7:15 to play. Kramer rang up two touchdown passes, the second to Rashad with only 95 seconds left, narrowing the score to 23–22. When the Vikes got the ball back, at the 20-yard line, there were only 23 seconds left—and no time outs. Kramer's first play was a lateral pass— a playground special that gained 34 yards to the Browns' 46-yard line, before the ball carrier, Ted Brown, went out of bounds to kill the clock with five seconds to play.

Cleveland	7	6	3	7—**23**
Minnesota	0	0	9	19—**28**

Cle—Hill 18 pass from Sipe (Cockroft kick)
Cle—Sipe 2 run (Kick failed)
Minn—Senser 31 pass from Kramer (Kick failed)
Cle—FG Cockroft 32
Minn—FG Danmeier 24
Cle—C. Miller 1 run (Cockroft kick)
Minn—Rashad 12 pass from Kramer (Danmeier kick)
Minn—Rashad 46 pass from Kramer (Kick failed)

One good sandlot play deserves another, and Vikings coach Bud Grant smilingly says, "We drew it up on the field." Not quite, but it did send all the Vikings receivers to the same spot on the goal line, hoping for a tipped ball. Kramer then threw as high and as long as he could.

Rashad, though, hung back at the five-yard line. "I just thought it made sense to hang around that spot and look for the tip," he said later. "I knew the [end zone] flag was behind me, and I thought I had a lot of room."

The ball was indeed tipped, by defensive backs Thom Darden and Ron Bolton, and plopped into Rashad's left hand. He merely backed the final few feet into the end zone—though with just inches to spare.

The Vikings had pulled out their 28–23 victory, and there wasn't even a second left on the clock. Now that is a Hail Mary Pass worth giving thanks for!

Dallas	0	10	3	14	**27**
St. Louis	7	3	7	7	**24**

St. Lou—Morris 1 run (O'Donoghue kick)
Dall—Dorsett 4 run (Septien kick)
Dall—FG Septien 28
St. Lou—FG O'Donoghue 42
St. Lou—Tilley 42 pass from Hart (O'Donoghue kick)
Dallas — Thurman 78 pass interception (Septien kick)
St Louis — Gray 34 pass from Hart (O'Donoghue kick)
Dall—Hill 28 pass from White (Septien kick)

Opposite: *Falcon running back Lynn Cain leaps high over Cowboys' defense, 1981.* Below: *Falcon's William Andrews swarmed by Cowboys' Bill Row and Dexter Clinkscale, 1981.*

WHEN DREAMS COME TRUE

New York Giants vs. Dallas Cowboys

December 19, 1981

For the New York Giants and their kicker, Joe Danelo, dreams really do come true.

For 18 years, from an icy Sunday afternoon in Chicago in 1963 until an icy Saturday afternoon in 1981, the Giants and their millions of faithful fans had dreamed of returning to the NFL playoffs, where for season after season in the late fifties and early sixties they were almost a permanent fixture.

Five stadiums, four coaches, and three states later, it finally happened when, on December 19, 1981, Danelo kicked a 33-yard field goal some 6 minutes and 19 seconds into a sudden-death overtime period that gave the Giants a 13-10 victory over the Dallas Cowboys and sent the happy kicker from the fantasy of a pregame dream into its delicious reality.

It also saved him from a nightmare that stalks every kicker in pro football—of being responsible for losing big games for the want of making easy kicks. In this instance, nightmare piled upon nightmare for Danelo in that cold, windy afternoon as three very makable kicks went awry, including one in the overtime that could have given the Giants a victory four minutes earlier and prevented a near mutiny among the 73,000 fans huddled in a battle of survival at Giants Stadium.

None of them even were aware that the previous night Danelo had dreamed that he had kicked the winning field goal and stood exulting in his subconscious as the fans poured down their adulation.

It was a dream he had before every game, and such was the excellence of his art that he really never had cause to question that, when the time came, his dream world would not come to life.

Of course, the millions of Giants fans had been living in their own dream world ever since 1956, when their team won its last NFL championship. They had five more tries at other NFL titles from then until they lost 13-10 to the Bears in Chicago in 1963, failing in every final game. In that list of heartbreaks was the epic-making overtime loss to the Baltimore Colts in 1958.

Then came the drought—only two winning seasons and hardly a whiff of playoff hopes as a succession of coaches muddled through the football art, and the franchise rode a rollercoaster that always went farther downward than upward. In between, the team left its hallowed home in Yankee Stadium and became a three-season orphan at the Yale Bowl and Shea Stadium while a new sports palace in New Jersey was being built for them. They did little to warrant such luxury, and even the 1981 season seemed another hopeless exercise as the team stumbled around for the first eleven games, never exhibiting the kind of drive that seemed capable of taking them into the playoffs.

Then a bit of magic struck. Maybe it was the unfathomable football sense of a young second-string quarterback named Scott Brunner who, in the team's eleventh game, had to take the starting role when starting quarterback Phil Simms went out for the season with an injury. Perhaps it was the emotional drive supplied by a young rookie linebacker named Lawrence Taylor, who had helped to revive memories of past playoff times when the great Giants defenses keyed the team's success.

Whatever it was, this team suddenly caught fire. From a previous 5-6 record, it turned around and won three of its next four games. The final obstacle was the season's last game against Dallas— already crowned the NFC-East winner, and already a favorite to win the Super Bowl. The Cowboys gave the Giants everything they could muster, but what they hadn't counted on was the resilience of Danelo, the poise of Brunner, the fury of Taylor—and the fickleness of the weather that measured a five-degrees wind chill whipped to miserable fury by winds whose gusts reached 45 miles per hour.

The Giants needed all of that. In their first two possessions they overwhelmed the famed Doomsday II Defense, and drove right to the Cowboys' front door. The first drive ended when wide receiver Johnny Perkins dropped Brunner's apparent touchdown pass and Danelo, who in 1981 had made every field goal that he attempted from less than 30 yards, badly shanked a 21-yard attempt.

After the wind partially stifled Danny White's punt and set up the Giants to reach Dallas' 15-yard line on their next possession, Danelo banged his next try off the right upright of the goal posts. Defensive end Ed ("Too Tall") Jones was offside so the Giants' kicker got another try—and this one, from 27 yards, went wide.

Three tries, all with the wind at his back . . . three misses . . . and by a kicker who had made 14 of 15 kicks from inside the 40-yard line during the previous 15 games.

"I couldn't believe what was happening to me," he said later. "Here I was, in the biggest game of my life, and putting

Joe Danelo's moment of agony: a second field goal miss in the first quarter of Cowboy-Giant play game (final: Giants, 13; Dallas, 10).

on the worse performance of my career. Probably what saved me was the fact that the other players would come over to me at one time and another, tap me on the helmet, or put their arm around my shoulder, and tell me to hang in there.

"'You'll win this thing with your kicking, so don't worry,' Mike Dennis told me. I would have liked to have believed him at the time, but I couldn't think that far ahead. All I was doing was praying that I'd get another shot. It was killing me that I was letting down my teammates. I don't care what the conditions are, I shouldn't have been missing those easy kicks and all I wanted to do was to redeem myself."

That would all come in time.

The Giants finally got the game's first points early in the second half following another 29-yard wind-shattered punt by White. Brunner, more workmanlike than brilliant, executed a flea-flicker pass that was tipped by an onrushing Cowboys lineman but which nonetheless fell into Leon Perry's hands for a 16-yard gain. He tacked on another 13-yard pass to rookie tight end Dave Young, and then polished off the drive with a stunning 20-yard pass to Tom Mullady, who made a diving catch just inside the red pylon at the goal line.

That triggered the Cowboys and suddenly the game swung in their direction as the fourth period began. White completed an 80-yard march with a 4-yard TD to Doug Cosbie, and three plays later, Michael Downs intercepted Brunner's pass to set up Rafael Septien's 36-yard field goal. That gave Dallas a 10-7 lead with only 5:48 to play.

Everyone knew that with the league's least-potent offense the Giants would have to find some quick way to break open the rugged Cowboys defense. Those missed field goals hung like black crepe and there seemed no redemption. At least that's what the huge throng was feeling; none among them ever thought help would come from the fickle gusts of wind that whirled around the floor at Giants Stadium.

This is where the gods smiled on the long-suffering Giants. White, as he had done a hundred times all season, whirled away from center and tossed the ball a few yards backward to Tony Dorsett to begin the Cowboys' most devastating running play. The wind held up the ball and Dorsett never really got possession. As he fought to get it, the ball slithered from his hands and onto the ground where defensive end George Martin fell on it.

With just over two minutes to play and needing 42 yards, this was the Giants' last shot. Three plays later that shot came down to one play, fourth down and 13 yards for a first down from the Cowboys' 48-yard line. If they missed, the Cowboys

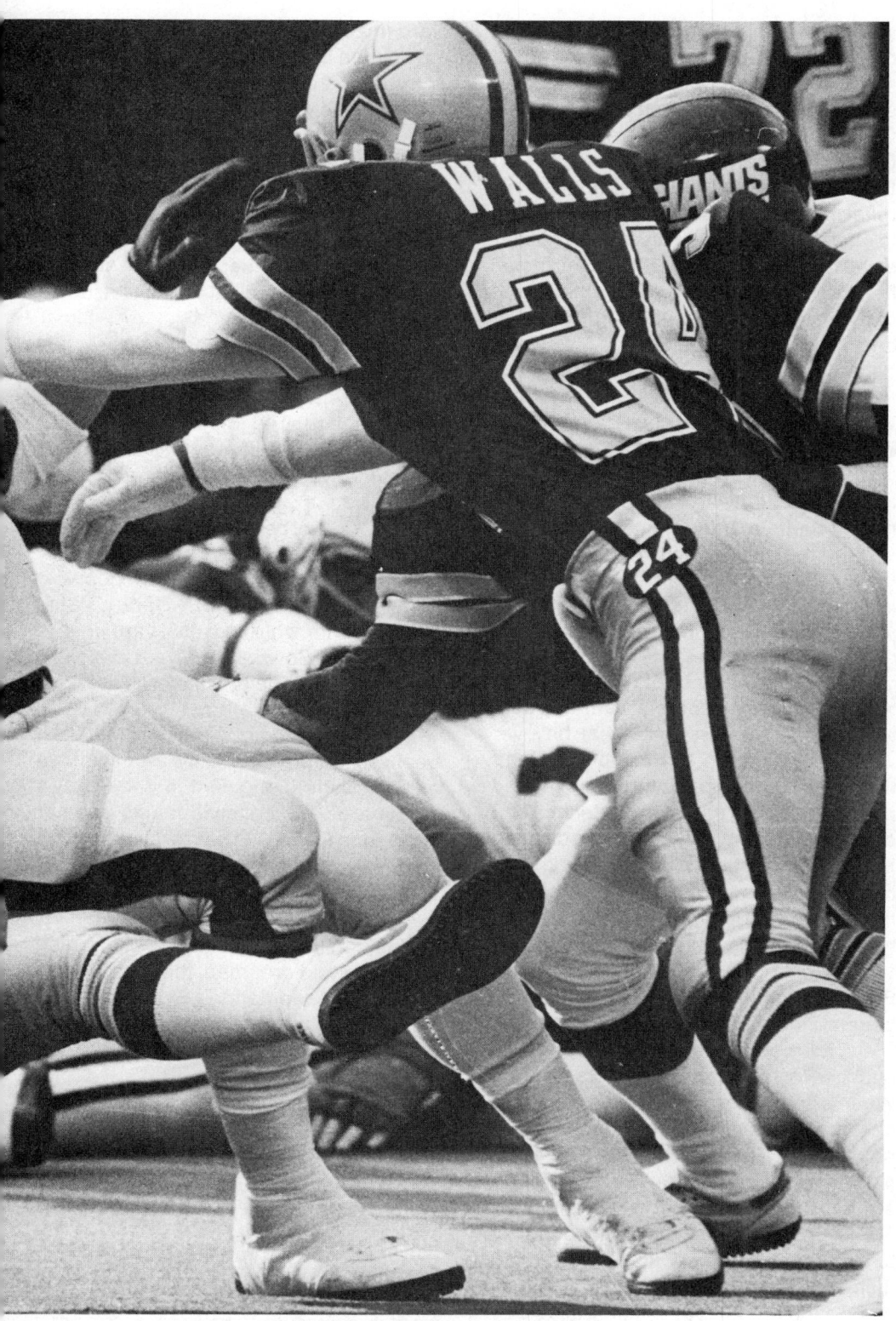

Solid reason for Giants' year of recovery: Rob Carpenter, running back, here succumbing to gang efforts of Cowboys.

243

would get the ball and easily run out the clock.

Brunner dropped back to pass, and seven Dallas defenders moved to cover five Giants receivers. Within seconds, the Cowboys' pass rush had closed in on Brunner. He deftly stepped up, momentarily relieving the pressure and enabling him to spot rookie wide receiver John Mistler in the middle of the field. Still on the move, he fired the ball, somehow laying it between a linebacker and a cornerback, and into Mistler's hands for a 21-yard gain to the Cowboys' 27-yard line.

Three plays netted two yards and with just 25 seconds to play, Danelo came on to try and tie the game. This time, the wind swirling in his face, the clock was his mortal enemy and there would be no more chances. It didn't matter. Brunner spotted the ball perfectly and the Giants' kicker sent a 41-yard kick squarely between the uprights, tieing the score and sending the game into its sudden-death period.

Here, the weather played a starring role. Dallas won the crucial overtime coin toss, but for the first time that he ever could recall, coach Tom Landry decided that rather than receive the kickoff—and possibly end the game on his team's first possession—the windy conditions dictated that his team would kick off. Giants' coach Ray Perkins had done the same thing at the start of the game, and wound up with two scoring opportunities as a result.

"There really was little choice," Brunner noted afterward. "The wind had become too much of a factor."

It certainly was for the Cowboys, because for the second time Dorsett found White's simple toss too difficult to handle as it got caught up by the wind. He again bobbled and lost the ball, this time at his 44-yard line, where Taylor fought through a pile of players to recover the fumble. The Giants had another golden opportunity to win and Brunner, with an incredible display of trickery, brought that closer as he bootlegged the ball inside Dallas' 20-yard line.

When Danelo trotted onto the field to try and win the game, he was seven yards closer to the yawning space between the yellow-painted goal posts than when he had kicked the tie-making field goal only minutes before. Everyone assumed this would be good too, and indeed as the ball headed toward the posts, the thousands at the other end of the stadium who had a clear look at its path let forth a mighty roar.

But the wind that had been so cruel to the Cowboys was playing no favorites, and it swept the ball toward the right, where it bounced off the upright. For Danelo, four tries, three misses, and still the game was not lost, proving that this was to be the Giants' day.

It was, too, because three plays later, rookie linebacker Byron Hunt, momentarily fooled on a pass play and out of position, scrambled to intercept a Danny White toss. Brunner whipped an 8-yard pass to Mistler to the Cowboys' 16-yard line. Now, it was time for Danelo to make the previous night's dream come true.

Staring at the goal posts which had been so unforgiving only four minutes earlier, Danelo blocked out the day's nightmares and calmly boomed another kick—one that could have traveled to the stars—but needed only 35 yards. This time, it was good!

Sure enough, just as he had dreamed, his kicking finally won the game ... and just as he had dreamed, the fans poured down their adulation. But why not? Eighteen years is a long time between playoffs ... and dreams.

Dallas	0	0	0	10	0	—	10
New York	0	0	7	3	3	—	13

NY—Mullady 20 pass from Brunner (Danelo kick)
Dal—Cosbie 4 pass from White (Septien kick)
Dal—FG Septien 36
NY—FG Danelo 42
NY—FG Danelo 33

TARGET PRACTICE FOR FOUTS

Miami Dolphins vs. San Diego Chargers

January 2, 1982

When the San Diego Chargers defeated the Miami Dolphins 41-38 nearly 14 minutes into an overtime quarter, millions around the nation sat transfixed before their television sets, still gasping at the almost unbelievable spectacle they had watched for nearly four hours.

For sheer drama, human emotion, strength, and endurance, there have been few games ever to match the semifinal NFL playoff game on January 2, 1982, between the Chargers and Dolphins at Miami's Orange Bowl. Here, the television eye was at its best, particularly when it focused on the agonizing countenance of Kellen Winslow, the superb tight end of the Chargers.

In 1982, a nation watched as Winslow was repeatedly hauled off the grass floor of the Orange Bowl, brought to the bench where he seemingly would lie for all time, almost too exhausted to lift his head or to raise his arms. "That may be it for Winslow," the announcers would intone time

Joe Rose goes over for his second Dolphin touchdown, completing a Miami comeback from early 24-point deficit.

and again. Yet when next seen he was catching another of his 13 passes.

His was not the only dramatic story that day. Off the Miami bench, with his team trailing 24-0 and seemingly out of the game even before the end of the first quarter, came Don Strock for David Woodley. Like his dogged opponents, he put on a marvelous display of gutsy football quarterbacking that had the nation as awestruck on his behalf as it was on Winslow's.

In the end, he not only overcame that 24-0 deficit, but he actually put his team into the lead and had it moving for a victory-clinching score late in the fourth quarter. He might have achieved the unachievable had it not been for two missed field goals—both very makable—that punctured his gallant efforts.

If ever there was a game for the masses, this was it. Yards and points came with computerlike speed. The Chargers produced an incredible 564 yards and the Dolphins had 466-1130 yards by two teams that were division champions and that supposedly had some defensive stability.

Miami, like other teams that thought they had some defensive strength, became target practice for the Chargers' superlative quarterback Dan Fouts—433 yards from 33 completions. Winslow's 13 catches produced 166 yards; Charley Joiner had 7 for 108; and Wes Chandler had 6 for 106. Though he was a quarter late arriving, Strock was every bit a match, completing 28 of 42 passes, or 67 percent, for 397 yards, and four touchdowns. He spread his weapons around because *only* two Dolphins had more than a hundred yards, Tony Nathan 108 on eight receptions and Duriel Harris 106 on six catches.

At the start, it was all Fouts and the Chargers. They polished off an opening drive when Benirschke kicked a 32-yard field goal. Three plays later, Chandler returned Tom Orosz' punt 56 yards for a touchdown and a 10-0 lead. The ensuing kickoff completely baffled the Dolphins

Wall of Charger defenders stops Dolphin fullback Andra Franklin in fourth quarter of brilliantly played game won in overtime.

as it plopped at their 28-yard line and the Chargers recovered. In seven plays, Chuck Muncie scored for a 17-0 lead. Miami's starting quarterback David Woodley then threw an interception, and four plays after that, Fouts hit James Brooks with the first of two touchdown passes. With the first quarter still not concluded, San Diego had what seemed like an insurmountable 24-0 lead—and Miami had run only seven offensive plays!

Shula, never one to shilly-shally with a decision, sent Strock into the game. "I just thought it had become the kind of game where Strock could do more than Woodley," Shula said later, and the day became unlike any other for Strock, who had toiled for eight seasons as a backup quarterback, mostly behind Bob Griese. He had proven his worth by bailing out both Griese and Woodley on several occasions, but asking him to overcome a 24-0 lead seemed a bit absurd.

On his first series, Strock came away with a field goal—not much, but it did reestablish in the minds of the shaken Dolphins that they could be effective. On his next possession, Strock passed one yard to tight end Joe Rose for a touchdown. Now it was 24-10, with more than 30 minutes still to play.

"We really wanted to get down to twenty-four-seventeen before the half," Shula and Strock both noted later. "We felt that would almost make it an even game, give them something to think about and still leave us plenty of time to win."

The Dolphins did that, all right, from the Chargers' 40-yard line. It was too far for a field goal so with six seconds to play in the half, Strock and Shula resurrected a give-and-go play that was the staple of the Fort Lauderdale Beach Touch League. This simply called for Strock to pass over the middle to Harris, who then would turn and lateral the ball to Nathan.

When Harris caught the ball, the Chargers converged on him. Just as he was being tackled, Nathan steamed by and took the quick lateral. There were no San Diego players in sight and the maneuver had caught them so off guard that Nathan loped the final ten yards into the end zone with the ball held aloft.

Chargers defensive back Glen Edwards later noted, "They really caught us with our pants down and everything went from there."

It certainly did. The Dolphins came back in the second half and drove for the tie when Strock hit Rose down the middle with a 15-yard touchdown pass. Suddenly, what had been unthinkable, almost unfathomable, had now become very plausible.

To its credit, San Diego did not fold, and many of the sporting pundits who had insinuated that the Chargers were all style and no substance began eating a slow lunch of those words. Fouts was indefatigable, driving his team right back with a 25-yard touchdown pass to Winslow, and the Chargers led again, 31-24. So what? Miami took the ball and Strock unleashed a 50-yard touchdown pass to tight end Bruce Hardy. It was 31-31 as the third quarter ended, but Miami had the ball, thanks to Lyle Blackwood's interception. On the first play of the fourth quarter, Nathan ripped twelve yards to give the Dolphins a 38-31 lead.

Miami got the ball again with 11:58 to play and Strock began another drive, eating up yards and minutes, and there seemed little that the Chargers could do about it. On second-and-seven, with 4:28 to play and Miami already at San Diego's 21-yard line, rookie fullback Andra Franklin struggled to get a couple of extra yards when defensive tackle Gary Johnson hit him from the side and linebacker Linden King jerked his arm, knocking the ball to the ground. Defensive back Pete Shaw fell on it at the Chargers' 18-yard line.

It was a crushing blow for Miami, but it was all that the intrepid Fouts needed; he cranked up a ten-play drive that went right down to the Dolphins' nine-yard line when Chandler caught a 19-yard pass. With 67 seconds to play, Winslow, who by this time had become the symbol of this frantic struggle, shook off his muscle cramps and exhaustion and reentered the game. Fouts sent him to the right side of the end zone, where he was immediately surrounded by Maimi defenders and it appeared that Fouts would have to dump the ball except ...

Except that Brooks, trailing the play a few yards deeper, caught it, and after Benirschke's kick the score was tied 38-38.

There were 58 seconds still to play, but Miami's chance for victory seemed to disappear when Strock's pass was intercepted by Willie Buchanon. But he fumbled and Tommy Vigorito recovered at the Chargers' 48-yard line. Strock redeemed himself with a 17-yard pass to Nathan, Vigorito ran for six more, and Shula then decided, with the ball at San Diego's 25-yard line, to run down the clock for one last play—a 42-yard field goal by Uwe von Schamann.

What the Dolphins didn't count on was the six-foot, five-inch frame of Winslow, anchoring an octopuslike arm that reached up and swatted the ball off its trajectory, forcing the teams into their overtime period.

San Diego wasted no time, taking the kickoff and driving to Miami's nine-yard line. Now it was Benirschke's turn—and a shanked 26-yard chip-shot field-goal attempt. The Chargers felt the rug go out from under still another time.

They had no corner on heartache, however, because, with 6:15 to play in the overtime, Strock's 21-yard pass to Jimmy Cefalo had the Dolphins at San Diego's 25-yard line. Three plays gained nine yards, and with the ball teed up eight yards closer, von Schamann tried again to win the game. This time, defensive end Leroy Jones broke through and blocked his 34-yard kick.

The Dolphins had at last used up their chances. Fouts knocked off 28 yards with two passes to Chandler, giving San Diego a first down at Miami's 49-yard line. Then, for the first time that long, long afternoon, the Chargers' quarterback had more than enough time to pass, and more than enough time to move around and wait for Joiner to find an opening in the middle of Miami's defense, where he caught a pass and picked up 39 yards to the Dolphins' ten-yard line.

That was it. San Diego coach Don Coryell had seen enough and he sent in Benirschke to end it—right through the center of the goal posts, at 13:52 of the overtime quarter with a 29-yard field goal.

"Without a doubt that was the most exciting game I've ever been involved with, maybe the best-played game ever between two football teams in a playoff," Fouts said afterward.

On the other end of the corridor beneath the Orange Bowl, Shula couldn't mask his bitter disappointment.

"This is going to be a tough one to live with," he said. "But these guys are men, as they proved out there on the field. They'll be able to handle it."

In time, yes, but it was a game that neither they, nor the millions who watched it, ever will forget.

San Diego	24	0	7	7	3	— 41
Miami	0	17	14	7	0	— 38

SD—FG Benirschke 32
SD—Chandler 56 punt return (Benirschke kick)
SD—Muncie 1 run (Benirschke kick)
SD—Brooks 8 pass from Fouts (Benirschke kick)
Mia—FG von Schamann 34
Mia—Rose 1 pass from Strock (von Schamann kick)
Mia—Nathan 25 lateral from Harris, 15 pass from Stock (von Schamann kick)
Mia—Rose 15 pass from Strock (von Schamann kick)
SD—Winslow 25 pass from Fouts (Benirschke kick)
Mia—Hardy 50 pass from Strock (von Schamann kick)
Mia—Nathan 12 run (von Schamann kick)
SD—Brooks 9 pass from Fouts (Benirschke kick)
SD—FG Benirschke 29

BELLES OF THE BOWL

San Francisco 49ers vs. Cincinnati Bengals

January 24, 1982

In 1980, the Cincinnati Bengals and San Francisco 49ers were two of the NFL's grubbiest charwomen, a pair of teams that won only a dozen of 32 games and certainly not considered worthy of an invitation to any of pro football's lavish postseason balls.

Ah, but what a difference a year can make!

Without any magic wands, those grubby charwomen became the belles of a Cinderella Super Bowl that no one ever thought could happen. And when the clock finally tolled midnight, it was the 49ers, after a 26-21 victory, who carried the gleaming silver Lombardi Trophy back to the City by the Bay, the first time in 32 seasons that the team had won the championship of the NFL.

More people than ever before—an estimated 102 million—watched this battle in Super Bowl XVI, and another 81,270 sat in the 70-degree comfort of the giant SilverDome in Pontiac, Michigan, while outside, arctic winds howled an icy gale.

Everything was new for this game— new teams, a new, non-warm-weather location, even a new uniform for the Bengals, whose first year of wearing their "stripes" had evoked as much comment as their rise from a 6-10 team in 1980 to a 12-4 AFC champion. Most were unsure how that happened, just as the 49ers were baffling everyone by coming from the same record to 13-3 and their first NFC title.

The Bengals were seen as a team loaded with talent—ten first-round picks

Ball stripping at its finest:
49er Eric Wright tackles Cris
Collinsworth and breaks up
19-yard Anderson pass completion.

and a veteran quarterback named Ken Anderson, who was the league's top-ranked passer and who, ironically, had been tutored in his early NFL seasons by 49er coach Bill Walsh, at that time a Bengals assistant coach. But it took the forceful personality of Forrest Gregg, raised in the regime of Vince Lombardi, to marshal all of that talent and get from it a brand of football that was at least the equal of the 49ers.

Everyone gave credit to Walsh for the 49ers' rise, and after three seasons as the team's head coach, some had termed him an "offensive genius" because he blended the talents of a third-year quarterback named Joe Montana with a team comprised mainly of middle-round draft picks and free agents, into one of the best offensive teams in the NFL. Walsh accepted all the praise, though he mildly disdained the "genius" tag in preference to "expert."

Expert or genius, it really didn't matter because for all of the 49ers' offensive reputation, it was their defense—coached by Chuck Studley, another former Bengals' assistant—that really won the game, and it did so in a four-play sequence at their goal line late in the third quarter that will forever stand as the hallmark of this game. That defense also was good enough to turn back Anderson from the five-yard line in the first three minutes of the game, thanks to an interception by Dwight Hicks following the Bengals' recovery of the opening kickoff.

The first big defensive play was almost as important—indeed some of the Bengals thought later it was the key—as the goal-line stand because Cincinnati, which had lost its loose and relaxed attitude in the final minutes before the kickoff, played the rest of the first half in a sort of stupor. Gregg said later that his team became tentative, more concerned about not making another mistake than about forcing the San Franciscans to make one. "A score right off the bat would have settled us down," he said.

That mental lapse was fatal for the Bengals. Montana took his offense on a 68-yard march following the interception, the key play being a third-down, 16-yard triple-option pass to tight end Charley Young. Montana finished the march with a one-yard sneak.

Early in the second quarter, Anderson had his team temporarily untracked and found Chris Collinsworth, his sensational rookie wide receiver, open at the 49ers' five-yard line. But defensive back Eric Wright stripped the ball from Collinsworth's grasp and Lynn Thomas recovered for San Francisco at the eight-yard line.

This time, Montana ran a beautifully controlled 92-yard scoring march—the longest in Super Bowl history—and finished it with an 11-yard pass to Earl Cooper, after the officials had marched off a 15-yard penalty for unnecessary roughness against the Bengals (it was later shown to have been caused by an illegal clip by one of the 49ers).

The bad luck of the penalty and the missed scoring chances that produced a swing of 28 points in San Francisco's favor—14 the Bengals could have scored, but didn't; and 14 that the 49ers did get—disarmed Cincinnati. Next, Montana ran a 13-play, 61-yard drive, climaxed by Ray Wersching's 22-yard field goal for a 17-0 lead.

The 49ers had baffled Cincinnati's defense with its variety of plays, including ten from an unbalanced line. "I think we were doing everything just about the way we wanted," Montana said, and that included a running attack that was better than anyone thought because it kept the Bengals' defense off balance and stifled its good pass rush.

But Walsh also had another trick. When his team had played the Detroit Lions in the SilverDome he noticed bouncing kickoffs were hard to handle because of the very hard surface. So he instructed Wersching to bounce every kickoff—and the most crucial came following Wersching's field goal, with just five seconds to play in the first half. Neither Archie Griffin nor David Verser could handle the ball and rookie Milt McColl of the 49ers recovered to allow Wersching to kick a 26-yard field goal for a 20-0 halftime lead.

The Bengals, who had lost to the 49ers 21-3 during the regular season when they suffered six turnovers, were being humiliated by their own ineptitude. Before the team left the dressing room to begin the second half, Gregg told his players, "Seattle had us down twenty-one-nothing in the first quarter. You came back then, you can come back now."

And they did. The defense, which had yielded 15 first downs in the first half, became a snarling, blitzing band of desperadoes. San Francisco ran only nine plays and got just four yards for the entire third quarter. On offense, Cincinnati went 83 yards to a touchdown from the opening kickoff. On third-and-five, Anderson ran up the middle and dove into the end zone for the score, and the Bengals trailed 20-7.

With 6:53 to play in the third quarter and facing third-and-23, Anderson lofted a 49-yard pass to Collinsworth to the 49ers' 14-yard line. Pete Johnson, the Bengals' 248-pound fullback, got a first down at the three, but with thousands of striped-clad Bengals rooters in a near frenzy, the 49ers then had their finest moments.

On first down, Johnson crashed behind all-pro tackle Anthony Munoz for two yards to the one. On second down, Anderson noticed 49ers linebacker Jack Reynolds edging toward the spot where the play would come—between Munoz and left guard Dave Lapham. He called out an audible to Verser, the wide receiver who was going in motion to that side of the field. It was for him to cut into the hole ahead of blocker Charles Alexander and Johnson, and cut down Reynolds.

But the cauldron of noise that bounced off the roof of the SilverDome obliterated Anderson's call, and Verser missed the change. Instead, San Francisco linebacker

Dan Bunz cut down Alexander, tackle John Harty grabbed Johnson low, and Reynolds, untouched by any blocker, stopped his momentum with a shoulder-high tackle. Had Reynolds been blocked, Johnson could have fallen over the goal line for a touchdown.

On third down, with still a yard to gain, Anderson rolled to his right, and Alexander went in the same direction. Verser was supposed to take a similar path, but deep in the end zone. He didn't, and seeing him too close, Alexander shortened the depth of his route, staying along the one-yard line instead of going just over the goal line.

At the same time, Ross came across to the other side of the field, unnoticed by the 49ers, who went with Anderson. Ken saw Alexander open near the goal line and threw him a pass which, 90 percent of the time, he would carry in for a touchdown. But he caught the ball at the one-yard line and was hit instantly around the shoulders by Bunz, killing his forward momentum and stopping the play for no gain.

Standing alone on the left side of the end zone was Ross!

Fourth down and the Bengals called a time-out to discuss their options. The 49ers had stopped their two most successful short-yardage plays to the left, so they decided on 46-M, sending Johnson, with Alexander again as a lead blocker, over right tackle. This play also had scored 90 percent of the time that it was called during the season.

It was important, though, for center Blair Bush to get a block on Bunz. But the 49ers' defense had placed three men over the middle of the line and Bush could not get out for the block. Mike Wilson, the Bengals' right tackle, moved his man off the line but, unmolested by any blocker, Bunz jammed Alexander in the hole and Johnson simply could not get through as Reynolds and the other 49ers linemen rushed to make the tackle.

Though there was talk at the time of

San Francisco having only ten men on the field during this sequence, films showed they had everyone needed.

The 49ers not only kept their 20-7 lead with that great defensive stand but they also bought five minutes of precious time, because that's how long it took the Bengals to score on their next possession. Anderson finished a seven-play, 53-yard drive by passing 4 yards to Ross.

There were ten minutes still to play, and with their lead now cut to 20-14, the 49ers were in grave danger of being swallowed up. They had not made a first down in the second half when, facing a second-and-15 situation, Montana called a rollout pass to flanker Mike Wilson, in which Wilson ran downfield 25 yards, then came back 5 yards to catch the ball.

"All year long when we showed anything twenty yards deep, it was a takeoff and go," Wilson said later. "I guess that their cornerback, Louis Breeden, figured I'd keep going."

Instead, when he came back, Montana's pass was on target and the 49ers not only worked themselves out of their doldrums with a 22-yard gain, but they also set in motion a five-minute drive that ended when Wersching kicked his third field goal for a 23-14 lead.

That meant the Bengals needed two scores in the final five minutes, and when Anderson was intercepted by Wright, the glass slippers began feeling a little tight for the Cinderella Bengals. Montana knocked off three more minutes as Wersching added a record-tieing fourth field goal for a 26-14 lead with 1:58 to play.

There was nothing for the 49ers to do but hold on, though the Bengals gave them a last furious ride as Anderson, who broke Super Bowl passing records with his 25 completions and 300 yards, ripped off a six-play scoring drive that ended with Ross' second TD pass, a record-setting eleventh catch.

There were 16 seconds left and the 49ers led 26-21 as Cincinnati kicker Jim Breech attempted an on-side kick. But the ball bounced into the willing hands of Dwight Clark and the glass slipper at last belonged to San Francisco.

"We didn't lose, we just ran out of time," said a crushed Forrest Gregg afterward, echoing the theme that he had heard Lombardi preach so often. Looking back, he may have been correct, because the time spent making up for that lost third-quarter touchdown plus the wasted first half, came back to haunt the Bengals at the finish.

Across the hall, Walsh said a silent "amen" to that—and a prayer of thanks for a defense that no one had trusted. It was a Cinderella story all the way.

San Francisco	7	13	0	6	—	26
Cincinnati	0	0	7	14	—	21

SF—Montana 1 plunge (Wersching kick)
SF—Cooper 11 pass from Montana (Wersching kick)
SF—FG Wersching 22
SF—FG Wersching 26
Cin—Anderson 5 run (Breech kick)
Cin—Ross 4 pass from Anderson (Breech kick)
SF—FG Wersching 40
SF—FG Wersching 23
Cin—Ross 3 pass from Anderson (Breech kick)

Game turning point: San Francisco gives Bengals four shots at the goal and turns them off cold. Above, hand-off to Johnson.

MADE TO BREAK RECORDS:

Mike Moseley and Ken Anderson

DECEMBER 19, 1982 AND JANUARY 2, 1983

During the 1982 season, both Mark Moseley, the placekicker for the NFL champion Washington Redskins, and Ken Anderson, the Cincinnati Bengals quarterback, performed two of the most amazing feats in pro football history by setting records that demanded both consistency and accuracy—and a touch or two of luck.

Anderson, a 33-year-old twelve-year NFL veteran, completed 20 passes in a row during a 35–27 victory by Cincinnati over the Houston Oilers in the season's final game on January 2, 1983, at the Astrodome. This broke the mark of 17 straight, set in 1974 by Bert Jones, then with the Baltimore Colts, and tied by Denver's Steve DeBerg only a few weeks before Anderson's feat. (Ironically, Anderson himself once held the old record of 16, which he set only a month before Jones broke it.)

In setting the consecutive completion mark, Anderson also finished the nine-game season with a pass completion percentage of 70.55, breaking a record of 70.33 that Sammy Baugh had set with the Redskins in 1945.

Anderson's season totals were 218 completions in 309 attempts (for 2,495 yards). Back in 1945, in a ten-game season during which the Redskins were conference champions, Baugh completed 128 of 182 passes (for 1669 yards). Even though Anderson played one less game than Baugh, he threw 127 more passes and completed 90 more. And despite the shortened season because of a players strike, there is no asterisk beside Anderson's name. The record is his.

Moseley, a 34-year-old who previously had been cut by two NFL teams and almost didn't make the final cut before the 1982 season began, kicked 23 straight field goals over a period of 12 consecutive regular-season games. Beginning with the fourteenth game of the 1981 season and lasting through the eighth game of the 1982 season, the record shattered the previous mark of 20 that had been set in 1978–79 by Garo Yepremian, while kicking for the Miami Dolphins and New Orleans Saints.

Moseley's recordsetter was a 45-yard kick in the final nine seconds of the December 19 game against the New York Giants and brought the Redskins a 15–14 victory. He went on to kick two more the following week against New Orleans for 23 in a row, finally seeing his string snapped in the final game of the season when he missed a 40-yard attempt late in the first half against the St. Louis Cardinals.

Moseley's streak began on December 6, 1981, when he kicked a fourth-quarter, 45-yard field goal against the Philadelphia Eagles, the team that had cut him after his 1970 rookie season. He added two more before the 1981 season ended, but Redskins coach Joe Gibbs was worried about his lack of consistency, particularly on kicks over 40 yards. He had made only 5 of 13 that season. As a precaution, Gibbs drafted Dan Miller from the University of Miami, and, for the first time since coming to Washington after being released by Houston in 1973, Moseley had to fight for his job.

As it turned out, he almost didn't make it. He had a mediocre preseason, and the team tried to trade him, without drawing much interest. In the end, it was a stroke of luck when Miller flubbed two easy kicks in the final preseason game and Gibbs decided to keep Moseley.

In the opening game of the season at Philadelphia, Moseley made all three field-goal tries, including a 48-yarder that tied the score on the final play of regulation time, then made a 26-yarder that won the game, 37–34, in overtime.

He was three-for-three the following week against Tampa Bay before the players went on their eight-week strike.

When the strike ended, he made a pair each in games against the Giants and Eagles, then added another in the Redskins' only loss of the season, against Dallas. He was now 12-for-12 and record-watchers trotted out Yepremian's streak as a target.

The following week, Washington

Record setter: Bengal quarterback Ken Anderson completed 20 passes consecutively in the season's final game, January 2, against Houston, played in the Astrodome. The former record was 17 straight set by Bert Jones of the Colts and tied by Steve DeBerg of Denver just weeks earlier.

played on an icy artificial surface at Busch Stadium in St. Louis, where Moseley's first kick, from 37 yards, went wide. But the Cardinals were offsides and he made good on the reprieve. He got lucky again in the second quarter when his 30-yard shot flattened out on takeoff and barely line-drived over the crossbar. He added kicks of 20 and 24 yards to account for all of his team's points in their 12–7 victory, the third time in his career that Moseley kicked four in one game.

The following week, December 19, Moseley not only had a chance to break the record but, more importantly, the Redskins needed a victory to assure themselves of a playoff berth. Moseley kicked his nineteenth consecutive field goal early in the second quarter, a 20-yard shot that ended a 44-yard drive. He tried Yepremian's record midway through the last quarter with a 31-yard kick that narrowed the Giants' lead to 14–12.

Washington got the ball for its last drive with 3:28 to play and quarterback Joe Theismann, who also was Moseley's kick holder, deftly moved his team to New York's twenty-five-yard line, where, with nine seconds to play, he set up for Moseley's decisive field goal. Not only would Mark get a chance to break Yepremian's NFL record, but also to win the game and put his team into the playoffs.

It was a worthy bit of drama—and Moseley made the most of it, bombing a forty-five-yard kick squarely through the uprights with such force that it even survived a slapped hand by Giants's linebacker Byron Hunt.

Moseley said that he also heard a hand hit the ball, "but the ball never really quivered. It was the best one that I hit all year.

"Above all," he added, "this record means more to me than any other I can

think of because I want to be known for my consistency. It's hard to be more consistent than hitting twenty-one in a row."

Everyone agreed, because at the end of the season, with his record established at 23 consecutive field goals and his team having the best record in the National Conference, he was chosen most valuable player.

On the same day, January 2, 1983, that Moseley missed on his twenty-fourth straight attempt, Anderson simply got into a groove that great baseball hitters always rave about—a time when every physical and mental action produces something positive.

In Ken's case, it began on his team's second possession of the game with a completion to Steve Kreider. Anderson had gone three-for-three in his first series, including TD pass to tight end Dan Ross. But on the second play of the next series, fullback Pete Johnson dropped an easy flare pass. Anderson, needing four yards for a first down, sent Kreider on a quick sideline hitch pattern that the wide receiver turned into a 25-yard gain. After four running plays, Anderson connected with Cris Collinsworth for a nine-yard gain that set up the Bengals's second TD and a 14–3 lead.

On Cincinnati's first series of the second quarter, Anderson went four-for-four, including two completions to Ross, who caught six passes for 75 yards during the streak, and for the only time during his record-setting run, did Anderson get three consecutive plays where he completed a pass.

Midway through the quarter, Anderson directed a 14-play, 80-yard drive, with 6 completions, 2 to running back Charles Alexander and 2 more to Ross. It was also during this run, after his tenth straight completion, that he overthrew Kreider, only to be saved by dual Houston penalties—pass interference and offsides. His next—and last—pass in that drive was a seven-yard completion to Isaac Curtis.

It was Curtis who also caught the next one, saving again Anderson's streak with a spectacular one-handed grab for a 44-yard touchdown play at the start of the third quarter and the only touchdown pass among all those completions.

By this time, all of the Bengals players—except Anderson, it seems—were aware that he had something going. On the sidelines, Kreider told his mates, "Hey, if you can touch it, you've got to catch it."

On Cincinnati's second possession of the third quarter, Alexander caught a pass, but then the Bengals had to punt. That made 15 in a row. Anderson got number 16 on a pass over the middle to Ross, tied the record on the next play with a quick sideline pass to Collinsworth for four yards; then he broke it with a four-yard turn-in to Kreider.

Then came a 17-yard completion to David Verser and another of 9 to Ross for 20 in a row. Archie Griffin's run was called back because of a holding penalty, and on a first-and-18 call, Anderson went back to Ross over the middle again. This time the ball landed about five yards short.

"I read zone coverage and he read man-for-man. We kind of mixed up communications," said Ross, who that day caught nine balls for 101 yards.

With the record disposed of—and already 23-for-24 Anderson then had a shot at his own single-game completion percentage of 90.2 (20 of 22 versus Pittsburgh in 1974), as well as breaking Baugh's total-season completion mark. He completed his next pass to Collinsworth, missed two more, then hit Curtis, who fumbled and lost the ball.

When Ken came out for his final series early in the fourth quarter, he di-

rected a ten-play, 76-yard touchdown drive that included an 11-yard completion to tight end M. L. Harris and one of 16 yards to Ross before Alexander scored the game's clinching touchdown.

That made 27 of 31 passes, good enough to squeak past Baugh's season total, but just one completion short of breaking his own single-game record.

"He was smoking," Collinsworth says. "He was so relaxed and so loose. If we could get him to loosen up his tailbone more, he'd do that every game."

December 19, 1982, at Washington, D.C.						
New York	7	7	0	0	—	14
Washington	0	3	6	6	—	15

NY—Perkins 28 pass from Brunner (Danelo kick)
Washington—FG Moseley 20
NY—Woolfolk 1 run (Danelo kick)
Washington—Washington 22 run (Kick failed)
Washington—FG Moseley 31
Washington—FG Moseley 42
Attendance: 50,030

January 2, 1983, at Houston						
Cincinnatti	14	7	7	7	—	35
Houston	3	10	0	14	—	27

Cin—Ross 1 pass from Anderson (Breech kick)
Hou—FG Kempf 35
Cin—A. Griffin 10 run (Breech kick)
Hou—Craft 9 run (Kempf kick)
Hou—FG Kempf 37
Cin—Johnson 1 run (Breech kick)
Cin—Curtis 44 pass from Anderson (Breech kick)
Hou—Casper 5 pass from Neilsen (Kempf kick)
Cin—Alexander 4 run (Breech kick)
Hou—Craft 3 run (Kempf kick)
Attendance: 26,522

34-year-old Mark Moseley, previously cut by two NFL teams, set a record for consecutive field goals over a period of 12 regular season games: 23 straight. Moseley began his streak in the fourteenth game of the 1981 season and wound it up in game eight of the 1982 season.

THE HOGS MEET THE KILLER BEES: SUPER BOWL XVII

Washington Redskins vs. Miami Dolphins

JANUARY 30, 1983

It sounded like a Hollywood sci-fi film, but what more than 103,000 fans at the Rose Bowl and more than 111 million on national television saw on January 30, 1983, was simply Super Bowl XVII.

When it ended, John Riggins's performance had earned him pro football's version of an Oscar and the two teams had concocted their own thrilling plot.

The Washington Redskins capped a day of big plays with a tingling 27–17, come-from-behind victory over the Miami Dolphins and one of the best Super Bowls yet played. Riggins was named the game's most valuable player after a record-setting 38 carries and 166 rushing yards, including a 43-yard run for the winning touchdown early in the fourth quarter.

Riggins, a 245-pound fullback, had dominated the defenses of three previous playoff opponents. He worked behind an offensive line that averaged 270 pounds per man and was nicknamed the Hogs—center Jeff Bostic, guards Russ Grimm and Fred Dean, and tackles George Starke and 295-pound Joe Jacoby.

Miami's answer was a defense called the Killer Bees, because of the last-name initial of six of its starters—linemen Doug Betters, Bob Baumhower and Kim Bokamper, linebacker Bob Brudzinski and safeties Lyle and Glenn Blackwood. But more than a gimmick, the Killer Bees were the top-rated defense in the NFL, who had eliminated San Diego and the New York Jets en route to the Super Bowl.

There were many who felt they could do the same to the Redskins, despite the presence of Riggins, who in three playoff games already had gained 444 yards in 98 carries, not too far off his nine-game season total of 553 yards.

Yet his first real running wouldn't come until the game came on the line in the fourth quarter. In the meantime, the first half of the game became a symphony of big plays by some of the other principals, beginning with a 76-yard touchdown pass from Miami quarterback David Woodley to wide receiver Jim Cefalo on the Dolphins' second possession.

When Miami got the ball again and began another drive, Redskins defensive end Dexter Manley sacked Woodley and forced him to fumble and lose the ball. Riggins then knocked off five straight runs for 22 yards to set up Mark Moseley's 31-yard field goal. This was answered midway through the second quarter by a 20-yarder from Miami's Uwe von Schamann for a 10–3 Dolphins lead.

The outcome of the game really was settled during that Miami drive, because the Redskins' defense, which had not received all of the notoriety heaped upon the Bees, had begun to shut down the Dolphins' offense. It forced Miami to kick its field goal after the Dolphins had a first down inside the ten-yard line, and for the remaining 36 minutes of the game coach Don Shula's offense got just 32 yards, and Woodley never completed another pass.

Washington quarterback Joe Theismann was doing a good job coping with the Killer Bees. Gibbs had determined not to allow the Miami defense to find a set pattern. Every Redskins offensive formation was disguised by some form of movement from the time the huddle broke until the ball was snapped; and he further unhinged them with a series of "gadget" plays such as reverses, screen passes, reverse screen passes—even a cross-field screen to Riggins, who never participates in such things.

Using all of this, Theismann got his team a 10–10 tie with 2:09 to play in the half as he ended an 80-yard drive by looping a 4-yard touchdown pass to wide receiver Alvin Garrett.

But in one final burst, Miami regained the lead for the last time as Fulton Walker took Jeff Hayes's ensuing kickoff at his 2-yard line, ran to the 20, veered sharply left and in a flash zipped to a record-setting 98-yard touchdown return. It was the first kickoff ever returned for a TD since the Super Bowl series began.

Theismann and his mates seemed undaunted by this explosion, and in the remaining 94 seconds of the half, they set the tone for the total offensive domination they would exact in the final two quarters by moving 77 yards to Miami's 16-yard line, where time ran out before they could get any points.

One of the most brilliant second efforts by a quarterback in pro football history: Joe Theismann has his pass deflected for what seemed a sure touchdown and recovers quickly enough to knock the ball loose from an unbelieving Bokamper.

Even so, at halftime the game had exceeded everyone's expectations with its mix of big plays and a neatly packaged rhythm of good offense and defensive action. Shula still felt that his team had control, though it was clear that the Redskins had begun to dominate both sides of the line of scrimmage. It wasn't until the Dolphins ran four possessions in the third quarter, sandwiched around Moseley's 20-yard field goal, and came away with just 28 yards in total offense that the Miami brain trust knew it needed a big play to get untracked. And they almost got it in the final two minutes of the third quarter.

Washington had a first down at its 18-yard line when Theismann tried to throw a 5-yard hitch pass to wide receiver Charley Brown. Nose tackle Kim Bokamper broke through and tipped the ball backward toward the end zone, and he scrambled to catch it. For a moment it appeared that he would have an easy touchdown, but somehow, Theismann got his right hand between Bokamper's arms and as Kim was about to clasp the ball on the goal line, Joe knocked it away.

Besides saving what probably would have been Miami's winning touchdown, Theismann's move also allowed Washington to maintain an offensive surge that had begun two plays earlier when Riggins reeled off 13 yards in two carries. Until then, the Dolphins had held him to just nine yards in five third-quarter carries and it had begun to look as if Miami had succeeded in neutralizing the Redskins' prime weapon.

But early in the fourth quarter, Riggins took over for keeps. This time, the Redskins started a drive from near midfield as two of John's runs gained eight yards and Clarence Harmon added another yard to bring up fourth-and-one at Miami's 43-yard line.

Miami didn't think the Redskins would risk a fourth-and-one, but when Washington went into an offensive huddle, the Dolphins called time out.

"They changed defenses," recalls Grimm, the Redskins' left guard. "They were in their basic three-four when they called time out, and then changed to a six-zero, with six down linemen filling the gaps."

The Redskins also did some disguising, showing the Dolphins a formation that forced cornerback Don McNeal to run across the field to cover the tight end who went in motion. He then had to stop and get back to the other side of the field, slipping to his knees right in front of Theismann, who was calling signals. Theismann hurried his snap count, and then handed the ball to Riggins heading to the left behind Jacoby's block. McNeal, because of his slip, was just a fraction of a second late in getting to the hole and couldn't get a full shot at stopping the Washington fullback.

Riggins didn't stop until he ended his 43-yard TD run that gave the Redskins their first lead of the game, 20–17, with ten minutes still remaining.

Washington's defense again forced Miami to punt after three plays, and as the Dolphins came off the field, Shula sent his "relief pitcher," quarterback Don Strock, to warm up. Strock had a fine record of reviving dormant Miami offenses and coming away with victories.

But he never got the chance. The Hogs and Riggins took over the game. Starting at the Dolphins' 41-yard line with almost nine minutes to play, Riggins ran five straight times for 18 yards. He sandwiched another around a couple of runs by Harmon and a Theismann pass that got a first down at Miami's nine-yard line.

The Redskins had eaten six minutes off the clock and Riggins got two more runs before the two-minute mark—38 carries for the day.

Super Bowl hero, John Riggins of the Redskins, piled up a record-breaking 166 yards in rushing, leading his team to its glorious win. Here Dolphins' Kim Bokamper and Larry Gordon combine to stop John.

On the next play, Theismann finished his day with a six-yard rollout pass to Brown for the clinching touchdown.

Strock came on and missed three straight passes . . . a final symbol of the Dolphins' frustration . . . and a final tribute to the job that Riggins and the Hogs had done.

Miami	7	10	0	0	—	17
Washington	0	10	3	14	—	24

Miami—Cefalo 76 pass from Woodley (von Schamann kick)
Washington—FG Moseley 31
Miami—FG von Schamann 20
Washington—Garrett 4 pass from Theismann (Moseley kick)
Miami—Walker 98 kickoff return (von Schamann kick)
Washington—FG Moseley 20
Washington—Riggins 43 run (Moseley kick)
Washington—Brown 6 pass from Theismann (Moseley kick)
Attendance—103,667

FIELD GOAL MASTER: JAN STENERUD

Green Bay Packers vs. Tampa Bay Buccaneers

December 12, 1983

No kicker in professional football history ever has kicked more field goals than Jan Stenerud, and that's not too bad for someone who was recruited from his hometown in Fetsund, Norway, to begin a sports career as a collegiate skier.

Kicking for the Green Bay Packers at the age of 41, and as the oldest active NFL player during the 1983 season, Stenerud broke George Blanda's career record of 335 field goals, and like any skier who ever has attacked a mountain, he did it with a verve and a measure of excitement that made the feat truly memorable.

Five times during that season, Stenerud had kicked field goals in the final minute, or in overtime, and won games for the Packers, including the night against Tampa Bay Buccaneers when he broke Blanda's record. The first of his four field goals that night tied the record; the second broke it in the final 42 seconds of the third quarter; and then he capped this most satisfying achievement with a pair that enabled the Packers to tie the game in the final seconds of regulation play, and then win it in the overtime period.

Yet, that had been Stenerud's way since he first came to the NFL in 1967 with the Kansas City Chiefs, for whom he kicked for 13 seasons, and for the Packers, who took him off the discard pile and breathed new life into his career.

Like all of pro football's great kickers, his physical skills are superb and his psyche seemingly made of sponge rubber, because he has survived the end-

less run of do-or-die situations that often turn ordinary kickers' knees and feet into wobbly rubber and their minds into twisted metal. He has seen the top: his 48-yard field goal in the Chiefs' Super Bowl IV victory over Minnesota still is a record; and he has felt the bottom: two missed field goals in a 1971 playoff game against Miami helped the Dolphins win 27–24 in the second overtime period of the longest NFL game ever played.

Stenerud was introduced to football at Montana State University, which he was attending on a skiing scholarship (he had been ranked sixth among all of Norway's skiers) when he began "fooling around" with a football, kicking it soccer style. When word reached football coach Jim Sweeney that Stenerud's kicks were traveling more than 50 yards, Sweeney invited him to join the team, and before Stenerud's collegiate career had ended in 1966, he was drafted by both Atlanta and Kansas City, in the days of AFL-NFL competition, and wound up signing with the Chiefs.

Kansas City released him prior to the 1980 season, and many teams that subsequently gave him a trial during that season weren't impressed with his skills. Finally, the Packers, desperate for a kicker, signed him, and from then until his record-setting kick, no kicker in the NFL had a better percentage.

When the 1983 season began—Stenerud's seventeenth in pro football—he needed only 19 field goals to break Blanda's all-time record, and with his

Having set a new record for kicking a total
of 336 field goals, Stenerud, in the same
contest, kicks the game winner.

82.4 percent accuracy rate (compared to 63.9 during his years at Kansas City) the only question seemed to be when—not whether—he would set the record. But no one, including Stenerud, was prepared for the virtuoso performance he would conduct during that epic season.

Consider:

• On opening day at the Houston Astrodome against the Oilers, he got 2 field goals—the second of 24 yards on fourth down with nearly 6 minutes played in an overtime period that gave the Packers a 41–38 victory. He now needed only 17 for the record.

• Two weeks later in Los Angeles, the Packers recovered a fumble by the Rams' Eric Dickerson at LA's 19-yard line with less than a minute to play and the game tied, 24–24. Two plays later, with one second remaining, Stenerud hammered home his second field goal of the game, 36 yards, and gave the Packers a 27–24 victory. He now had 321, still 15 away from the record.

• Stenerud raised his total to 324 when the Packers played Washington in a Monday-night game at Green Bay, and again he notched 2 more field goals, of 47 and 20 yards. The second came with just 54 seconds to play, and it stood up for a wlld-and-woolly 48–47 Green Bay victory that was assured only in the last second after Mark Moseley—acclaimed as the NFL's best kicker at the time—missed a 47-yard field goal on the game's final play.

• Seven weeks later, when the Packers played the Chicago Bears for the first time in the 1983 season, Stenerud's field goal totals had reached 333. He got 334 that day on the final play of the game, a 19-yard shot that ended a 5-play, 78-yard drive after the Bears seemingly had nailed down a victory on Dennis McKinnon's 59-yard punt return for a touchdown with 1:50 to play.

He was just two field goals away from breaking Blanda's record when the Packers traveled to Tampa Bay the following week for a Monday-night game. With millions around the country watching on television, Stenerud tied the record on the Packers' first possession when, 4 plays after an interception at the Bucs' 24-yard line, he drove a 33-yard field goal through the uprights, number 335 of his career.

The score was tied, 3–3, late in the third quarter when Green Bay got the ball at its 49-yard line. Five minutes later, the Packers faced a fourth down at the Bucs' 14-yard line, and on came Stenerud to try what he, and millions around the country, knew would be his record-breaking kick.

"Oh, I knew what was happening," he said later. "I knew that I had tied the record in the first quarter, and I just

wanted one more try to break it and get the whole business behind me. It was a goal that I had set for a couple of years, because I really wanted one of George Blanda's records.

"On top of that," he added, "I hadn't kicked well for about ten days before this game, and I was a little nervous going in. I didn't know how I would react, but when I kicked the first one, that eased some of the pressure. But I really wanted that second one, probably more than I ever wanted any single kick in my life."

And he got it—32-yard beauty at 14:32 of the quarter that belied any nervousness for such an epic-making effort.

The kick gave Green Bay a 6–3 lead, and the story should have ended right there. But it didn't.

Tampa Bay went ahead midway through the fourth period on Jack Thompson's 4-yard TD pass to Adger Armstrong, but the Bucs' kicker, Bill Capece, missed the extra point, so the Packers trailed 9–6. Four plays later, Tampa Bay got the ball again after an interception and, with an opportunity to sew up the game, Capece then missed an easy field goal.

That gave Green Bay one last shot, and Lynn Dickey drove his team to the Bucs' 5-yard line where, with 28 seconds to play, on fourth down, Stenerud calmly tied the score with a 23-yard kick.

The Packers won the coin toss in overtime, got the kickoff, and 11 plays later, Stenerud put the capper on the night by again kicking a 23-yard field goal—number 337 of his career—for a 12–9 victory. It was the fifth time during the 1983 season that his field goals had won a game.

"Somebody wrote the script perfectly for me," he said afterward. "I felt very lucky. I'm not a religious man, but I should get down on my hands and knees and give thanks."

| Green Bay | 3 | 0 | 3 | 3 | 3—12 |
| Tampa Bay | 0 | 3 | 0 | 6 | 0—9 |

Green Bay—FG Stenerud 35
Tampa Bay—FG Capece 22
Green Bay—FG Stenerud 32
Tampa Bay—Armstrong 4 pass from Thompson (Kick failed)
Green Bay—FG Stenerud 23
Green Bay—FG Stenerud 23

"It's good!" Packers' Jan Stenerud watches his field goal clear to break the old record set by George Blanda.

ALLEN STYMIES THE HOGS

Los Angeles Raiders vs. Washington Redskins

January 22, 1984

An oyster, inside and out, is a rather drab creature. But open one and find a pearl, and suddenly it's transformed into something very rare.

That is how it was in January 1984 when the Los Angeles Raiders and the Washington Redskins played in Super Bowl XVIII—a game that had the potential for being the very best of these NFL championship games, but one that was oyster-gray until Marcus Allen uncorked a dazzling 74-yard touchdown run on the final play of the third quarter that really sealed a momentous 38–9 victory by Los Angeles over the favored Redskins.

No runner ever had steamed that far in Super Bowl competition, and when the game ended, no running back ever had gained so many yards in one of these games as had Allen, who finished with 191 yards in 20 carries. His other 19 runs included a dandy cut-back, 5-yard touchdown slant earlier in the third quarter and his record-setting last carry of 39 yards that made him the Super Bowl's all-time one-game rusher. These, however, paled next to his 74-yard journey, which will stand as one of the most electrifying plays in NFL championship game history.

Moreover, it was a play that never was thought possible against the best rushing defense in the NFL. In one of the more ironic twists to this game, during all the pregame hoopla Allen had never really been considered a threat, given the all-out publicity blitz heaped upon the high priest of NFL rushers, John Riggins, and his Washington offensive line,

nicknamed the Hogs. After all, the media reminded us, it had been Riggins who, a year before, had set a Super Bowl rushing record of 166 yards, including a 44-yard game-winning TD run. And, it was Riggins who had taken center stage throughout the 1983 season, when Washington was unabashedly acclaimed the best team in the NFL.

After they had won the AFC championship, Allen and the Raiders were simply football's number two.

The two teams had played earlier in the season, and Washington had roared from a 35–20 deficit with just seven and a half minutes to play and defeated Los Angeles, 37–35. In the final minute Joe Theismann fired a six-yard TD pass to Joe Washington for the victory. Allen had missed that game because of an injury, but Riggins had battered the Raiders' defense for 91 yards in 27 carries.

Even from a season in which he gained 1,014 yards rushing and in which he sometimes complained of not getting the ball enough, there really was nothing to foretell that Allen would be the indomitable force when the Raiders played for the NFL championship. In fact, from the very beginning of his professional career, Marcus Allen, Heisman Trophy and all, seemed to be the great player that no one—save the Raiders—really wanted.

He was a back, 6–2, 210 pounds, who had set an NCAA season rushing record of 2,342 yards in his senior year at Southern California en route to winning the Heisman, Maxwell, and Walter Camp trophies—the top awards given to a collegian—and then being ignored by nine of the NFL's worst teams until the Raiders made him their first-round selection on the tenth pick of the 1982 draft.

His speed is questionable, the by-passers claimed. So questionable that Allen became the league's rookie of the year during the strike-abbreviated 1982 season. In 1983, his thousand-yard season helped the Raiders to a 12–4 record and into the Super Bowl.

Perhaps because every individual Raiders player must be a part of the silver-and-black football machine that is the Raiders organization, no one really expected anything dramatic from this running back. Yet everyone knew that if the Raiders' offense was to function with its required balance, Allen still had to be reckoned with. Stop him, the Redskins said, and they would have the opportunity to go after LA quarterback Jim Plunkett and force him to do what he does not do very well—carry the team's

offense with his passing. Washington was very confident that its top-ranked rushing defense could do the job.

It didn't, and the Raiders let it be known on the first three plays that Allen was very much a key to their success as he gained 13 yards on 2 runs and a pass. By the end of the first half, he led all rushers with 51 yards on 11 carries.

Los Angeles also had stunned the Redskins by taking a 21–3 lead. In typical "organization" fashion, one score had come on Plunkett's 12-yard pass to Cliff Branch, another on Derrick Jensen's block and recovery for a touchdown of a Jeff Hayes punt early in the first quarter. The third had come on a 5-yard interception return by reserve linebacker Jack Squirek of a foolish screen pass by Theismann with just 21 seconds to play in the first half.

Instead of just allowing the clock to run out when they had the ball at their own 5-yard line, and behind 14–3—still

Marcus Allen, new Super Bowl record-holder for most yards gained, flies for second quarter first down, leaving Redskin pursuers to bite the dust.

very much in the game—Redskins coach Joe Gibbs tried to resurrect a play that had gained 67 yards in the season's earlier matchup between the two teams.

Raiders' defensive coach Charley Sumner played a hunch when he saw the Redskins' offensive set and rushed Squirek into the game with orders to guard running back Joe Washington, who flared out to his left while three other wide receivers tried to draw off the defense with deep patterns. Squirek did just as he was told, and Theismann threw the ball almost without looking, enabling the Raiders' linebacker to snap it out of the air and vault into the end zone for a crushing TD.

The Redskins took the opening kickoff of the second half and for the only time that day looked like the team that had so dominated opponents throughout the season. Driving 70 yards in 9 plays—the last 4 by Riggins—Washington had a touchdown. Mark Moseley's extra point was blocked, so Washington trailed, 21–9. For a moment at least they had plugged themselves back into the game.

The Raiders, while stunned at the

The Raiders' Allen sets another Super Bowl record when he runs for the longest touchdown in the 18-game history.

suddenness of that surge, were not severely shaken and proved that with a 9-play drive of their own—including a 38-yard pass-interference penalty against defensive back Darrell Green—that was ended when Allen started running toward his right, saw a big opening in the middle, and easily cut into the space for a 5-yard TD run, and a 28–9 lead.

Still vivid, though, was the memory of the Redskins' sudden awakening earlier in the season, and Washington's hopes for a replay were rekindled late in the third quarter when Branch lost the ball at the Raiders' 35-yard line. There still was time in the third quarter for Washington to narrow the score to 28–16 and set the stage for a final charge.

In three plays, those hopes came down to a fourth-and-one at LA's 26-yard line. Riggins, as usual, got the ball and tried the same off-tackle play that he had run for the game-winning touchdown in Super Bowl XVII. This time, the Raiders' defense had plugged the holes, and Riggins tried futilely to find room to the outside. No deal. Linebacker Rod Martin and other defenders swarmed over him just a half foot shy of that previous first down.

Out came the Raiders, and in the span of 12 seconds, they put the game away for good with a play called "17 Bob Trey," designed for Allen to run to the left and cut inside a block by guard Mickey Marvin. Marvin did his job, the hole was there, but not Allen.

"I was out of position and I didn't get to the hole," he said later. "Then all I saw were Redskins, and after messing up, I knew I had to do something fast. So I just turned around and went the other way."

Simple enough, except that generally a back will try to sweep the field with such a maneuver, and Allen saw that route cut off by a bevy of Redskins, and he felt the arms of defensive back Ken Coffey lunging at his legs. At the same time, a big hole opened in the middle of the defense, so he cut into it and veered sharply to the left, against the frantic pursuit the Washington players had begun.

"I was lucky to get away from Coffey," he says, "and then there was this big hole up the middle, the only place I could go. I ran by Darrell Green, but he was still tangled up with one of our wide receivers, and there was no one in front of me.

"'Maybe,' I thought, 'I can score.'"

He thought correctly, because no one laid a hand on him as he completed that record-setting 74-yard run, a remarkable play that erased the previous Super Bowl record of 58 yards set by Tom Matte of the Baltimore Colts in Super Bowl III. Matte did not score on his run.

Allen's touchdown doomed the Redskins, even though in the fourth quarter he carried just three more times—his final run was a 39-yard sprint, again on a cutback to the left, that got him the rushing record.

"I didn't realize I had the record—I didn't even think about it—until I came out of the game and looked at the scoreboard where my statistics were being flashed," he recalls.

Allen quickly pointed out that such a record really was the result of the great work done by the Raiders' offensive line that so outshone the much-publicized Hogs. "They either were neutralizing Washington's defensive line or pushing them where they wanted to go.

"Then it was just up to me to find the holes. I rely on cutting back and I did a lot of that."

Right into the record books with a gem of a performance.

Washington	0	3	6	0—9
Los Angeles	7	14	14	3—38

LA—Jensen blocked kick recovered in end zone (Bahr kick)
LA—Branch 12 pass from Plunkett (Bahr kick)
Wash—FG Moseley 24
LA—Squirek 5 run interception (Bahr kick)
Wash—Riggins 1 run (Kick failed)
LA—Allen 5 run (Bahr kick)
LA—Allen 74 run (Bahr kick)
LA—FG Bahr 21

"AWFUL TOUGH TO BEAT"

Chicago Bears vs. New Orleans Saints;
Los Angeles Rams vs. Houston Oilers

October 7, 1984; December 9, 1984

Walter Payton's leap began just past the line of scrimmage, and as his body hurtled through the air over a mass of New Orleans Saints' and Chicago Bears' players, he tucked the football tightly into his middle, and rolled himself into the tightest package possible. When he landed among a raging group of defenders who fought against black-jersied Bear blockers, the most hallowed of all of pro football's individual records—Jim Brown's career rushing mark of 12,312 yards—had been broken.

And by a man whose nickname is Sweetness, but whose style on the field is absolutely explosive.

The record, which Brown set over nine seasons with the Cleveland Browns, ending in 1965, had been assaulted by the game's best runners for nearly two decades, but never conquered. Many believed that it had become an impenetrable barrier.

No longer.

Payton, who seemed to sneak up on the mark since having joined the Chicago Bears as a No. 1 draft pick from Jackson State University in 1975, shattered it in the sixth game of the 1984 season, and may put it out of anyone's reach by the time he finally retires.

Of course, there always will be challengers—other Walter Paytons—and already Eric Dickerson has taken aim on the mark. In 1984, he obliterated another of the NFL's most cherished rushing - records when he finished the season with 2,105 yards. That broke O. J. Simpson's record of 2,003 yards (described earlier in this book), which was considered almost unbreakable when it was established back in 1973.

More about Dickerson's mark later; to Payton go top honors in this great generation of running backs. Still, to many who saw him play, Jim Brown always will be the greatest runner in pro football history, and his supporters point out that Brown set his career mark in fewer seasons (9 versus·10) and games (119 versus 136) than Payton.

Prior to 1984, many had ceded Franco Harris the honor of breaking Brown's record. The running star of the Pittsburgh Steelers since 1972, Harris was just 362 yards away from the mark, while Payton trailed by almost 700 yards when the 1984 season began. But Harris fell short because his legs had grown unreliable after 12 seasons. His failure to agree on a generous contract offer from the Steelers, who were willing to give him enough work to break the mark, caused him to be cut from the team, and he eventually landed with the Seattle Seahawks without the benefit of any training camp work. Sadly for Harris, when the 1984 season came and went, he was out of football and still looking up at Jim Brown—and now at Walter Payton.

Payton, on the other hand, began and ended the season a physical marvel and in perfect shape to assault Brown's record. He can bench press almost 400 pounds, and leg press more than 600. His upper arms are enormous, like a lineman's, and his thighs bulge with layers of muscle. His abdomen is rock solid, his neck thick and strong, and he always seems to go out of his way to punish would-be tacklers.

Like Brown, he is a perfectly sculpted human being, a man who caused his coach; Mike Ditka, to remark, "When God said He would make the best football player who ever lived, He probably had two men in mind: Jim Thorpe and Walter Payton."

In his own quiet way, Payton took dead aim on the record after finishing the 1983 season with 11,625 career rushing yards, 325 behind Harris and 687 behind Brown. First, he got what he called his "11,000-yard checkup," by having both knees arthroscoped to clean out the accumulated debris from nine years of work for the Bears, on teams far less talented than those that supported Brown and Harris.

Then he took after his friend Franco.

"I've always needed motivation, so I decided to pass Harris *before* he set the record," Payton recalls. "I knew it was an utterly unrealistic goal, but so was man walking on the moon at one time."

In the fourth game of the season, Payton had crept to within 34 yards of Harris after having gained 250 yards in each of his first three games. Two dozen carries and 116 yards later, he was ahead of Franco for good, having bumped him to third place on the all-time list with a 9-yard gain in the second quarter of a game between Seattle and the Bears.

Ahead lay Jim Brown and his record—and the 222 yards needed to break it. The following week when Payton played against the Dallas Cowboys and gained 130 yards in the first half, it ap-

Payton explodes over the top to score a second-quarter touchdown.

peared that he might set the record. But he got the ball just 5 times in the second half to finish the game with 155 yards—only 67 between him and that seemingly impenetrable barrier.

The following week, October 7, the Saints came into Chicago's Soldier Field, and as Payton stood poised for this landmark event, you'd have thought that Toddlin Town would be agog at the prospect. Alas, the city was totally taken up by the Cubs, who that day were playing for their first National League championship in 40 seasons.

When the day ended, the Cubs again had broken the hearts of Chicago, but Payton had broken Jim Brown's record.

In the first half, he bashed and scratched for 65 yards, just 2 shy of the record. The Bears got the second-half kickoff, and on first down, Payton gained a yard. One yard to go—two for a new record.

In the huddle, quarterback Jim McMahon called, "Toss-twenty-eight-weak." That sent the No. 2 back—Payton—sweeping toward the left side of Chicago's offensive formation.

At the snap of the ball, left tackle Jim Covert and tight end Emery Moorhead blocked the Saints' defenders toward the middle. Left guard Mark Bortz pulled out and teamed with flanker Dennis McKinnon and fullback Matt Suhey to lead Payton around the New Orleans' defense.

Walter skittered along, holding the football in his right hand in front of him, and he thought to himself, "Don't fumble." Then, seeing the Saints' defenders beginning to close in, he leapt just as he passed the line of scrimmage—and landed in the NFL's history book. Only 49 seconds of the second half had been played, but in that brief span of time, Payton had wiped away 20 years of looking at a great record.

The game was stopped and a cavalry charge of photographers and team-mates hurtled toward him. Instinctively, Payton took off, heading for the Saints' bench, where he shook hands with New Orleans' coach Bum Phillips, and then he circled the group and headed toward his own bench, where he was mobbed by his teammates. Watching from a private box were his wife, Connie; son, Jarrett; his mother; and a group that included his high school and college coaches.

When he finally got back into the huddle, he said to McMahon, "It's over with. Now let's go for the win."

That was pure Payton, and he continued his assault on the Saints' defense as Chicago went on to win 20–7. Finally, with 30 seconds to play, Ditka took him from the game, having gained 154 yards in 32 carries for a career mark of 12,400 yards.

When the 1984 season ended, Payton won his sixth NFC rushing title with 1,684 yards for a career total of 13,634 yards. At age 30, there is no telling what numbers he will make the new "impenetrable barrier," but his first target will be 16,000 yards. "Whatever it is, I'm going to make it awful tough for someone to beat," he says.

That's what Dickerson said when he finished the 1984 season with his record—and he may be the one who Payton had in mind, because in his first two NFL seasons, Eric had gained nearly 4,000 rushing yards, and had become the first player in NFL history to twice rush for more than 1,800 yards in a season.

In 1983, he had shattered the rookie rushing mark of 1,808 yards and then, in 1984, broken Simpson's single-season record in his fifteenth game of that campaign. The Juice had set his record in 14 games back in 1973.

In 2 of his 1984 games, Dickerson, a 6-foot 4-inch, 218-pounder who has run 100 yards in 9.2 seconds, gained more than 200 yards, including the record-setter against the Houston Oilers when he picked up 215, his season's best. He also had 9 other games of more than 100 yards, including 1 of 149 when his Rams played Payton and the Bears. Payton got 60 yards.

After the season's fourteenth game, a 149-yard effort against New Orleans, Dickerson had 1,792 yards, with Houston and the San Francisco 49ers still to play. On Tuesday before the Oilers' game, Dickerson visited Simpson at his California home; O. J. said to him, "Get the record this week against Houston and get it over with, otherwise you'll wind up needing eighty or a hundred against the 49ers in the final game of the season. Add that to the playoff implications of that game (the Rams were fighting for a wild-card berth), and the burden may be too much."

On December 9, the Rams and Oilers played in Anaheim Stadium, and even Rams' coach John Robinson noticed a change in Dickerson's usual pregame demeanor.

"I don't know when I've seen a man more ready for a game," he said later. "He had a fierce look in his eye."

Dickerson played the same way, relentlessly banging away at Houston's defense as his line tore open huge holes, or provided him with alleys for his patented cut-back moves that so frustrate defenders who think they have him cornered.

Finally, with 3:30 left in the game, Rams' quarterback Jeff Kemp tossed Dickerson the ball on a sweep to the right, and when that play ended, Dickerson had gained 9 yards—and a season total of 2,007—5 more than the record.

He was mobbed by his mates, and Robinson told him, "Okay, that's enough. Take the rest of the day off."

He did, and the following week he finished the season against the 49ers with 98 yards, for a final total of 2,105 yards, 102 more than Simpson had amassed in 1973.

While certainly proud—and relieved—to get the record ("I even started to dream about it because people kept

Dickerson deftly evades Oilers' Keith Bostic on his way to the end zone.

reminding me how much I needed each week"), Dickerson still takes a bow in Simpson's direction.

"He's the best because he did it in fourteen games, and I did it in fifteen," Dickerson says. "So there's a difference that people always will bring up. I hope I can do it in fourteen games someday."

How long will that be?

"I don't know," he replied. "I'm like Walter Payton. I hope I can get it so far out there that the next guy who tries to break it, will break his neck . . . except me, of course."

Of course.

October 7, 1984, at Chicago:

New Orleans	0	7	0	0— 7
Chicago	6	7	0	7—20

Chi—FG B. Thomas 48
Chi—FG B. Thomas 46
NO—W. Wilson 15 pass from Todd (Anderson kick)
Chi—Payton 1 run (B. Thomas kick)
Chi—McKinnon 16 pass from McMahon (B. Thomas kick)

December 9, 1984, at Anaheim, Calif.:

Houston	3	10	3	0—16
Los Angeles	17	3	0	7—27

LA—Dr. Hill 57 pass from Kemp (Lansford kick)
Hou—FG Cooper 21
LA—Dickerson 7 run (Lansford kick)
LA—FG Lansford 35
Hou—FG Cooper 42
Hou—Moriarty 4 run (Cooper kick)
LA—FG Lansford 19
Hou—FG Cooper 18
LA—Dickerson 6 run (Lansford kick)

49ers STRIKE IT RICH

San Francisco 49ers vs. Miami Dolphins

January 20, 1985

In pro football it is a commandment that offense wins games, but *defense* wins championships—even when matched against the most productive passer—and passing attack—in NFL history.

Dan Marino, the record-setting quarterback of the Miami Dolphins, knows that now.

Joe Montana, the efficient, resourceful quarterback of the San Francisco 49ers, knew it all along, as well as the fact that when a team combines the two, the results can be astounding, which is what happened to him and his teammates during their smashing 38–16 victory over the Dolphins in Super Bowl XIX.

This game was projected to be one of the best ever played because Marino, the 6-foot 4-inch, 215-pound second-year pro from Pitt, was coming in with a passing attack that had been all but unstoppable throughout the 1984 season. It would be matched against a 49ers team that was proficient in all phases of the game, as illustrated by its 17–1 record during the regular season and playoffs.

But ballyhoo and impressive statistics don't win championships, though in the week prior to the game, Marino had become this Super Bowl's central attraction. Among his other achievements in 1984, he had, after all, passed for 48 touchdowns and more than 5,000 yards. No one had ever done that before.

Included among his statistics were 2,965 yards and 26 touchdowns accumulated by the "Marks Brothers"—Mark Duper and Mark Clayton—his favorite wide receivers, who had the speed to run through secondaries and perfectly complement Marino's magnificent arm.

Of course, in the frantic excitement of the game, those numbers seemed to mask the fact that Marino was just 23 years old, with only 2 years of pro experience but none in the pressure-cooker environment of a Super Bowl; and that his team had serious shortcomings, such as a mediocre running game and a very ordinary defense.

Regardless, everyone had decided that Marino would produce the victory—or he would be responsible for the defeat. As it turned out, he did neither. Instead, Joe Montana and the 49ers were responsible for everything that happened that day—both good and bad.

Montana was at his very best in this game. Lost in the glare of Marino, had been the considerable talents of the 49ers' quarterback—talents that included running an offense that utilizes dozens of formations in every game and chipping away with short- and medium-range passes—and the solid running of Wendell Tyler and Roger Craig. Nothing spectacular, mind you—just deadly efficient.

Montana's forte was efficiency. He had earned MVP honors in the 49ers Super Bowl XVI victory—and he did so again in this game—because of his ability to make the complexities of his offense look so easy.

The 49ers' defense was just as complex, using some 125 different looks that found room to work in 9 defensive linemen and a 4-man secondary that was chosen intact to participate in the Pro Bowl. Marino would be their test, it was decided, but on Super Sunday that defense never was better. It was, in fact, the ultimate difference.

Still, the Dolphins and Marino struck first, driving 45 yards in 7 plays for Uwe von Schamann's 37-yard field goal midway through the first quarter. Marino looked as impressive as advertised, completing 4 of 5 passes for 38 yards, including a 25-yarder to running back Tony Nathan on his first play.

However, when the 49ers got the ball for the second time, crucial parts of the game story became clear. First, Montana's running ability became a factor. When the Dolphins' defense continually ignored him in their pass coverage and rushed three linemen, that gave Montana room to run if he couldn't find an open receiver. He did just that for 15 yards on a third-and-seven situation that got a first down at Miami's 33-yard line.

On the next play, Montana sent three receivers into the left of Miami's defense and hit the middleman, Carl Monroe, with a pass for the game's first touchdown. On the drive, Montana completed all four of his passes, and it was obvious that his offense, fanning receivers to all areas of the field, was becoming too much for the Dolphins' defense.

However, the 49ers' defense had not yet solved the Marino riddle—and incredibly, the Dolphins offered the quickest possible solution on their next possession when they ran a no-huddle offense. The intent was to keep the 49ers' special defensive substitutes, including pass rushers Fred Dean and Gary Johnson, and two defensive backs on the bench.

This move became a two-edged sword because Marino swept the Dol-

phins 70 yards in 6 plays for a touchdown, completing 5 passes for 65 yards, including a 2-yard TD pass to tight end Dan Johnson. However, the 49ers had anticipated something like this, and had readied a special defense to use against Marino if his passing became too effective. Defensive coordinator George Seifert immediately installed a four-man pass rush featuring Dwaine Board, Jeff Stover or Michael Carter, plus Dean and

Johnson. Only Keena Turner remained at linebacker, but in came defensive backs Jeff Fuller, who played a combination linebacker-safety spot, and "nickel back" Tom Holmoe to join cornerbacks Dwight Hicks and Eric Wright and safeties Carlton Williamson and Ronnie Lott.

Seifert also had designed new stunts for his defensive line in order that they could put pressure on center Dwight Stephenson, the Dolphins' best offensive lineman. The Niners tried to tie him up on every play and thereby open the middle, and at the same time to prevent him from helping his mates combat San Francisco's great pass rush. This left the remaining four Dolphins' linemen one on one with the three other pass rushers, and either Turner or Bryant, who blitzed on nearly every play.

The effect was awesome. When Marino tried to pass, he had to sift through six pass defenders—and the ability of those backs was such that he needed as much time as possible for his receivers to try and get free. However, with Dean, Johnson, and company coming at him so hard on a pass rush, there simply wasn't much time for waiting.

The end result: 4 sacks—Marino had been sacked only 14 times all season—and so much pressure that in key situations, he began to throw his passes into the ground, or to the wrong side of his receivers; ultimately, he was often forced just to heave the ball to escape the punishment he knew was coming on nearly every play.

Meanwhile, back on offense, Montana flourished, thanks in part to other Miami failings, such as the inability of punter Reggie Roby to keep San Francisco from getting good field position.

This first happened early in the second quarter when Roby punted only 37 yards to his own 47-yard line. Four plays later Montana put the 49ers ahead to stay with a 19-yard run and a 3-yard pass to Craig, the first of Roger's 3 rec-

ord-setting TDs. The neatly conceived play sent tight end Russ Francis into the middle of the Dolphins' defense, taking the linebackers with him, and Craig simply came into the open area for his pass.

When Marino missed a key third-down pass by underthrowing to wide-open Nat Moore, the Niners started another scoring drive, helped by Dana McLemore's 28-yard return of Roby's ineffective 40-yard punt. Montana polished off this 6-play, 55-yard drive with a 6-yard scoring run after primary receiver Dwight Clark was covered in the end zone. The 49ers now led 21–10.

They upped the lead to 28–10 on their next possession after Marino's third-down sideline pass to Duper, who was forced to turn to the inside to get the ball, was knocked away on a spectacular play by Hicks. This time, Montana received a big break from a botched fumble call by the officials. Wide receiver Freddie Solomon caught a pass that was shaken loose and recovered by Miami, but it was ruled that he did not have complete possession of the ball.

Replays showed that he did, and instead of getting the ball with a chance to get back into the game, or at least to thwart the 49ers, Miami watched its victory chances fade—5 plays later Craig zipped 2 yards for his second touchdown, with nearly 13 minutes played in the second quarter.

"Moving the ball came a lot easier than we expected," Montana said later. "The approach we had, running and mixing in play-action passes, was excellent. But Miami really helped us since I didn't get a lot of pressure from their pass rush because they use their linebackers and defensive backs to try and cover all receivers.

"When they went to the nickel defense, they would try and double cover certain receivers, but the middle was always open, and no one covered me. So we'd send our backs or tight ends into the middle, or I'd have a clear field to run. All of this just evolved as the game went on."

Miami fired one last salvo following the 49ers' fourth TD, when Marino moved his team 85 yards in a dozen plays, the biggest a 30-yard completion to tight end Joe Rose to the Niners' 12-yard line. On third down from the 13, he lofted an "Alley Oop" pass to Clayton in the corner of the end zone, but Lott batted it away. So Von Schamann kicked his second field goal.

With 12 seconds left in the half, the Dolphins kicked off, but Guy McIntyre, 49ers' offensive guard, caught the ball on one knee at his 18-yard line. He hesitated a moment, and as he got up to run, Joe Carter knocked the ball loose and Jim Jensen picked it up and started for the end zone. McIntyre redeemed himself somewhat with a tackle that saved the TD, but Von Schamann easily kicked another field goal, and Miami now trailed 28–16 at the half.

The consensus at halftime was that this bit of lightning was all Miami needed to get back into the game. But it didn't work that way. On the first series, Miami lost ten yards, including nine on Dwaine Board's third-down sack of Marino. When the Dolphins got the ball again, Board and Manu Tuiasosopo sacked him twice. In between, Montana clinched his MVP day, first by scampering 15 yards in the crucial play on a 53-yard drive that ended with Ray Wersching's field goal; and then on his next possession, taking his team 70 yards in 5 plays, 1 a 40-yard pass to Tyler, another a 16-yard TD throw to Craig.

The huge, largely partisan 49ers' crowd at Palo Alto, California, saluted him with a thunderous ovation—and for good reason. By game's end, he had set Super Bowl records with 35 completions, 331 yards passing, and 59 yards rushing, the most by any QB. His offense also had gained a record 537 yards.

49er Roger Craig squeezes out a few more yards before being thrown for a spin by Dolphin corner-back William Judson.

The 49ers' defense had allowed only 25 yards rushing—Tyler himself got 65 rushing and another 70 receiving—and only 289 passing, 110 of those in the second half when the Dolphins and Marino were trying desperately to get back into the game. The secondary allowed Duper just 1 catch for 11 yards while Clayton had 6 catches, the longest just 27 yards.

"Sometimes I didn't throw the ball well; sometimes I didn't have time; and sometimes guys didn't get open," Marino noted afterward, the frustration, pain, and fatigue from the pounding and emotionally gruelling day showing on his handsome face—and perhaps saying more than his words.

All Montana did was smile. So did his defense—the King Maker.

| Miami | | | 10 | 6 | 0 | 0—16 |
| San Francisco | | | 7 | 21 | 10 | 0—38 |

Mia—FG Von Schamann 37
SF—Monroe 33 pass from Montana (Wersching kick)
Mia—D. Johnson 2 pass from Marino (Von Schamann kick)
SF—Craig 8 pass from Montana (Wersching kick)
SF—Montana 6 run (Wersching kick)
SF—Craig 2 run (Wersching kick)
Mia—FG Von Schamann 31
Mia—FG Von Schamann 30
SF—FG Wersching 27
SF—Craig 16 pass from Montana (Wersching kick)

OVERTIMES ARE FUN TIMES

Giants vs. Eagles; Falcons vs. Eagles; Raiders vs. Chargers; Chargers vs. Broncos; Seahawks vs. Broncos; Broncos vs. Raiders; Raiders vs. Chargers

1985

Overtimes in the National Football League are fun times.

Sometimes.

Depending, of course, on whether your team wins or loses, the lure of sudden death in football is almost irresistible, and true to the great theater that it presents, it never seems to disappoint those who seek the dramatic.

Judging by what happened during the 1985 season, it would seem that fans in Denver, Los Angeles, San Diego, and Philadelphia thrive on the special brand of artistry from games in overtime.

Sometimes.

The Broncos had four of them during the season, a quarter of Denver's schedule that had to be decided after 60 minutes of play. They won two . . . but the two they lost, to the Los Angeles Raiders, wound up costing them the AFC Western Division championship and a trip to the playoffs.

The Raiders, on the other hand, had three overtime games. In addition to their victories over Denver, they lost a wild-and-woolly game to the San Diego Chargers. San Diego, conversely, also lost a wild-and-woolly affair to Denver.

For sheer dramatic impact, the Eagles bowed to no one, losing an overtime game to the New York Giants when an intercepted pass was returned for the winning touchdown; then they beat Atlanta in another overtime contest on a 99-yard, record tying touchdown pass. In the game they lost 16–10 to the Giants, Philadelphia had forged a tie with less than four minutes to play when defensive back Herman Edwards grabbed a tipped pass

from Giants' quarterback Phil Simms and easily ran three yards for the touchdown. Paul McFadden, the Eagles' kicker, had had a chance to win the game in regulation time, but had missed a 43-yard field goal.

Philadelphia won the coin toss to start the overtime period and took the kickoff. On the second play, Eagles' quarterback Ron Jaworski tried a pass, which was tipped from its trajectory into the hands of New York cornerback Elvis Patterson at Philly's 29-yard line. Patterson, a replacement for all-pro player Mike Haynes, had earned the nickname "Toast" because he had been burned so often the previous year in pass situations. Not this time, though.

"The first thing that came to my mind was to catch the ball," he recalled. "The second was to look over the field for a route to the end zone. I stepped inside to avoid a tackler, then broke to the outside, and Lawrence Taylor gave me an escort all the way home."

Six weeks later, the Atlanta Falcons were in Philadelphia and trailed the Eagles 17–0 in the fourth quarter. But the Falcons forged the overtime when Mick Luckhurst tied the score with a 27-yard field goal with 2:32 to play. Like McFadden earlier in the season, Luckhurst could have won it for his team with a 42-yard kick in the final 9 seconds.

Atlanta got the ball first but didn't get a first down. When Falcons' punter Rich Donnelly put his punt out of bounds at the Eagles' one-yard line, it looked as if Philadelphia was in a hole that could ultimately lead to disaster. But on the second

A jubilant Elvis Patterson after intercepting Ron Jaworski's pass and returning 29 yards for the Giants' winning touchdown.

play—the first was an incomplete pass—Jaworski called a quick slant pass to Mike Quick, a mercurial wide receiver.

"We just wanted to get some breathing room for our offense," Quick said later. What he got was a 99-yard touchdown play that happened in large part because safety Scott Case of Atlanta tried—and missed—an interception. Cornerback Bobby Butler, also on the coverage, never had a chance to back up the play.

"When Quick gets by you like that, you might as well stop and look back to see if there are any flags," Butler said. "You know you're not going to catch him. He looked like he was training for the 1988 Olympics."

In addition to giving the Eagles a 23–17 win, the play also was the sixth 99-yard TD in NFL history. You can't go any farther than that on a scrimmage play.

The same day, ironically, in San Diego, the NFL's most renowned "little man," Lionel James, was achieving the second highest all-purpose yardage total for one game in NFL history—345 yards, the last 17 being a touchdown run less than four minutes into overtime that gave the Chargers a raucous 40–34 victory over the Raiders.

The touchdown was James' second of the game and capped a day in which both the Chargers and Raiders accumulated 1,047 yards of total offense, 593 by San Diego, which broke a 7-game losing streak against the Raiders. Perhaps it was fitting that James, the smallest offensive performer in the NFL at 5 feet 7 inches, became the game's biggest man. "People who say I'm too small give me determination to prove them wrong," the 172-pound back says. He backed up his words not only in this game but at season's end, when he had set an NFL all-purpose (running, pass receiving, kickoff, and punt returns) record of 2,535 yards.

The Chargers had forged a tie when, with less than a minute to play, Charlie Joiner caught a 14-yard TD pass from quarterback Dan Fouts, who completed 26 of 41 passes for 436 yards and 4 touchdowns in the game. San Diego then won the coin toss and in 7 plays, including a key 23-yard pass to Pete Holohan and Gary Anderson's 23-yard run, went 80 yards for the final score.

But those who live by the overtime sword also can die from it . . . sometimes excruciatingly so. Five weeks after that momentous win over the Raiders, San Diego thought it had caught a break against the Denver Broncos when, in overtime, an offsides penalty nullified a block of Bob Thomas' field goal by Dennis Smith. So the Chargers, five yards closer, lined up to win the game a second time.

But this time, Smith and cornerback Daniel Hunter switched from the left to the right side of the line for their rush on Thomas. "The first time Hunter told me they were blocking him out and he didn't think he could get to the ball," Smith said. "So on the second one, I told him to go outside and try to open a seam for me. He did, and I was able to get between the tight end and the wingback and get my hand on the ball."

Incredibly, he blocked Thomas' kick a second straight time—and the third

Denver's quarterback John Elway scrambles for a first down against Raiders' Jeff Barnes.

time in the game—except this time, there was no penalty. Hence, the Chargers could not avoid disaster as Denver cornerback Louis Wright scooped up the deflected kick and raced 60 yards untouched for the Broncos' 30–24 victory.

Blocked kicks were epidemic in this game. A blocked Denver punt helped San Diego take a 24–21 lead with 78 seconds to play, but Denver went 48 yards in 7 plays, the last being Rick Karlis' 34-yard field goal with 5 seconds to play that got the overtime.

Karlis knows that kickers are the real victims of overtime. In 1984, he had cost the Broncos a game against Seattle when his field goal that would have sent the game into OT bounced off a goalpost upright. Earlier in the 1985 season, he

had redeemed himself when he kicked a 24-yard field goal at 9:17 of overtime to help the Broncos beat the Seahawks 13–10, the first of Denver's four overtime games that season.

But Karlis could be only an innocent bystander in the Broncos' last two overtime games. Following Denver's win against San Diego, the team went to Los Angeles and got ambushed by the Raiders 31–28 at 2:42 of sudden death on Chris Bahr's 32-yard field goal. On the sidelines Karlis only nodded, knowing what it was like as Bahr missed a 40-yarder on the last play of regulation.

"On the one I missed, it went right by about a foot," Bahr recalled. "I was a little surprised it didn't come left a little. The wind should have pushed it back. But the last one was right down the middle."

It got to go "right down the middle" because, like Quick's pass play for the Eagles, a small play became a very big one. On second-and-nine at the Raiders' 35-yard line, quarterback Marc Wilson hit wide receiver Dokie Williams with a pass designed to gain about 12 yards. But Williams broke free of Denver's Mike Harden at the 47-yard line and wasn't caught until he reached the Broncos' 23-yard line. A five-yard face mask penalty added five yards, and all Bahr had to do was to kick the winning points three plays later.

The teams played each other again in Denver three weeks later, this time in the snow. Both teams were tied for first place in the AFC West, and in the end, first place and a trip to the playoffs all came down to a wrong call when the coin toss for overtime took place.

Denver won the toss and had planned to kick off to get a brisk wind at their backs. Instead, co-captain Barney Chavous elected to receive, as is usually the custom in overtime games because there is no second chance if the other team scores first.

"When we lost the toss, I knew we'd be okay," Bahr said. "The wind was the deciding factor."

The Raiders' defense never gave Denver a yard, nor allowed the Broncos beyond their own 20-yard line. When quarterback John Elway got the ball for his third series of downs, he tried to pass on first down. Defensive linemen Howie Long and Greg Townsend flushed him from the passing pocket, and Long stripped the ball from his arms as he was being tackled. Townsend fell on it, and on the next play, Bahr kicked a 26-yard field goal with 4:55 gone in the overtime period, for a 17–14 victory.

It was that easy . . . that dramatic . . . the great lure of overtime.

Sometimes.

September 29, 1985, at Philadelphia

New York	0	0	10	0	6 —	**16**
Philadelphia	0	0	3	7	0 —	**10**

Phila—FG McFadden 41
NY—FG Atkinson 49
NY—Bavaro 26 pass from Simms (Atkinson kick)
Phila—Edwards 3 interception return (McFadden kick)
NY—Patterson 29 interception return (No kick)

November 10, 1985, at Philadelphia

Atlanta	0	0	0	17	0 —	**17**
Philadelphia	0	14	3	0	6 —	**23**

Phila—E. Jackson 8 run (McFadden kick)
Phila—Jaworski 1 run (McFadden kick)
Phila—FG McFadden 30
Atl—Washington 18 pass from Archer (Luckhurst kick)
Atl—Riggs 1 run (Luckhurst kick)
Atl—FG Luckhurst 27
Phila—Quick 99 pass from Jaworski (No kick)

November 10, 1985, at San Diego

Los Angeles	7	6	14	7	0 —	**34**
San Diego	7	3	10	14	6 —	**40**

SD—Chandler 10 pass from Fouts (Thomas kick)
LA—Hester 35 pass from Wilson (Bahr kick)
SD—FG Thomas 34
LA—Hawkins 1 run (Bahr kick)
SD—FG Thomas 23
LA—Allen 1 run (Bahr kick)
SD—James 34 pass from Fouts (Thomas kick)
LA— Hester 54 pass from Wilson (Bahr kick)
SD—Anderson 21 pass from Fouts (Thomas kick)
LA—Christenson 24 pass from Wilson (Bahr kick)
SD—Joiner 14 pass from Fouts (Thomas kick)
SD—James 17 run (No kick)

November 17, 1985, at Denver

San Diego	7	7	0	10	0 —	**24**
Denver	7	0	0	17	6 —	**30**

SD—Anderson 98 kickoff return (Thomas kick)
Den—Watson 4 pass from Elway (Karlis kick)
SD—James 6 pass from Fouts (Thomas kick)
Den—Lang 2 run (Karlis kick)
Den—Lang 4 run (Karlis kick)
SD—FG Thomas 36
SD—Spencer 2 run
Den—FG Karlis 34
Den—L. Wright 60 blocked FG return (No kick)

October 20, 1985, at Denver

Seattle	0	0	7	3	0 —	**10**
Denver	7	0	3	0	3 —	**13**

Den—Winder 36 run (Karlis kick)
Den—FG Karlis 45
Sea—Largent 9 pass from Krieg (Johnson kick)
Sea—FG Johnson 39
Den—FG Karlis 24

November 24, 1985, at Los Angeles

Denver	7	14	0	7	0 —	**28**
Los Angeles	7	7	14	0	3 —	**31**

Den—Watson 16 pass from Elway (Karlis kick)
LA—Allen 61 run (Bahr kick)
Den—Willhite 9 pass from Elway (Karlis kick)
LA—Christensen 17 pass from Wilson (Bahr kick)
Den—Kay 6 pass from Elway (Karlis kick)
LA—Junkin 3 pass from Wilson (Bahr kick)
LA—Wilson 1 run (Bahr kick)
Den—Sewell 3 run (Karlis kick)
LA—FG Bahr 32

December 8, 1985, at Denver

Los Angeles	0	0	14	0	3 —	**17**
Denver	7	7	0	0	0 —	**14**

Den—Wright 5 pass from Elway (Karlis kick)
Den—Winder 1 run (Karlis kick)
LA—Christensen 3 pass from Wilson (Bahr kick)
LA—Allen 15 run (Bahr kick)
LA—FG Bahr 26

PLAYING THE WINNING NUMBER

Bears vs. Giants, Rams, Patriots

1986

The Chicago Bears of 1985 had the right number: 46.

That was the designation of their defense—the "46 Defense," which many compared to the best ever put on an NFL playing field—and the number of points they scored in defeating the New England Patriots (46–10) and winning their first Super Bowl, and their first NFL title since 1963.

Though they had the game's most productive running back in Walter Payton (he had gained more yards than any rusher in pro football history) and some gutsy offensive players, like quarterback Jim McMahon and wide receiver Willie Gault, it was the defense that caught everyone's attention because it almost did what it bragged it could do: become the first NFL champion ever to shut out every opponent in a playoff series.

The Bears made good on the boast in the first two playoff games, beating the New York Giants 21–0, and then coming back the following week and beating the Los Angeles Rams 24–0. No one had ever done that before—shut out both opponents to win a conference playoff—and when the Bears got to New Orleans to prepare for Super Bowl XX, their fiery linebacker Otis Wilson told everyone they would shut out the Patriots, too—just about guaranteed it, in fact.

That boast went out the window in the game's first minute after Payton fumbled on the second play . . . and the Pats recovered at Chicago's 19-yard line. Tony Franklin's 36-yard field goal broke the Bears' spell—but New England never budged off the 3-point mark.

For the rest of Super Bowl XX, though, as in the two previous games, it would be hard to find a better defensive performance in any playoff. Chicago, which led the NFL in total defense and was first in rushing defense during the 1985 season, made that ranking stand up. None of their three opponents ever totaled 200 yards in any game. If anything, the Bears got better as they went along, allowing New York 181 yards in the first playoff game, the Rams 130 in the NFC title game, and then hammering the Pats to the tune of 123 yards, including a minus 19 at halftime.

People the nation over were rattling off the quick-and-easy answer: the 46 Defense, as if anyone save perhaps the Bears themselves, and its originator, defensive coordinator Buddy Ryan, really knew how it worked.

In essence, it's a variety of the 4–3 defense, an alignment not used too much in pro football anymore. It has four defensive linemen—ends Dan Hampton and Richard Dent, and tackles Steve McMichael and William (Refrigerator) Perry—and three linebackers—Otis Wilson and Wilbur Marshall on the outside, and Mike Singletary as the middleman. However, it's where the players line up, along with the four defensive backs, that's the key. Both outside linebackers, Wilson and Marshall, will be on one side, normally the strong side of an offensive formation with the tight end. Dent rushes from the weak, or open, side and also drops back in pass coverage.

Strong safety Dave Duerson plays close to the line of scrimmage and also has responsibilities as a linebacker. Singletary, on the other hand, often will have pass coverage duties as a strong safety and is protected by his line so he can move to make tackles on running plays.

From that alignment, many things can happen. Throughout the playoffs, the Bears stunted and shifted their players, with Dent often wheeling around the massive Perry and coming right up the middle to pressure the passer. Normally blocked by the offensive left tackle, Dent found his opposition thinking someone else would do the job on these maneuvers. Often it didn't happen, and he wound up with a total of six sacks in the three games and was picked as the Super Bowl's most valuable player.

· The architect of this defense was Buddy Ryan, who already had been to Super Bowls as defensive coach of the New York Jets and Minnesota Vikings. The Bears, though, were his ultimate conception, and he never doubted for a moment that his players could be in the forefront of a championship season.

All of the Bears seemed to feel that way, from the very first day of training camp, and a 15–1 season record was evidence that this was a dedicated team. Their only loss had come on a Monday night against the Miami Dolphins, and many of the Bears had hoped for a re-match in the Super Bowl.

But New England, which had lost to the Bears 20–7 early in the season, had messed up that dream by upsetting Miami in the AFC championship game, settling a score of their own: It was the first time that any New England team had won in Miami since 1966, the first year of the Dolphins' existence.

Before the Bears got to New Orleans, though, they had had to win the NFC title, which had eluded them in 1984, when they fell to the San Francisco 49ers 23–0. But there would be no slips in 1985.

The final blow—Henry Waechter brings Steve Grogan to his knees in endzone for additional 2-point safety to make a lopsided final score of 46–10 for Super Bowl XX.

The first test was the Giants, winner of the NFC wild–card playoff against San Francisco. New York, recalling a similar matchup against the Bears for the 1963 NFL title, vowed it would be different: That day the Bears won 14–10 on frozen Wrigley Field turf that completely negated New York's great passing game, led by quarterback Y. A. Tittle and wide receivers Del Shofner and Frank Gifford. This time, New York rolled into frozen Soldier Field with its all-time rushing leader, Joe Morris, who had set a club record 1,336 yards in 1985, and complemented by the passing of Phil Simms, who had erased Tittle's season marks.

But if the faces and the dates had changed, the Bears really had not. Twenty-two years later, Chicago's defense held Morris to just 32 rushing yards in 12 carries after he had averaged nearly 84 yards per game during the season. When Perry squashed him on a second-quarter tackle, the 5-foot 9-inch runner was never the same, and the Giants lost their most imposing weapon.

With no running game to protect him, Simms was at the mercy of the Bears' pass rush, and it got him six times. Dent had three and a half of those sacks, and the Giants wound up with just 149 yards passing, most of those in the fourth quarter, when the Bears were killing the clock.

The Bears turned back New York's only serious scoring threat in the final 39 seconds of the first half. The Giants had a first down at Chicago's two-yard line, but three passes into the end zone—the Giants had no time-outs left—were incomplete, though one of Simms' balls should have been caught by wide receiver Bobby Johnson. Whatever life the Giants had left expired on fourth down when kicker Eric Schubert's 19-yard field goal bounced off the left upright of the goalpost.

Chicago's defense had things in hand from the beginning, when New York punter Sean Landetta miskicked a ball from his end zone, just skimming it with his foot. Defensive back Shaun Gayle picked up the mini-punt and ran five yards for a touchdown.

McMahon passed 23 and 20 yards for touchdowns to wide receiver Dennis McKinnon in the second half, and the Giants never got a whiff of the Bears' end zone. Singletary rated his defense an 8½ for their job.

He raised his mark to 9½ after the Bears totally dominated the Rams the following week to win the NFC title. Again, Chicago took on one of the game's best runners, Eric Dickerson, who the previous week had set a league playoff record with 248 yards against the Dallas Cowboys. On a cold and blustery day in Chicago, he got just 46 yards in 17 carries, after averaging 77 per game during the season.

So good was the Bears' defense that Los Angeles ran only nine plays in Chicago's territory all day, and that included three controversial ones at the end of the second half, when the Rams allowed the clock to expire while just nine yards from the end zone—with a time-out still remaining.

In the meantime, the 46 Defense had rendered the Rams' quarterback, Dieter Brock, like Simms the week before, powerless to cope with its intricacies. He got only 44 yards from his passes and was sacked 3 times. On one sack, by Dent, the ball was stripped from Brock's hands and picked up by Marshall, who ran 52 yards for the game's final touchdown early in the fourth quarter.

In winning its conference, the Bears' defense had allowed two of the NFL's best running backs a total of just 78 yards, and two of its most productive offenses just 311 yards. McMahon, for his part, did what he had to—running 16 yards for a TD against Los Angeles and

passing 22 to Gault for another after changing a play sent in to him by head coach Mike Ditka.

So, when it came to the Super Bowl, the Bears were brimming with confidence. They had dedicated themselves to winning this game, and throughout the week, they talked of little else. McMahon, perhaps, talked a little too much, and the 308-pound Perry couldn't say enough about a season in which he had become a cult hero of sorts.

New England, though, was still seen as dangerous. The Pats had come from nowhere to get to the Super Bowl, primarily on a crunching running game led by Craig James and an opportunistic band of warriors who snapped up a half dozen enemy fumbles and turned them into touchdowns in three playoff games.

The big question was, could quarterback Tony Eason and coach Raymond Berry figure out the 46 Defense? During the week, Eason never exuded much confidence, saying he went to sleep wondering what Buddy Ryan was going to do and woke up thinking the same thing.

Going into the game, Berry thought he had the answer. His team, following Payton's lost fumble, threw three straight passes and missed on all three, though a second-down pass to wide receiver Stanley Morgan should have been caught for a touchdown. When Berry's team, now tied 3–3, got the ball again, he tried three more passes, and the last resulted in Eason's being sacked by Dent.

Running had gotten the Pats to the Super Bowl.

"I wanted to come out throwing," Berry said afterward. "I wanted to get their attention. . . . We wanted to run the ball, too, and have a balanced attack. But I wanted to get the passing game going."

It never worked . . . but neither did the running game. Chicago's defense was right in the thick of the Bears' record-setting point totals. The defense made 5 plays that either resulted directly in, or led

to, 26 of their points. Seven of those came on Reggie Phillips' 28-yard interception return of a tipped pass in the third quarter; and another 2 came on Henry Waechter's sack of Pats' quarterback Steve Grogan in the end zone for a safety in the last quarter.

Dent's second sack of Eason in the first quarter led to Kevin Butler's second field goal—and marked the end of Eason for the game. Dent then forced James to fumble, and this led to the Bears' first TD, by fullback Matt Suhey. And when Marshall recovered a fumble by Morgan, this set up a thundering one-yard TD by the Refrigerator, making the score 44–3.

When the carnage had ended with a 46–10 victory, James, who had gained more than 1,200 yards during the season, and 258 in three previous playoff games, had just 1 yard, and the Pats had netted only 7. The Bears had sacked Eason three times and Grogan four more in allowing their puny total of 123 yards, second lowest in any Super Bowl game.

And after the game, Singletary was asked for a rating: "In order to be successful today," he said, "we needed a 10. And we came as close to a 10 as we have all year."

Thanks to a 46.

January 5, 1986, at Chicago

New York	0	0	0	0	—	0
Chicago	7	0	14	0	—	21

Chi—Gayle 5 run with punt (Kevin Butler kick)
Chi—McKinnon 23 pass from McMahon (Butler kick)
Chi—McKinnon 20 pass from McMahon (Butler kick)

January 12, 1986, at Chicago

Los Angeles	0	0	0	0	—	0
Chicago	10	0	7	7	—	24

Chi—McMahon 16 run (Butler kick)
Chi—FG Butler 34
Chi—Gault 22 pass from McMahon (Butler kick)
Chi—Marshall 52 run with fumble (Butler kick)

January 26, 1986, at New Orleans

Chicago	13	10	21	2	—	46
New England	3	0	0	7	—	10

NE—FG Franklin 36
Chi—FG Butler 24
Chi—FG Butler 24
Chi—Suhey 11 run (Butler kick)
Chi—McMahon 2 run (Butler kick)
Chi—FG Butler 24
Chi—McMahon 1 run (Butler kick)
Chi—Phillips 28 interception return (Butler kick)
Chi—Perry 1 run (Butler kick)
NE—Fryar 8 pass from Grogan (Franklin kick)
Chi—Safety, Waechter tackled Grogan in end zone

The Bears' swarming "46 Defense" swamps Eric Dickerson during NFC championship game.

287

THE DRIVE

Denver Broncos vs. Cleveland Browns

JANUARY 11, 1987

The Drive: 98 yards, 15 plays, and a game-tieing touchdown with 39 seconds to play. Further details are almost unnecessary. The Drive means an epic performance by Denver Broncos' quarterback John Elway, against the Cleveland Browns in the 1986 AFC championship game.

Elway's Drive now fits with other such epics in NFL history, the 68-yard move that was directed on that same Cleveland Stadium field—and in the same direction—by Otto Graham of the Browns that ended with Cleveland winning its first NFL title game in 1950 in the final 16 seconds, the 86-yard march that Johnny Unitas of the Baltimore Colts masterminded to get a tie with seven seconds to play against the New York Giants in the 1958 NFL Championship Game, forging pro football's first overtime game.

Ironically, Unitas and Elway then proceeded to march their teams to winning touchdowns the first time they had the ball in the overtime period, Elway directing a 60-yard drive that ended with Rich Karlis kicking a 33-yard field goal for a 23-20 victory by the Broncos.

Drives are special in pro football, and they should be snipped, framed and forever treasured because they reveal the true essence of any great quarterback. As Elway remarked after his team's victory, "You know how you think the night before about doing great things in a game? Well, this is the kind of game you dream about."

Indeed, it is the kind of game that requires a blend of execution, mental toughness, great physical endurance, intelligence, and unanticipated events that contribute luck.

On the second Sunday of 1987, a raw, windy day so typical of Cleveland's winters in the face of Lake Erie's blasts, the Browns were a solid favorite to beat the Broncos, mainly because of their great defense which had named itself The Dawgs, reinforced by thousands of fans who howled and barked, and threw dog bones and biscuits into the end zone. They were an intimidating group whose noise was so great that Elway often could not be heard in the privacy of his own huddle.

Elway rolls out during Denver's thrilling overtime win over Cleveland for AFC title.

The howlers were just one part of the crowd of 79,915 who jammed the old stadium and who had watched their team score first on a six-yard pass from quarterback Bernie Kosar to Herman Footent, but then fall behind 13-10 going into the final quarter. Kicker Mark Moseley got them a tie with a 24-yard field goal with 15 minutes to play, and wide receiver Brian Brennan almost brought down the old stadium when he caught a 38-yard pass from Kosar; and after turning defensive back Dennis Smith around and literally screwing him into the ground, pranced ten more yards for a 48-yard TD play that gave Cleveland a 20-13 lead with just five minutes and 43 seconds to play.

As far as the Cleveland fans were concerned, that was the ball game; and there were millions more watching across the nation on television that day who probably agreed. The Dawgs' defense had pretty much controlled Elway and the Broncos offense by allowing just 216 yards.

Denver then proceeded to dig itself into a hole, by thoroughly fouling up the ensuing kickoff, finally falling on the ball at their two-yard line. A hundred or so yards up the field, they could see the fans shaking fists, and they could hear them howling and barking.

But Elway hears nothing but the beat of his own particular drummer, one that had produced a sometimes erratic beat over his first four NFL seasons that caused some to find him suspect in big games, but which also had caused others to call him the sport's pre-eminent player, a force all by himself in any game. He was, beginning the moment that he stepped into his huddle that had formed at the very back of the Broncos end zone. "We have a long way to go, so let's get going," he told his teammates. "We'll do whatever it takes."

On the Browns' sideline, where pure elation reigned among the players who rightly felt they were in a commanding position now to win the game and make their first Super Bowl trip, coach Marty Schot-

tenheimer recalled a prophecy which starkly came to life in the next minutes.

"Elway provides a dimension that's difficult for our defense to address because he can turn a negative into a positive," he had said before the game. "The onus of stopping him rests with our secondary because if I tell our defensive linemen to try to contain him, instead of applying pressure, they'll stand around like three or four traffic cops."

Elway wasted no time in making Schottenheimer a prophet. His first play was a five-yard swing pass to running back Sammy Winder that got him away from his end zone. Winder then took a toss and gained three more yards, bringing up the first of three third-down plays the Broncos had to make—and the Browns needed to stop to regain the ball.

"Winder is a great wedge runner," Elway said, "so we handed him the ball and he got just enough for a first down over left guard."

Two plays later, Elway began an 11-play sequence in which he became the only Bronco to control the ball. On second-and-seven at the Browns 15-yard line, he dropped back to pass, felt too much pressure and saw the Browns had left a gaping hole on the right side of their defense. He scrambled free and took off for an 11-yard gain—the type of play many think makes him the most dangerous quarterback in the NFL, terrorizing secondaries with his passing skills, and then sucker punching them with his ability to run.

Denver had a first down at their own 26-yard line, and Elway got them another with a 22-yard swing pass to Steve Sewell to the 48-yard line. A lot of the joy had gone out of Cleveland Stadium, though the clock had also ticked inside the three-minute mark, and Elway still had to get a touchdown just to tie the game.

He stabbed at the Browns' defense with a 12-yard pass to Steve Watson into the middle of Cleveland's defense—three plays, three first downs as the clock hit

1:59, and the ball on Cleveland's 40-yard line.

"That was our only breakdown on the drive," coach Dan Reeves said later, "but it was a temporary one because we tried to get some different receivers into the game and that led to too much confusion on John's part, which in turn led to the sack."

With a third-and-18 staring him in the face, and with the Dawg House at the far end of Cleveland Stadium raging, Reeves called Elway to the sidelines. "'You don't have to get it all on one play,' he told me, "because we're going on fourth down if we have to,'" Elway remembers. "We called a 'release 66' pass with Orson Mobley as the primary receiver, about 10 yards over the middle.

Elway and Coach Dan Reeves discuss strategy during time-out with third-and-18. Ensuing pass to Jackson was good for 20.

"But when we lined up, I saw their strong safety (Ray Ellis) was playing very, very deep and that we had a chance to go for the whole 18 yards. So, instead of looking for Mobley, I looked for Jackson."

That was Mark Jackson who zoomed down the left sideline. He almost never had a chance to make the play because, with Elway lined up deep in a shotgun formation to receive the ball, center Bill Bryan's snap deflected off the leg of Watson, who was passing between him and Elway as a man in motion.

Elway quickly snapped up the loose ball, took one look toward Jackson and fired a perfect pass for a 20-yard completion to the Browns' 28-yard line, with 79 seconds left to play.

Elway then sandwiched a 14-yard pass to Sewell around a couple of incompletions to Watson; and on second-and-10 at Cleveland's 14-yard line, he broke from his passing pocket and scrambled nine yards to the Browns' five-yard line.

It was third-and-one, and Elway ended this astounding odyssey with a five-yard laser shot to Mark Jackson in the end zone for the tie-making touchdown. The ball was thrown low and away so that Jackson had to reach for it—and no Cleveland defender could even touch it. As it was, the ball's velocity was so severe, it was a wonder that Jackson was able to catch the ball.

"I thought their cornerback would bump Jackson at the line of scrimmage," said Elway, "but when he didn't, it was Mark against the safety, one-on-one. No problem."

Jackson said that as he was running his pass route he could hear the crunching of dog biscuits beneath his feet, thrown into the end zone by the rabid Browns rooters, who were stunned into total silence by his touchdown play.

The overtime was almost anti-climatic compared to the drive that forged it; Elway made short work of Cleveland, after Karl Mecklenberg and Rulon Jones had stuffed Fontenot on a third-and-two run at Cleveland's 38-yard line.

The Browns punted, and starting on his own 25-yard line, Elway took just nine plays to get the winning points. The biggest was a third-and-ten at the 50-yard line, when he was flushed from the pocket and decided to run. He saw he couldn't make the first down marker, and peeking downfield, realized that Hanford Dixon had left Watson to cover his run.

"I just floated a little 'touch pass' over Dixon's head because Steve was all alone," Elway recalled. Watson caught it and was finally downed after a 28-yard gain to the Browns 22-yard line. Elway knew he had field goal range for Karlis, so he called three running plays by Winder that gained seven yards to the 15-yard line.

On fourth down, Elway trotted off the field, his job done. He passed Karlis, hobbling over the icy turf with his kicking foot unsheathed of shoe and sock, and told him, "Just as in practice."

"I tried to tell myself it was just another kick, just as in practice," Karlis said. "I tried to fix a smooth spot to kick the ball, but was digging a hole instead and said, 'To hell with this. Let's just kick it and get out of here.'"

And he did...33 yards with 5:48 elapsed in the sudden death period.

A kick won the game, The Drive was forever.

At Cleveland, January 11, 1987. Attendance: 79,915

Denver	0	10	3	7	3	—	23
Cleveland	7	3	0	10	0	—	20

Cle—Fontenot 6 pass from Kosar (Moseley kick)
Den—FG Karlis 19
Den—Willhite 1 run (Karlis kick)
Cle—FG Moseley 29
Den—FG Karlis 26
Cle—FG Moseley 24
Cle—Brennan 48 pass from Kosar (Moseley kick)
Den—M. Jackson 5 pass from Elway (Karlis kick)
Den—FG Karlis 33

22—FOR—25

New York Giants vs. Denver Broncos

JANUARY 25, 1987

Phil Simms has seen it all.

In 1979, when he was the New York Giants' first round draft pick it was Phil who? From there, the career roller-coaster ride got wilder until, on a crisp, late January evening, he was chosen as the MVP of Super Bowl XXI, leading the Giants to a 39-20 victory over the Denver Broncos, having helped the Giants to their first NFL title in 30 years.

It is a nice touch for anyone who has suffered as much personal and physical agony as Simms had to endure for most of the first five of his eight NFL seasons. He couldn't even convince the team's fans in their Super Bowl year that he was a worthy quarterback. Indeed, though teammate Lawrence Taylor, a linebacker, was named as the NFL's most valuable player for the 1986 season, it was Simms who did more to bring his team to the Super Bowl, and then to secure the victory with the finest passing performance in NFL playoff history.

The statistics tell much of the story in his record-setting, award-winning performance; 25 passing attempts and 22 completions for a record .880 percentage. He passed for 268 yards and three touchdowns, 6-for-6 on his team's first touchdown drive, 10-for-10 in the second half, when the Giants scored 30 points, and he threw two touchdown passes. It was an unflappable, almost magical overall performance that fueled the Giants to such a dominating game that they buried the Broncos, just as they had buried the 49ers (49-3) and the Redskins (17-0) in the playoffs. In fact, the Giants defeated opponents nine straight times to reach the playoffs.

Super Bowl MVP Phil Simms rolls left during Giants convincing victory over the Broncos.

True, the Giants' defense also did its part in getting to this game; it helped stave off the ambitious, and thoroughly underdog Broncos in the first half with a goalline stand. And, true, it was running back Joe Morris, who had set a team record 1,516 yards during the season, who lashed Denver's defense in the second half and opened up some opportunities for Simms to display his perfect passing.

But in the end, it was Simms who engineered the show, and who simply took advantage of all that was offered to him in the way of open receivers, the bounce of the ball, and some ill-timed misfortune for the Broncos. No other NFL quarterback ever did better; not Otto Graham, Johnny Unitas, Joe Namath, Terry Bradshaw, nor Joe Montana, when a championship was on the line.

At the start, it appeared as if Denver's John Elway would have the stage to himself. Fresh from leading his team to an astounding overtime victory over the Browns in the AFC title game just two weeks before, Elway came out smoking and got his team a quick 3-0 lead, when Rich Karlis kicked a record-tieing 48-yard field goal. Alas, that was the last good thing that Karlis did on a summery afternoon, but the way that Elway was in stride, no one could envision such personal disasters.

Some months before, the Giants had beaten Elway and the Broncos 19-16 with a last-second field goal, but the Denver defense, with its myriad shifts and formations, had not surrendered a point to Simms' offense. At that time, they played an almost exclusive man-for-man defense against the Giants, and Simms had more than his share of problems, until he hit a 45-yard pass that set up the winning field goal.

When Denver opened the Super Bowl game with the same basic scheme, Phil was ready. The Broncos were not; they expected Joe Morris to be the key weapon, and had geared themselves to shutting him down. Instead, Simms came out throwing, and by completing his first six passes, including one of 10 yards to Stacy Robinson on third down, and another of 17 to tight end Mark Bavaro to the Broncos six-yard line, he totally unglued Denver's defensive schemes.

"We didn't know if we should put our pass defense in on first down, and our run defense on second," noted Broncos linebacker Karl Mecklenberg. "They were outguessing us."

Simms was also confusing them because he sent tight end Zeke Mowatt in motion, and then got him lost among the Denver defense so that he was wide open

for a six-yard tie-making TD.

Elway was equally undaunted. He was 4-for-4 the next time he got the ball, helped by 18 yards in penalties. With a five-yard pass to Vance Johnson, he had his team at New York's four-yard line. He then did the one thing that the Giants' defense had sworn he wouldn't do, he ran for a touchdown on a quarterback draw, and had the Giants on the defensive, as well as behind 10-7.

The next time he had the ball, Elway hit Johnson with a 54-yard pass to the Giants 22-yard line, and soon had the Broncos to the one-yard line with a seven-yard toss to Steve Sewell, as he nailed five-of-seven passes in that drive.

Here, though, a combination of Giants' defense and some questionable play-calling by Denver coach Dan Reeves took its toll. The Broncos knew beforehand they would have to take advantage of every scoring opportunity to stay in the game against such an overpowering opponent. Elway tried to run a keeper to the right on first down, and was thrown for a yard loss by Taylor; Gerald Willhite was stopped in the middle for no gain by Harry Carson; and linebacker Carl Banks, the Giants' dominant defensive player throughout the playoffs, threw Sammy Winder for a four-yard loss on a sweep to the left.

It was now left for Karlis to salvage something, but incredibly he shanked a 23-yard field goal to the right—his first miss in 11 attempts. The Broncos sagged.

When Denver got the ball the next time, late in the second quarter, they seemed to lose all heart because Karlis missed another easy field goal, this one from 34 yards, with just 13 seconds to play, and Denver ahead 10-9. Again, the Giants' defense kept the Broncos out of the end zone after a 31-yard pass to Steve Watson and one of 11 yards to Willhite gave them a first down at the 21.

In between that disaster, Elway and the Broncos also got nailed for a safety by defensive end George Martin, playing fulltime at age 33. Ironically, it was also Martin who had intercepted a pass and rolled more than 70 yards for a touchdown in that earlier regular season game.

Denver, though, really was a victim of bad officiating and faulty technology on the safety. On the previous play, tight end Clarence Kay dove to catch a pass from Elway that would have given the Broncos a first down, but officials ruled incorrectly that he had trapped the ball. The NFL's Instant Replay was called up to verify the call, and the verdict was "inconclusive."

Simms connects again in a near-perfect performance—22 completions in 25 attempts, an .880 record percentage.

However, out in CBS' control room, there was a replay tape that clearly showed the ball had been caught—only the technician did not see it until some ten minutes afterward, and thus did not replay it for consideration by NFL officials, as they considered Kay's "non-catch."

That really was it for the Broncos, and as the Giants trooped into their locker room in the Rose Bowl, tackle Brad Benson thought, "Well, they played about as well as they could, and we haven't played worth a damn. We can still win this thing."

And the Giants did...with as great a second half of football that ever has been played in any NFL Championship Game, and the man directly responsible was Simms, though he had one big assist from sub quarterback Jeff Rutledge, who pulled off the play of the game.

This was a "gadget play," on fourth down at the Giants' 46-yard line, when New York needed one yard for a first down on their initial second-half drive. Coach Bill Parcells, in a frenzied bit of play-calling, decided to put in Rutledge with his punt team, and allow him either to draw Denver offsides as he hunkered under center waiting for a snap, or else take the snap and try to sneak for the first down.

The Broncos caught on to the ploy and did not substitute their punt return team. Then it became a waiting game. Rutledge under center waited for Denver to go offside. Denver sat patiently waiting for Rutledge to make his move. Finally, with two seconds left on the 30-second clock, Rutledge got the ball and dove for two yards and a first down.

After that, it was easy. Simms passed for 22 yards to Lee Rouson, and then polished off the drive with a 13-yard TD pass to Bavaro, giving New York the lead for good. "You could feel a surge of power and confidence through the whole team after that," Simms said. "We had control and we knew it."

They certainly did. On their next possession, Phil McConkey returned a punt 25 yards to Denver's 36-yard line and Raul Allegre kicked a 21-yard field goal, for a 19-10 lead. Denver punted after the next kickoff—the Broncos had only two yards of offense in the third quarter in three possessions against the Giants defense—and Parcells pulled out another gadget, this one a flea-flicker pass. Simms handed the ball to Morris as if he was sweeping left, and Joe tossed it back to his quarterback, who then hit McConkey with a 44-yard pass to the Broncos' one-yard line. Morris easily scored on the next play for a 26-10 lead.

When New York got the ball back early in the fourth quarter, they nailed down the victory with a 52-yard drive that ended with McConkey—the spiritual and emotional leader of the team—diving to catch a tipped pass to Bavaro in the end zone. Ironically, this drive was set up when Elvis Patterson, the most suspect of all the Giants' defensive backs, intercepted Elway. New York led 33-10.

It hardly mattered that Karlis regained his field goal touch with a 27-yard shot and that Elway passed 47 yards to Johnson for a TD in the fourth quarter, or that he completed 22 of 37 passes for 304 yards. The Giants' defense allowed only 52 yards of rushing, and sacked Elway three times. Even John couldn't do it all on this day.

"I was like a fastball pitcher," Phil Simms said. "I had great location all day. Almost every pass landed exactly where I wanted it. I've never played better."

And neither has anyone else.

At Pasadena, January 25, 1987. Attendance: 101,063

Denver	10	0	0	10	—	20
New York	7	2	17	13	—	39

Den—FG Karlis 48
NY—Mowatt 6 pass from Simms (Allegre kick)
Den—Elway 4 run (Karlis kick)
NY—Safety (Elway tackled in end zone by Martin)
NY—Bavaro 13 pass from Simms (Allegre kick)
NY—FG Allegre 21
NY—Morris 1 run (Allegre kick)
NY—McConkey 6 pass from Simms (Allegre kick)
Den—FG Karlis 28
NY—Anderson 2 run (Kick failed)
Den—V. Johnson 47 pass from Elway (Karlis kick)

THE MONKEY OFF THEIR BACKS

New Orleans Saints vs. Pittsburgh Steelers

NOVEMBER 29, 1987

The New Orleans Saints team was founded on All Saints Day in 1966, but until the eleventh week of their twenty-first season, the team had one devil of a time gaining respectability. It wasn't until the defeat of the Pittsburgh Steelers, 20-16, on November 29, 1987, that the Saints finally were assured of their first winning season. No NFL team ever had been so deprived. Neither had any group of fans, because an entire generation of the New Orleans population had been born and grown to maturity without ever knowing the Saints as a winning team. Instead, many knew the team as the ignominious "Aints."

Respectability was "in" during 1987 in other places as well, most prominently in Indianapolis, where the Colts broke a nine-season losing streak to win the American Football Conference's Eastern Division title with a 9-6 record. New Coach Ron Meyer and a blockbuster trade that brought all-pro running back Eric Dickerson to Indianapolis were the chief reasons the Colts had their first winning season since 1977, when their 10-4 record won them the AFC-East title as the Baltimore Colts.

Then there were the Buffalo Bills and Houston Oilers, two teams who had tasted more success during the past decade than the Colts and Saints, but who had swooned back to losing seasons for which they were better remembered. In 1987, the Oilers finished second in the AFC-Central and made the playoffs as a wild-card entry; and the Bills were surprising contenders for most of the year in the AFC-East.

But no one could displace the Saints as "most deserving." Consider that the team had only two 8-8 seasons to break that intolerable run of mediocrity and failure since John Mecom was granted a NFL franchise on November 1, 1966, and that they were the first NFL team ever to have fans show up wearing bags over their heads. The team was torn apart in 1980 by drug problems, just when it appeared they were about to become winners; and in 1983, a field goal by the Los Angeles Rams in the final two seconds of the final game of the season prevented them from getting that elusive winning season.

If losers, at least the Saints were different. They won a game in 1970, when Tom Dempsey kicked a NFL record 63-yard field goal (see pages 142-145); a former astronaut, Dick Gordon, who had piloted Apollo 12 to the moon, was team vice president; top 1981 draft pick, George Rogers, NFL Rookie of the Year,

Quarterback Bobby Hebert exemplified the sound strategy of coach Jim Mora which featured unspectacular but steady offensive movement.

who set a rushing record, was shipped off to the Redskins after admitting involvement with drugs; and the team went through 13 seasons and six head coaches before they were even able to play .500 ball for a season.

It really wasn't until New Orleans automobile dealer Tom Benson—who has a proclivity for boogeying around the sidelines at the Super Dome—bought the team, that the Saints got serious about the football business. Benson rooted out many of those who had been part of the Mecom era, and brought in Jim Finks to run the football operation. Finks was a proven winner: general manager of two of the Minnesota Vikings' four Super Bowl teams and builder of the other two; who ran the Bears, as they ended a 14-season playoff drought in the late seventies; and who had stepped into major league baseball and helped steer the Chicago Cubs in 1984 to their first National League playoff since 1945.

"I had no great desire to go back into the football business," says Finks, who, when called by Benson, was in the advertising business. "But I always thought that New Orleans could be an ideal franchise if handled right."

Finks's biggest—and best—move was bringing in head coach Jim Mora before the 1986 season. Mora had been a NFL assistant coach before winning two championships in the United States Football League. He was a methodical builder, a peg-by-peg planner, who had the kind of toughness Finks knew the young Saints players—and the older ones who were accustomed to losing—needed to become successful. He disdained the flash and dash so closely associated with New Orleans and its own particular style, and built a very plain, conservative, no-frills team that counted on its defense to control the game and the offense to do enough to win, but never so much that there was clear danger of losing.

Special teams became just that—special; big plays on defense were spread around, from five-foot, nine-inch linebacker Sam Mills—who had played for Mora in the USFL—to Pro-Bowler Rickey Jackson. Kicker Morten Andersen was handed as many scoring opportunities as quarterback Bobby Hebert. Mora came up with Reuben Mayes in the 1986 draft to key his running game, and supplemented him with Dalton Hilliard, both very effective in the 1987 turnaround season.

For the first part of 1987, it didn't appear as if the Saints were going to improve upon Mora's 7-9 record in 1986, splitting their first six games—the final a 24-22 loss to the San Francisco 49ers when Andersen missed a 52-yard field goal with seven seconds to play. After the game, Mora tore into his players and anyone else within earshot.

"We ain't good enough to beat those guys. We're close, we're close but close don't mean spit," he fumed. "Good teams don't say 'could have' and 'would have.' I'm sick of coming close and saying 'would have' and 'should have.'"

He didn't have to say it again. Beginning the following week, with a 38-0 victory over Atlanta, the Saints rolled. En route, they even beat the 49ers, this time 26-24 on Andersen's 40-yard field goal with less than two minutes to play. The following week, they roared from behind and defeated the defending NFL champion New York Giants 23-14, and then traveled to Pittsburgh.

On that day, it came up Steeler weather—cold, wet, and dismal, as the Steel City can be in the late fall, and that gloom seemed to grip the Saints and shake them. They muddled through the first half with only Andersen's 25-yard field goal. The Steelers' Dwayne Woodruff picked off one of Herbert's passes and ran 33 yards for a second quarter touchdown, and with just 46 seconds to play in that quarter, Walter Abercrombie ended a 75-yard march with a touchdown, for a 14-3 halftime lead.

In a sense, the Saints had the Steelers right where they wanted them—ahead in the ball game, because New Orleans rattled off the game's next 17 points. Mayes finished off a 13-play, 86-yard drive with a five-yard touchdown run in the third quarter; in the fourth, Herbert passed 19 yards to Eric Martin, after David Waymer recovered a Steelers fumble. Rookie cornerback Milton Mack then intercepted a Steelers pass, to set up Andersen's 32-yard field goal with six-and-a-half minutes to play.

In New Orleans, the gods of frustration don't give up easily; the Steelers then marched right down to the four-yard line. On fourth down, and just inches away from the end zone, Mills—who was scoffed at as a NFL prospect before Mora brought him to the Saints from his Stars' USFL teams—slashed through a narrow gap and stopped Steelers' fullback Frank Pollard to thwart the scoring drive.

The Saints ran three plays, then took a deliberate safety with 65 seconds to play. After the free kick, the Steelers cranked it up again, and in just 27 seconds, they were at New Orleans' 14-yard line. On the next play, Pittsburgh quarterback Mark Malone hit Calvin Sweeney at the three-yard line. It looked like the Saints' first winning season would have to wait for another week.

"At that point, the old Saints would never have survived," Rickey Jackson said afterward. "We would have blown it."

But not the new Saints. On the next play, linebacker Pat Swilling sacked Malone back to the 11-yard line, and then Waymer intercepted a pass intended for Sweeney, as the Steelers' receiver slipped and fell.

So, New Orleans had its eighth win in a 15-game season—one game was lost because of the player strike—and the winning year was guaranteed. But that wasn't enough for defensive lineman Tony Elliott, who had been through five frustrating seasons.

"We've won eight games twice before," he said after the Steelers' win. "That's all this is, our eighth win. Some are

The Saints' ground game centered around draft choice Reuben Mayes and Dalton Hilliard (above), both very effective in turnaround 1987.

going to say it's really not a winning season. We want to remove all doubts by winning nine.''

So they did...the following week, beating Tampa Bay 44-34; and they kept on winning until they finished the season with a 12-3 record, the second best record in the NFL. It doesn't really matter that the Saints lost to the Vikings in the first round of the playoffs. Mora put it into perspective after the Steelers game.

"People can no longer say, and write, and talk about the Saints being the only team not to have had a winning season. Now we've got the monkey off our backs.''

And it only took 21 seasons.

At Pittsburgh, November 29, 1987:

New Orleans	3	0	7	10—**20**
Pittsburgh	0	14	0	2—**16**

NO—FG Andersen 25
Pitt—Woodruff 33 interception (Andersen kick)
Pitt—Abercrombie 5 run (Andersen kick)
NO—Mayes 5 run (Andersen kick)
NO—Martin 19 pass from Herbert (Andersen kick)
NO—FG Andersen 32
Pitt—Safety (Hansen stepped out of end zone)

SECOND QUARTER EXPLOSION

Washington Redskins vs. Denver Broncos

JANUARY 31, 1988

Given time to set up, Williams proved virtually unstoppable.

Let's say "magnificent" as the only way to describe the Washington Redskins' second quarter explosion in Super Bowl XXII that buried the Denver Broncos, 42-10. It was 15 minutes in which Washington scored five touchdowns, 35 total points, while amassing 356 yards on 18 offensive plays.

Many individual records were established in San Diego's Jack Murphy Stadium on this Super Sunday, but above all, it was the awesome display of offense that stamped this game as special among all the games played for the championship.

The Redskins, on this day, didn't come close to setting a championship game scoring record—the Bears beat the Redskins 73-0 for the 1940 NFL title, and a later edition of the Bears routed the New England Patriots, 46-21, in Super Bowl XX. But neither of those teams scored five touchdowns in just 15 minutes. It is rare indeed to find any team in NFL history that put up five touchdowns on just 18 offensive plays. That is as close to perfection as a team is likely to come.

The men in the middle of this explosion were the Redskins' quarterback, Doug Williams; running back Tim Smith, working behind an offensive line long known as the Hogs; and a "smurf" of a wide receiver named Rick Sanders.

Williams, the first black quarterback to start in a Super Bowl contest, was the in-and-out play caller for the Redskins for most of the 1987 season, cementing the starting job just before the playoffs began, and looking anything but threatening when Washington defeated Chicago and Minnesota to reach its third Super Bowl in just five years.

The media made a big deal of Williams's lackluster performance prior to the game. Redskin coaches became fearful that their quarterback might come to question himself, forgetting the job at hand.

Their worry was needless. Williams, with a smile, had willing answers, displaying no sign that he was bothered in his role of pioneer. "I wasn't the quarterback of the Washington Redskins because I was black. That's the important thing," he said. "It was a relief to get on the practice field and be able to work hard and concentrate on the game. I didn't allow the questions to affect me."

He was also constantly being compared—and put down as a result—to Denver's marvelous quarterback, John Elway. There was little doubt that Elway was the best in the NFL, and that he would have to carry the Broncos, if they were to win. There also were few doubts that he could shoulder those burdens successfully—his team was a three-and-a-half point favorite.

Those odds appeared about right when Elway passed 56 yards to Ricky Nattiel for a touchdown on the first offensive play, and then got the Broncos a 10-0 lead on his next possession, with Rick Karlis's 24-yard field goal. It was pure Elway to this point, as he mesmerized an obviously too-tight Redskins defense, while the Broncos were holding Williams in his first four se-

ries to a scant 53 yards, and sent him limping to the sidelines with a badly twisted knee.

For a few moments, Washington coach, Joe Gibbs, and his staff believed their plans to beat a very average Broncos defense might never be implemented. The Redskins had been certain they could run the ball effectively against the smaller Denver defense, especially if they started the quicker Tim Smith, a rookie, ahead of veteran George Rogers. If Williams could complete half of his passes, they would beat a weak secondary.

Gibbs had decided to start Smith the night before the game, but didn't tell him until just before the kickoff. ("We didn't want him throwing up all over the locker room," cracked offensive coach, Joe Bugel.) Gibbs even allowed Rogers to be introduced with the starting Redskins offense, before sending in Smith on the first series.

"George had been gimpy all week, but more than that, I wanted to use Timmy's speed to run outside because I figured Denver's defense would try to pinch us off inside," Gibbs said.

First, the Redskins had to climb back into the game. They did it on their first play of the second quarter, when Williams limped back into the game, and hurled a record-tying 80-yard touchdown pass to Sanders. The play started as a seven-yard toss, but Denver cornerback Mark Haynes came up and bumped Sanders off his route. Sanders quickly adjusted, went deep, and broke past Haynes to catch the ball in the clear at the midfield. He easily ran in for the touchdown.

"That was the turning point," Gibbs said. "You could feel our team come alive. We caught fire."

And how! Look at what happened on the next four possessions:

(1) The first four Redskin plays netted 37 yards, 20 on two runs by Smith, before Gary Clark ran the same pattern as Sanders and got behind Steve Wilson to catch a 27-yard TD pass. Washington took the lead, 14-10.

Tim Smith bursts through Denver's line on the now-famous "counter-gap," designed against a quick defense, and Washington's most consistently successful play of the day.

The Broncos had a chance to stem this flood on their next possession, but Karlis, who had missed a couple of first-half field goals against the Giants the previous year, watched his 43-yard attempt sail wide.

(2) On the first play following the missed field goal, Williams passed 16 yards to Clark to the Redskins' 42-yard line. On the next play, he called a counter-